The Future of Social Insurance

The Future of Social Insurance

Incremental Action or Fundamental Reform?

Peter Edelman
Dallas L. Salisbury
Pamela J. Larson
Editors

NATIONAL ACADEMY OF SOCIAL INSURANCE
Washington, D.C.

The Future of Social Insurance: Incremental Action or Fundamental Reform?
may be ordered from:

BROOKINGS INSTITUTION PRESS
1775 Massachusetts Avenue, N.W.
Washington, D.C. 20036
Tel.:   1-800/275-1447
         202/797-6258
Fax: 202/797-6004
Internet: www.brookings.edu

Library of Congress Cataloging-in-Publication data

The future of social insurance : incremental action or fundamental reform? /
Peter Edelman, Dallas L. Salisbury, Pamela J. Larson, editors.
  p. cm.
Includes bibliographical references and index.
  ISBN 0-8157-0213-2 (pbk. : alk. paper)
  1. Social security—United States. I. Edelman, Peter B. II. Salisbury, Dallas L.
III. Larson, Pamela J.
  HD7125.F8795 2002
  368.4'3'00973—dc21   2001006494

9 8 7 6 5 4 3 2 1

The paper used in this publication meets minimum requirements of the American
National Standard for Information Sciences—Permanence of Paper for Printed
Library Materials: ANSI Z39.48-1992.

Typeset in Times Roman

Composition by AlphaWebTech
  Mechanicsville, Maryland

Printed by R. R. Donnelley and Sons
  Harrisonburg, Virginia

Preface

This book is based on papers delivered at the thirteenth annual conference of the National Academy of Social Insurance, held January 24–25, 2001, at the National Press Club in Washington, D.C. The conference examined emergent ideas for Social Security, Medicare, unemployment insurance, retirement income, and health insurance.

The Academy received financial support for this conference from the Robert Wood Johnson Foundation and the John D. and Catherine T. MacArthur Foundation, the California Health Care Foundation, the Daimler-Chrysler Fund, and the AFL-CIO.

As with all activities organized under its auspices, the Academy takes responsibility for ensuring the independence of this book. Participants in the conference were chosen for their recognized expertise and with due consideration to the balance of disciplines appropriate to the program. The resulting chapters represent the views of the authors and do not necessarily reflect the views of the officers, board, or members of the National Academy of Social Insurance.

The editors would like to thank all the conference participants for sparking lively discussion and debate. We also commend the Academy staff for helping to design stimulating sessions and for facilitating the smooth running of the conference, in particular, Elizabeth Dulaney, Daniel Mont, Terry Nixon, Kathryn Olson, Virginia Reno, Katherine Robie, and Cecili Thompson.

We appreciate the efforts of all those who made this book possible: the authors for their attention to the task of turning their presentations into chapters; Cecili Thompson of the Academy staff, who organized the process; Kerry Kern, who copyedited the manuscript; Inge Lockwood, who proofread the pages; Shirley Kessel, who provided the index; and Janet Walker and the staff of the Brookings Institution Press.

Contents

PART I

Introduction

1

Overview

Dallas Salisbury, Peter Edelman,
and Pamela J. Larson

A T THE TIME the National Academy of Social Insurance (NASI) planned the conference on which this book is based, the primary battles were ongoing in both major political parties. That early point in the campaign evidenced great clarity: the visions of the two major parties of the future of social insurance were quite different. The Democratic Party platform called for incremental action on both Social Security and Medicare, while the Republican Party platform talked of fundamental reform. What did they mean? What would be the implications of each direction for programs and people? What changes in the economy and the retirement income system should be considered in any reform debates to come? This overview presents a capsule look at the full conference, while the chapters that follow provide full detail of the conference discussion.

What Role for Social Insurance in the New Economy?

Economist William Dudley of Goldman Sachs in chapter 2 presents his definition of the New Economy and, given that definition, considers what the implications might be for social insurance. Dudley highlights two major conclusions. First, the New Economy bolsters rather than undercuts the case for social insurance. Second, the New Economy, because it is associated with more rapid productivity growth, actually makes a social safety net more affordable. In essence, he suggests that fundamental reform is not economically necessary if the New Economy turns out to be enduring, because the nation could actually afford Social Security in a form not significantly different from how it exists today. Fundamental reform might be justified based upon a change in policy, but not by economics alone.

Issues in Social Security Reform

A central issue in the debate over Social Security reform is related to rates of return. One question is whether the Social Security Trust Fund could be earning a higher rate of return if invested in the private equity markets. Another question is what the effective rate of return is for the individual beneficiary on the taxes they have paid to Social Security. In chapter 3 economist Richard Berner of Morgan Stanley Dean Witter speaks to the first issue based upon a comprehensive study undertaken in 1999.[1] Berner concludes that "investing a major portion of the likely future flow of Social Security receipts in equities would not assure the solvency of the trust funds through 2075." He assumes that, under the proposed reforms discussed by the presidential campaigns, annual flows would start at between $75 and $190 billion in the first year of the program. Such flows would be small in the context of the total private market, and the markets should easily be capable of absorbing these flows without disruption or significant impact on equity prices. Berner argues that a gradual program of equity purchases could eventually yield an overall return to the trust fund that is 1 percent to 2 percent higher than the current full investment in special nonmarketable Treasury securities. This could be done without increasing the riskiness of returns to the program, and such prefunding would increase national saving and increase economic returns.

A second issue in the reform debate relates to the social insurance aspect of Social Security. That is, lower income earners receive benefits that replace a higher percentage of past salary in retirement than do higher earners. Fundamental reform of Social Security, particularly the addition of individual accounts to the program, would replace this nonproportional replacement rate with a common percentage of salary going into every worker's account. Analyst Kilolo Kijakazi of the Center on Budget and Policy Priorities reviews in chapter 4 what Social Security now provides to low-wage earners and underlines the government's role in reducing poverty among elderly individuals. Kijakazi stresses that "the Social Security program has been a constant upon which most workers have been able to depend to receive income for themselves and their families when they retire, become disabled or die. The program has been one of the nation's most effective defenses against poverty." She argues that "as the country moves forward toward reforming Social Security, it is important that solutions be adopted to reduce poverty further among those who still are vulnerable in their old age." Kijakazi suggests

1. Richard Berner, "Implications of Investment of a Portion of Social Security Funds in Financial Markets," report prepared for the Committee on the Investment of Employee Benefit Assets, June 1999, mimeograph.

changes that would expand the present national commitment to retirement income security. Rather than creating individual accounts within Social Security, she proposes creating a federally matched retirement savings plan targeted to low- and moderate-wage earners in addition to Social Security.

Public officials listen to economists such as Dudley and Berner, and policy researchers such as Kijakazi, and ask a natural question: What does the public think about incremental action or fundamental reform? Researchers Fay Lomax Cook of Northwestern University and Lawrence Jacobs of the University of Minnesota provide in chapter 5 a comprehensive picture of public views on Social Security. They note that "proponents of divergent proposals for reforming Social Security often rest their claims on a set of working hypotheses about the public's confidence in the program and support for current arrangements and for reforms." These have to do with the public's confidence in the future of Social Security, support for Social Security, and desire for privatization and incremental reform of Social Security. Cook and Jacobs then present a history of surveys on each of these three working hypotheses. Cook concludes that "neither of the first two working hypotheses about public opinion stand up to hard data." Jacobs looks at the third hypothesis and concludes that identically worded or very similarly worded questions in a number of different polls show the evidence on public support for reform to be a bit ambivalent. Jacobs observes, "The challenge is whether policymakers are willing to respond to the public's preferences or whether Democrats or Republicans will substitute their own preferences and those of their supporters."

Howard Fluhr, a business executive from the Segal Company, provides a comprehensive comment on the first group of papers, noting: "As in any debate, the advocates are choosing the 'facts' that support their positions. If the policymakers understand and utilize research-based facts, they are more likely to come to sound solutions. We need to try to overcome the natural inclination to accept what supports our beliefs and to dismiss what does not."

Policy advocate Cecilia Muñoz of the National Council of La Raza provides a comment as well, highlighting why these issues are so important. She notes that Latinos "will largely be relying on Social Security as they retire. Their lack of pensions and the ability to save are both the result of low income and lack of information, access, and know-how with respect to the way that savings and investments work."

Journalist Robert Rosenblatt of the *Los Angeles Times* provides a comprehensive comment that touches on each of the presentations from the perspective of a journalist. Commenting on the role of economics and market returns, he notes: "I believe what is happening in the market is somewhat irrelevant to the debate unless the market crashes. If it crashes and is down for a prolonged period of time, then the talk about privatization fades away. But if the market stays level or goes up, it is a live issue. People who believe in privatization believe in it as a matter of faith. It does not matter how much economic analysis you produce. If you believe that privatization is a good idea, if you believe that it gives individuals more control over money and more control over the future of their retirement, then you believe in privatization." Rosenblatt goes on to note that Kijakazi "has given a lot of valuable information on improving the welfare of the poorest segment of society with new benefits. Adding a minimum benefit, having an upward adjustment in Supplemental Security Income, and improving the survivor benefit. All of those could add to the well-being of a lot of people." Rosenblatt notes that these ideas have been around for a long time, but have never been implemented because there is no impetus to reform Social Security generally. "Commission after commission says it is a good idea, but nothing happens." Third, he moves to the issue of public opinion and concludes: "President George Bush believes in privatization. He will trumpet this under the reform banner. It then becomes an issue, and then people will have to decide if this is something that they like or not."

The Future of Retirement Income

Social Security is often described as one "leg" of a multilegged retirement income stool. Employment-based pensions, personal savings, and continued work are discussed as the other legs. For decades a "pension" was thought of as a monthly annuity, but Congress enacted the Employee Retirement Income Security Act of 1974 (ERISA) and included an expanded definition of pensions to include "defined contribution" plans to which a percentage of pay is contributed, investment earnings are added or subtracted, and a single-sum distribution is made to the individual worker. As a result of this trend, documented in chapter 6 by economists Jack VanDerhei and Craig Copeland, the concerns of analysts about the economic well-being of future retirees have heightened: Will the money be managed in such as way as to provide long-term supplementation of Social Security? Copeland concludes that future retirees will have less than half as much relative income from defined benefit plan annuities. For those born in 1964, the last year of the baby boom, 80 percent of their retirement pension wealth will come from individual retirement account (IRA) rollovers and defined contribution plans. As a result, the long-term well-being of future retirees will be far more dependent on decisions they make postretirement about how fast to spend retirement assets. Based upon the data presented by VanDerhei and Copeland, it becomes clear that the "new" retirement system will lead to better-off retirees if they preserve money as they get single-sum distributions, invest the money prudently, and do not spend the money too fast. They could end up worse off by spending the money too quickly.

Economist Jeffrey R. Brown of Harvard University focuses in chapter 7 on how the nation might take this new retirement asset reality and turn it into retirement income success. He notes that the key issue is longevity risk, or—to put it more simply—how people make retirement financial planning decisions when they do not know how long they are going to live. He gives the example of a sixty-five-year-old male, who on average can expect to live another sixteen years, but who also has a one-in-eight chance of dying before the age of seventy. Brown then highlights the more optimistic statistic that a sixty-five-year-old male has about a one-in-six chance of living to age ninety or above, and the numbers are even more favorable for women. Brown provides a review of annuity forms, the pluses and minuses of annuities, and makes recommendations on public policy actions that could help ensure streams of income from single-sum payments. While Brown raises the issues, he does not explore the contradiction between the move to individual responsibility represented by the growth of defined contribution plans and proposals for individual accounts in Social Security and the paternalism represented by mandated annuities. That is handled in the comments that follow.

Analyst Ann Combs, then of the American Council of Life Insurers, notes that "government regulation, both real and as perceived by the employer community, is in fact stifling employers' willingness to offer defined benefit plans. Defined contribution plans may be the only practical option for smaller employers who employ an increasing share of the work force." She observes that defined contribution plans provide meaningful retirement benefits to all covered workers, not just to those who spend an entire career with one employer, which is the group that benefits greatly through the traditional defined benefits system. She agrees with Brown's conclusion that wealth accumulation is fine but believes it is not enough to guarantee retirement income security and proposes a broader focus for the pension debate. "Asset accumulation is essential, and we need to improve incentives for people to save for their retirement. . . . The more difficult challenge . . . is to create incentives for employees to elect annuities. If we can create a demand for annuities, employers will respond by trying to meet employees' needs for a cost-effective annuity product. And even if the employer does not step up to the challenge and offer the annuity, then the employee would still have the ability to roll into an IRA and purchase an annuity."

Finance writer Al Crenshaw comments on the need to educate people not only about the choices they may have, but also about the long-term consequences of these choices and how they could be affected by ups and downs in the market. He observes that "coming off about twenty years of perhaps the best investment climate any of us will ever know . . . has turned the attitude of a growing block of people about retirement planning away from social insurance and toward wealth accumulation." He notes that some employers have dropped their defined benefit pension plan after determining that their 401(k) plan was what attracted new workers. He cites the discontent with investment returns by people with annuities or those at the full wage base for Social Security.

Crenshaw believes that people are ignoring the risks of outliving their retirement money and the risk that they will invest poorly. He recommends that we educate people about "the long-term consequences of [their retirement income] choices and the way they could be affected by the ups and downs in the market."

Economist Heidi Hartmann of the Institute for Women's Policy Research believes that "Social Security should be kept as a social insurance system because the private marketplace really is not taking care of our retirement needs." She notes that VanDerhei and Copeland usefully document the shift away from defined benefit and toward defined contribution retirement plans and contribute a precise estimate of what the distribution of income will be in retirement. She commends Brown's discussion of annuities and the role that they might play in protecting people against risks, such as the risk of living too long. She believes that, for the most part, Social Security and defined benefit pension plans are playing that role now, with Social Security being challenged and these pension plans disappearing.

The messages are clear. First, Social Security makes the difference between poverty and income sufficiency for a majority of retirees. Second, the New Economy is not likely to change this for the better. Third, moving Social Security money to the equity markets, in the amounts discussed in most proposals, will have marginal impact. Fourth, a majority of the working population is accumulating retirement assets at work. Fifth, most of those assets will flow to workers in single-sum payments upon job change or retirement, placing all future risk upon the individual for decisionmaking regarding investment, speed of withdrawal, and other vital aspects. Sixth, available data suggest that few will choose to purchase annuities to smooth the income stream unless changes in policy, market incentives, and education are significant.

The Future of Unemployment Insurance

During his campaign for office, President Bush talked of a slowing economy and the prospect of increased unemployment. After an extended period of decreasing unemployment, relatively flush unemployment fund reserves, and discussions of spending those reserves for other purposes, the prospect of rising unemployment was new. As a result, it is a worthy topic for exploration in this volume.

Economist Janet Norwood, who as chair of the Advisory Council on Unemployment Compensation oversaw the most recent comprehensive review of unemployment insurance, provides a review of the history of the unemployment insurance program and of the new challenges facing the program as the labor force changes to include more women and more multiple-job-holders. Norwood also reviews the program issues raised by welfare reforms enacted in the 1990s that make many who have traditionally been covered by welfare ineligible for unemployment insurance. She recounts the major recommendations issued in the mid-1990s by the Advisory Council on Unemployment Compensation and comments on the absence of action on them by Congress. Norwood concludes that "we have an opportunity now to strengthen the entire unemployment insurance program as a federal-state cooperative program that produces results for workers who lose their jobs through no fault of their own." She argues that unemployed workers have a right to a modernized unemployment insurance program, one that recognizes changes that have occurred in the makeup of the work force and in employment conditions. Norwood provides a list of reforms that would ensure that the unemployment insurance system will continue to assist unemployed workers in periods of economic distress and be better able than it is now to help workers who need it in the future.

Eric Oxfeld, of UWC Strategic Services on Unemployment and Workers' Compensation Inc., adds the perspective of business when he comments that "business supports unemployment insurance as a program that provides limited wage replacement to workers who are seeking suitable new employment, who have a strong attachment to work, and who lost their jobs because their employer no longer had work for them. That has been the precept of the unemployment insurance program since its inception. In the view of employers, there is no reason why that should change." Oxfeld details reforms supported and opposed by the business community and responds directly to the recommendations of the commission summarized by Norwood.

Economist Wayne Vroman of the Urban Institute provides a review of the funded status of the unemployment insurance program and future prospects, examines data on the current use of the program, and describes a project under way that looks at interstate variation in receiving unemployment insurance benefits. The study suggests that there are identifiable reasons why recipiency varies so much by state and that recipiency is systematically different in some regions of the country compared to others.

Charity Wilson of the AFL-CIO provides a worker's advocate perspective on the commission report described by Norwood. She notes that worker advocates had accomplished "two major goals: to address the issues of low-wage workers for eligibility and to address the issue of administrative financing." While people tend to think that worker advocates always emphasize eligibility and benefit levels, Wilson maintains that "there has to be a system to serve those people to help get them back to work, into training, or into education programs" and emphasizes the need for timely adoption of the recommendations in order to both improve and secure the unemployment insurance program.

Reflections on Welfare Reform

Welfare reform has been going on since 1996, and the discussion in chapter 9 makes clear just how differently people can view outcomes data and interpret success or failure. Two former congressional staff, Wendell Primus and Ron Haskins, provide in chapter 9 a dialogue in which they agree on the data but disagree on whether positive outcomes are the result of welfare reform or a strong economy. As a result, the discussion also provides an enlightening look at what the future might bring, including disagreements over what a possible economic downturn might bring, whether enough has been accomplished to deem welfare reform a success, and how Congress and the administration should assess the data as they consider the extension of welfare reform provisions.

The Future of Medicare

Economist Marilyn Moon of the Urban Institute provides a detailed report in chapter 10 of the recently completed work of a NASI study panel on the long-term financing of Medicare. The panel concluded that benefits of the program should not be cut and new revenues must be part of the debate to secure Medicare's long-term funding. The panel also concluded that action should be taken as soon as possible, rather than waiting until cash flow turns negative. Moon concludes that the program is sustainable and that Medicare is not a doomsday story.

In chapter 11 Sheila Burke of the Smithsonian and Harvard University reports on the ongoing work of a NASI panel on Medicare governance and management. The panel is seeking to define what problems are facing Medicare's current structure of governance—its accountability and its management. Burke lists the kinds of questions the panel is exploring: "What is working? Why is that particular aspect of it working? What was envisioned in 1965? What has become of the program since then? What changes have been made? What are the pluses and minuses of the current organizational structure of the Health Care Financing Administration (HCFA)?[2] What are the alternative models? Should the same agency that controls Medicare be in charge of Medicaid?" The panel is scheduled to make recommendations in each of these areas, producing a report by the end of 2001.

Economist Mark Schlesinger of Yale University chairs the NASI study panel on Medicare and markets. At the time of the NASI conference this panel was in the earliest stages of its work, so rather than project conclusions, Schlesinger presents in chapter 12 his perception of the challenges the panel faces. He sees three core problems. First, Medicare provides inadequate financial security. Second, Medicare has not improved the American health care system's ability to deal with the health care issues of people with chronic illness. Third, Medicare fails to deal with increasingly clear disparities in outcomes associated with differences in coverage between rich and poor, well educated and less educated, and whites and racial and ethnic minorities. Schlesinger's assessment is that Medicare has problems to which markets may not be a ready solution and, in fact, may produce exactly an opposite result. "To make Medicare work well, you have to expand benefits to eliminate the disincentives for disenrollment of healthy enrollees. To make Medicare work well, you need administrative capacity to adequately monitor quality of care in these managed care plans. To work well, it demands a more active and capable role for HCFA, not a less active one. That is not going to be an easy message to sell." The work of the panel is ongoing, but Schlesinger suggests that its core mission is to put the understanding of the role of markets for Medicare on a more realistic, evidentiary basis.

Gerard Anderson of Johns Hopkins University reports in chapter 13 on the work to be undertaken by a NASI study panel on Medicare and chronic care. The panel's charge is to examine how Medicare can ensure access to appropriate care for people with complex, chronic, and long-term health conditions and disabilities. Anderson notes that the Medicare program's focus has historically been on acute episodes rather than insuring against the costs of meeting the needs of beneficiaries with one or more chronic conditions. Anderson hopes that the panel will "show why caring for people with chronic diseases should be the major priority of the Medicare program." He notes that this will require a fundamental change in how the Medicare program and society views itself.

2. HCFA was renamed the Centers for Medicare and Medicaid Services in June 2001.

Philanthropic Initiatives in Health Security

In chapter 14 Lauren LeRoy of Grantmakers in Health provides an overview of the issues of access and insurance coverage. She notes that "when you look at this in the framework of the future of social insurance, the history related to the underinsured and the uninsured has been incremental and has involved both government at all levels and the private sector." Leroy explained that "those who seek to improve access and expand insurance coverage cannot neglect the importance of basic education on the issue of the uninsured. It is imprudent to assume that people truly understand the causes and dimensions of uninsurance simply because of the persistence of the problem."

She notes that, because of the lack of a comprehensive national response, wide variation in coverage can be seen across the country. This reflects an interplay of the various public and private options that are available in different geographic areas. "Economic performance and the impact of welfare reform have varied across the different states and regions. . . . [creating] an evolving profile of who has insurance coverage and what that coverage includes, both nationally and within different states."

LeRoy observes that most of the uninsured do get medical care, but "they get it by paying out of pocket, by going to safety net providers, or by obtaining primary care in more costly emergency room settings. It comes at a relatively high cost to them, given their incomes, and in ways that are ultimately inefficient and costly to the health system and to our society." Leroy then describes the types of initiatives private foundations can and do take to help the uninsured, expand the number of insured, and educate all sectors on the importance of expanding health insurance coverage and access.

In chapters 15 and 16 two foundation executives describe initiatives that illustrate the lessons learned. Ruth Reidel of the Alliance Health Care Foundation reports on efforts in San Diego County, California, to expand health insurance coverage through a public and private sector partnership. She outlines the many facets of that program to achieve increases in coverage, including research, public relations, media public service announcements, development of a low-cost health insurance product, small business education and enrollment assistance, and aggressive action by all partners.

Henrie M. Treadwell provides a comprehensive report on Community Voices, the community health initiatives of the W. K. Kellogg Foundation. She underlines the difficulties of making progress, noting that design, organization, and delivery must be considered along with financing because financing creates the possibility of financial access, but does not make people aware of or enroll them in coverage for which they qualify. She notes that financing alone does not shift the focus of services away from budget-breaking tertiary sickness care to primary care, broad-based prevention, and facilitated self-management of chronic conditions, nor does it fill significant gaps in covered benefits, such as oral health and mental health services and pharmaceuticals.

Treadwell goes on to say that the United States cannot expect to fill gaps in any type of insurance simply by better educating people, as the structure of the U.S. economy requires low-wage workers. "The solution to adequate social insurance lies, therefore, in protecting *all* people—not just "people like us"—from the temporal and lifelong costs associated with preserving health."

She notes that the Community Voices program works to address and integrate the complex needs and issues affecting those who work with no benefits, who are paid too little, and who are paid without income verification. "To improve health security and ultimately a system of social insurance, the adequacy and reliability of any current 'system' of employment insurance should be considered to determine if basic reform is needed relative to employment policy and practice. Far too many people work but have no network of insurance of any type available to them, short of national programs for which they may or may not qualify."

Treadwell asserts that philanthropy cannot and should not direct community action. Its appropriate role is to support the work that people in communities feel they need to implement to achieve their own goals. But, she added, "philanthropy can, and should, shine a light on documentable evidence of human suffering, human misery, and a diminution of the human condition and of the human spirit."

Treadwell concludes by tackling the public policy nexus: "The public, not-for-profit, and marketplace sectors have an option, and perhaps a moral and ethical responsibility, to examine, implement, and expand the work that people in communities have validated."

Jack A. Meyer of the Economic and Social Research Institute comments that health policy leaders are often tempted to fall into the "either/or" syndrome when discussing safety-net efforts and expanding health insurance coverage or to think that the problem is merely a lack of money, when it is a problem of financing and better allocating money toward primary and preventative care. He urges foundations to finance qualitative research to yield case studies that "bring to life the impact of these initiatives on real people and their lives." He adds that "foundations have fallen short on probing the relationship between demonstration projects and the need for national reform." Foundations need to support people who help answer the question of why the United States does not treat health care contributions in a social insurance framework like the European countries do.

James Tallon of the United Hospital Fund emphasizes that the activity subset reported on in this part of the book is that of "community-oriented initiatives within a broader context of other policy and other programmatic initiatives undertaken by a range of philanthropic organizations." Tallon discusses the fragmented financing system for health care, the importance of the issue of maintaining the present fully voluntary system of enrollment for health insurance versus moving to a system of automatic enrollment, and the importance of the structure of the delivery system for care. He notes other challenges to expanding coverage, including difficulties in the individual insurance market and renewed health care cost inflation that is driving premiums up. Tallon concludes by noting that community strategies "give voice to the problem, include communities in developing solutions, and design the delivery systems in a way that links the resources of that community to underserved populations. This is a powerful mix." But Tallon ends on a note of skepticism about the danger that policymakers will not hear the message that the financing problem can be solved through community strategies alone.

The Future of Social Insurance

Susan Dentzer of the *NewsHour with Jim Lehrer* provides a journalist's view of Social Security and Medicare issues and reform proposals. Dentzer recounts a number of past actions and a combination of unintended consequences and costs. For example, the creation of Medicare was based upon initial future cost projections that were off by several hundred percent, and Medicare + Choice was to extend the health maintenance organization (HMO) opportunity, but now the focus is on how to slow the rate of HMO withdrawal from the program. Dentzer comments that, when looking ahead, "even the most die-hard believer in the necessity of reforming Social Security and Medicare would acknowledge that there is a great deal of opportunity for mischief there. There are opportunities for many bad or unworkable policies to be adopted."

Dentzer discusses the long-term consequences of not thinking through the consequences of proposals and notes that many questions remain about any reform proposals. How will people living in the real world respond to them? Is it conceivable that reforms could to any degree accomplish each side's sought-after economic, ideological, or other goals?" Dentzer uses the 1988 election debate over long-term care and the way in which that issue has "fallen off the table" to underline the degree to which those who believe that reforms are needed must persist energetically to keep an issue on the agenda of policymakers.

Conclusion

The conference objective was to provide a balance of perspectives on the issue of comprehensive reform or incremental action in Social Security, Medicare, unemployment insurance, and efforts to reduce the health uninsured. As this overview and the chapters in this volume show, the objective was not met.

Why? Because those selected as authors from the private sector, who it was assumed would argue—based upon past writings—for a move away from social insurance through comprehensive reform, did not. Those from the nonprofit sector, who it was assumed would argue—based upon past writings—for a move to expand social insurance through comprehensive reform, did not. In the former case the chapters reveal a broad support for the "safety net" of public social insurance and strengthening present systems through incremental action. In the latter case there seemed to be recognition that the prospects for incremental action were far better than comprehensive reform, even when they preferred comprehensive reform.

The result is a book that is useful for the present policy environment, in which the political parties effectively share power in the nation's capital, thus making comprehensive reform that either eliminates or greatly expands social insurance highly unlikely.

2

The New Economy: Bolstering the Case for Social Insurance

William C. Dudley

MOST OF THE CHANGES in the U.S. economy associated with the "New Economy" concept bolster rather than undercut the case for social insurance. More rapid technological change means greater creative destruction and the risk of premature obsolescence to companies and workers of capital, job skills, and earnings power. The shift toward defined contribution plans means more of the investment risk falls on the individual worker. Both changes underscore the need for maintenance of a sturdy social safety net.

Fortunately, these same changes imply that the United States can afford such a safety net. After all, the New Economy has generated a rise in productivity growth. If this proves to be sustainable, that will generate the resources needed to shore up the solvency of the current social insurance system.

Finally, faster productivity growth implies that real wages will rise more quickly. This suggests another mechanism to bolster the solvency of Social Security, that is, loosening the link between real wage growth and Social Security benefits a bit. If that were done, the payroll tax deficit that exists over the next seventy-five years for the Social Security system could gradually be whittled away over time without a downward adjustment in the real value of benefits.

What Is the New Economy?

The New Economy means different things to different people. To some it means an economy that is like the Six Million Dollar Man of TV fame—stronger, faster, better, and not subject to limits. In this characterization, the bull market in equities continues forever. But there is no growth rate fast enough or unemployment rate low enough to countenance a monetary policy response designed to rein in either the pace of economic activity or the equity market.

To others, the New Economy means the technology sector and the Internet— a source of rapid productivity and the locus of the investment boom that has characterized the past few years.

To still others, the New Economy is a sham. They cite Robert Solow's famous observation: you can see computers everywhere, except in the productivity statistics.

My view of the New Economy lies in between. On one hand, the optimistic view is already in the process of being proven incorrect. The stock market has retrenched and the investment boom threatens to fizzle.

But, on the other hand, the pessimistic view that the New Economy is a sham does not seem correct either. That is because two developments can be identified that make the economy now much different than it was in the past: (1) the economy has become less cyclical, and (2) productivity growth has increased.

The New Economy: Less Cyclical

Although it seems somewhat foolhardy to observe that the economy has become less cyclical on what may turn out to be the eve of recession, empirically the observation still appears to be valid. After all, this has been the longest economic expansion in U.S. history, and it followed another unusually long-lived expansion from 1982 to 1990. In fact, the United States has been in recession for only eight months during the 1982–2000 period. That is a frequency of about 4 percent of the time. Prior to 1983 the United States was in recession about 25 percent of the time. No wonder the stock market has performed well over this time period!

Moreover, the reasons for the improvement in economic performance can be identified. First, luck has clearly played a role. The "peace dividend" allowed defense spending to be cut, thereby freeing up resources for the private sector. In addition, most of the shocks to the U.S. economy during the 1990s were well timed and in the right direction and magnitude. For example, the Asian crisis in 1997 helped slow the U.S. economy when it threatened to overheat, and this helped hold down inflation.

It is difficult, however, to attribute the economy's performance to just this factor. If it is assumed that the same probability distribution generated the last two business cycles as the other post–World War II expansions, then it can be shown that the probability of experiencing two such long-lived business expansions back-to-back would be less than 1 percent. In other words, it is very unlikely that the current situation can be ascribed to just good luck.

Second, policy innovations have been important, and the economy should remain less cyclical as long as these lessons stay learned. In particular, monetary policy generally has been more preemptive during the 1990s. As a result, inflation has been kept in check, and this has forestalled the type of aggressive monetary policy tightening that has precipitated economic down-turns in the past. And, by generating a large budget surplus, fiscal policy has freed up resources for the private sector. The control on spending and tax cuts implemented as part of the Budget Enforcement Act of 1990 played an important role in turning chronic budget deficits into surpluses.

Third, and most important, structural changes in the economy have oc-curred that have made it less vulnerable to forces that might precipitate an economic downturn. In particular, five major changes can be identified that have made the economy less cyclical than it was prior to the early 1980s:

—better inventory management

—globalization and trade liberalization

—more flexible markets for labor and capital equipment

—financial market deregulation and the growth of the capital markets at the expense of depository institutions

—improvements in corporate governance

Better Inventory Management

Just-in-time inventory management—an idea imported from Japan and then facilitated by improvements in information technology—has been an impor-tant structural change because it has made the economy less vulnerable to fluctuations in demand. Because businesses have better information, they can hold less inventory relative to sales and react more quickly to changes in demand. The use of just-in-time inventory management necessitates more frequent adjustments in production rates. But because the adjustments are made more often, they tend to be less severe in both magnitude and duration. As a consequence, the big swings in inventory accumulation rates that have often led to recessions in the past have become more muted, enabling the economy to avoid inventory-induced recessions.

The potential for just-in-time inventory management to smooth out busi-ness cycles is evident in the role inventory swings have played in previous recessions. Over the past three decades reduced inventory accumulation has always made a significant contribution to the decline in real gross domestic product (GDP), at times accounting for all of the fall in output, as shown in

Table 2-1. *How Inventory Swings Have Moderated*

Percent

Business Cycle		GDP decline	Inventory share of decline	Inventory swing as percentage of GDP
Peak	Trough			
April 60	February 61	−1.78	117.98	−2,19
December 69	November 70	−0.60	189.16	−1.13
November 73	March 75	−3.70	52.67	−1.95
January 80	July 80	−2.49	45.24	−1.13
July 81	November 82	−2.96	30.80	−0.91
July 90	March 91	−2.01	48.91	−0.98
Average		−2.26		−1.37

Source: Department of Commence. Author's calculations

table 2-1. And reflecting businesses' improved ability to manage inventories, the ratio of inventory to sales has been in a long secular decline, as shown in figure 2-1.

Globalization and Trade Liberalization

Globalization has been another important factor in muting the amplitude of swings in the business cycle. The U.S. economy has become much more open

Figure 2-1. *Just-in-Time Inventory Management in Action*

Inventory/Sales Ratio—Manufacturing

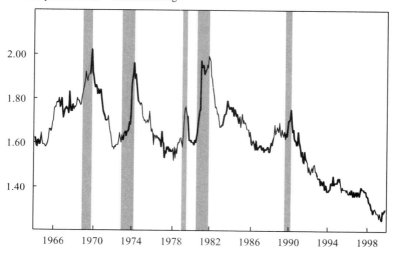

Source: Department of Commerce.

Figure 2-2.   *Import Penetration Climbs*

Percent

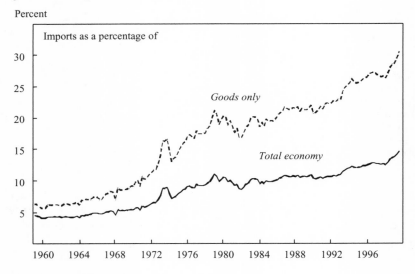

Source: Department of Commerce.

over the past few decades, and this has dampened cyclicality in two ways. First, when demand in the United States falters, an increasing proportion of the production adjustment is borne abroad rather than by U.S. producers, as illustrated by the rise in import penetration shown in figure 2-2. Second, although a more open economy means that the United States is more exposed to demand shocks from abroad, openness also dampens the volatility of production by diversifying the sources of demand more broadly.

The importance of a more open economy is clear: When the U.S. economy grows quickly, the net exports deficit tends to widen, siphoning off some of the strength; when it slows, the trade position improves, cushioning that decline. As shown in figure 2-3, the contribution of trade to real GDP growth is negatively correlated with the growth itself, demonstrating that the trade sector has a stabilizing influence on U.S. economic activity.

A more open economy has had the additional benefit of holding down inflation by increasing the competitive pressures on U.S. producers. For example, during the mid-1980s a strengthening dollar led to significant foreign competitive inroads that largely destroyed the informal domestic cartels between business and organized labor. Prior to this period, producers could afford to pay higher wages in exchange for labor peace because they could generally pass these increases along to consumers via higher prices. This

Figure 2-3. *Trade Sector Dampens GDP Swings*

Percent change, year ago

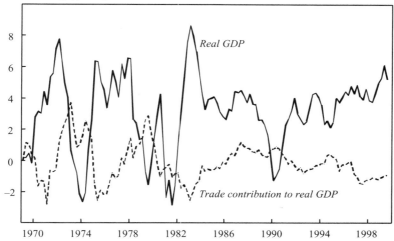

Source: Department of Commerce.

arrangement unraveled when increased foreign competition meant that domestic producers who raised prices would lose market share. The strategy of passing along higher labor costs to consumers was no longer viable. Over the past few years the gap between goods and services price inflation has widened because the strength of the dollar has increased foreign competitive pressure and constrained goods producers from raising prices.

Flexible Markets

Flexible markets for labor and capital equipment inputs have also helped to improve the U.S. economy's performance. On the labor side, the increased flexibility has occurred as businesses have become much more aggressive about restructuring their businesses. Since the mid-1980s the restructuring movement has spread from large integrated oil companies throughout manufacturing and is now under way in earnest among more regulated industries, such as telecommunications and electric power generation. The U.S. labor market has also become more flexible as employees, recognizing the change in the implicit labor contract with their employers, have become less loyal and more willing to change jobs for new opportunities. The growth of defined contribution plans, such as 401(k) plans, at the expense of defined benefit plans

Figure 2-4. *Capital Equipment Comes on Stream More Quickly*

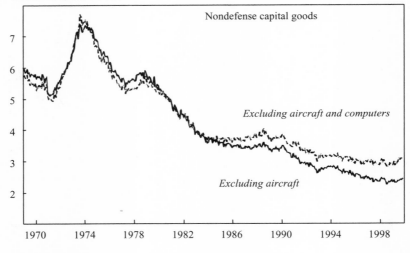

Months of unfilled orders

Source: Department of Commerce.

has also contributed to this process by reducing the cost of changing jobs. Two of the most visible aspects of heightened labor-market flexibility are the secular growth in the use of temporary workers and the increase in outsourcing of ancillary activities by U.S. companies.

On the capital equipment side, the big change has been a significant shortening of the time lag between orders and deliveries, as shown in figure 2-4. This is important because it has allowed capital equipment to be ordered and placed into production in time to break up bottlenecks that otherwise could have generated significant price pressures. In the past, a paper manufacturer might have ordered a new plant toward the end of the business expansion, only to find that the expansion had ended before the plant was operational. In this regard, besides helping to dampen inflationary pressures, the ability to deploy capital equipment more quickly has also helped to encourage greater investment. After all, the faster the equipment can be put into production, the lower the risk that it will not be fully utilized once put into place.

Financial Market Deregulation

The deregulation of the financial system is the fourth important structural change that has improved the U.S. economy's performance. Three aspects of this deregulation have been especially important: (1) the end of credit rationing to the housing industry that occurred with the elimination of interest-rate ceilings on deposits and the development of a market for securitized mortgages, (2) the growth of the capital markets at the expense of depository institutions, and (3) the shift to a floating exchange rate system.

The abolition of interest-rate ceilings on deposits and the development of the mortgage securitization market has made the housing sector much less cyclical by eliminating the credit rationing to housing that occurred when market interest rates rose above the ceilings set by Regulation Q (that is, the limits on the interest rates that depository institutions could pay on retail deposits). Before these changes, modest increases in interest rates above these ceilings severely curtailed the flow of funds to the mortgage market, as depositors pulled their monies out of banks and thrifts, forcing these institutions—then the primary conduit of financing to the housing industry—to cut off the flow of credit to housing. The development of mortgage securitization was important because it dramatically reduced the dependence of the housing industry on depository institutions for credit. Other types of companies, such as mortgage bankers, could originate mortgage loans knowing that these loans could be sold into the capital markets and would not need to be funded by deposits. As a result, annual fluctuations in housing starts have dropped by nearly two-thirds, while new home sales have lost more than one-third of their volatility. According to Department of Commerce figures, the variance housing starts declined from a standard deviation of 348,000 in the 1966–85 period to 139,000 for 1986–99; the variance of new home sales declined during the same periods from a standard deviation of 105,000 to 64,000 (both measures calculated using annual data).

Meanwhile, capital markets have gained share at the expense of financial institutions in intermediating flows of credit between borrowers and lenders, as shown in figure 2-5. This development has spurred significant innovations, such as mortgage securitization and the high-yield credit market, which have reduced the cost of borrowing. At the same time, the larger role played by capital markets has helped improve the conduct of economic policy, as these markets have often sent strong and clear signals about the credibility of economic policy. Thus, the costs of bad policy have become more visible, helping to push policymakers in the right direction.

A good example is the bond market's reaction to the Clinton presidency in early 1993. Bond market participants were skeptical about whether President Bill Clinton would follow fiscally conservative economic policies. As a result, bond yields remained high despite the persistence of considerable slack in the economy at that time. This created an incentive for a prudent fiscal course,

Figure 2-5. *Capital Markets Become Dominant*

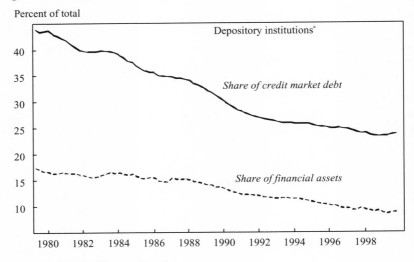

Percent of total

Source: Federal Reserve Board.
a. Commercial banks, savings institutions, and credit unions.

because the policymakers would reap a reward from credible deficit reduction in the form of lower long-term interest rates. On the monetary policy side, a similar episode occurred in 1994. For most of the year, bond-market participants worried that Federal Reserve policymakers were not tightening policy aggressively enough. Finally, when the Federal Open Market Committee voted to raise the federal funds rate target by seventy-five basis points (that is, .0075 percent) in one fell swoop in November, that was enough to reassure bond investors; as it turns out, this was enough to help the economy settle down to a more sustainable growth pace.

The transition to a floating exchange rate regime is a third aspect of financial market deregulation that has helped to increase competition and reduce the cyclicality of the economy. Now, a strong U.S. economy is often accompanied by a strengthening of the dollar, which increases foreign competitive pressure. This spurs productivity and dampens foreign demand for U.S. goods and services, helping to brake the pace of the economic expansion.

Improvements in Corporate Governance

The final important structural change has been a shift in corporate governance. In contrast to the 1960s and 1970s, managers' incentives are now closely aligned with shareholders' via the use of stock options and other

Figure 2-6. *Nonfarm Business Productivity Growth Climbs*

Percent change, year ago

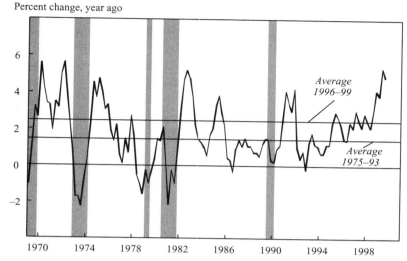

Source: Department of Labor.

remunerative devices tied to equity price performance. The shift in corporate governance has been important in increasing the efficiency of investment. Investment projects that fail to meet hurdle rates are not undertaken, raising the rate of return on investment. Instead, excess cash has been returned to shareholders via dividends and share buybacks.

The New Economy: Higher Productivity

The rise in productivity growth is the second aspect that characterizes the New Economy. Between 1973 and 1995 nonfarm business productivity rose at only a 1.4 percent annual rate. Since then there has been a sharp acceleration, with nonfarm productivity rising at a 2.5 percent annual rate between 1996 and 1999, and it is estimated that in 2000 productivity rose by more than 4 percent (see figure 2-6).

This upsurge in productivity growth has been driven primarily by two factors. First, a reduction in the cyclicality of the economy reduced the riskiness of new investment. As a result, businesses increased their investment spending sharply beginning in 1993. Second, the returns on new investment projects remained high despite the heavy spending. Thus the investment boom persisted for more than eight years—the longest boom in investment spending in U.S. history.

Figure 2-7. *Multifactor Productivity Has Increased*

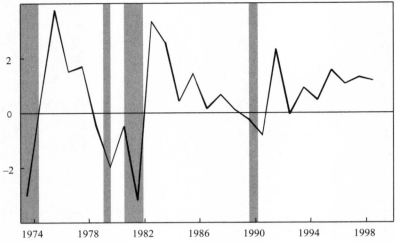

Percent change

1974   1978   1982   1986   1990   1994   1998

Source: Department of Commerce. Stephen Oliner. Daniel Sichel.

The consequence of this investment spending was a rise in productivity, which kept inflation low, made the Federal Reserve friendly, and sustained the business expansion. In essence, a virtuous circle was established in which investment helped sustain the business expansion, which thereby encouraged additional investment.

Productivity growth was aided by a fortuitous upswing in the pace of technological innovation. As a result, productivity got a boost not just from capital deepening (more capital per worker), but also from a rise in multifactor productivity (see figure 2-7). Multifactor productivity is the magic elixir of the economy. It measures the added output that is not due to adding more inputs. Although the level of multifactor productivity illustrated in figure 2-7 is not particularly high, the pattern through the business cycle is atypical. Rather than declining as the business expansion has become more mature, multifactor productivity growth climbed during the 1995–2000 period.

The New Economy and Social Insurance

What implications does the New Economy have for social insurance? In my view, there are four major implications.

First, by raising productivity, the New Economy has already helped to put Social Security on a more solid financial footing. Higher productivity growth has facilitated a more rapid rise in real wages and a lower sustainable unemployment rate. In my view, higher productivity growth pushes down the so-called nonaccelerating inflation rate of unemployment (NAIRU). Both factors have boosted the Social Security system's revenue faster than outlays.

The rise in trust fund assets has helped to push back the insolvency date of the Social Security Trust Fund (formally known as Old-Age, Survivors, and Disability Insurance), and the cumulative seventy-five-year payroll tax deficit has been cut. For example, from 1997 to 2000 the insolvency date was pushed back to 2037 from 2030, under the intermediate set of economic and demographic assumptions. Moreover, the cumulative long-run payroll tax deficit has been falling. For example, it declined to 1.89 percent in 2000 from 2.07 percent in 1999.

Second, if this productivity growth surge were to be sustained, then the costs associated with restoring the Social Security system to long-term solvency should prove to be affordable. After all, a rise in the sustainable trend of productivity growth to 2.5–3 percent per year from 1–1.5 percent leads to a doubling in the level of real GDP fifty years out. In that context, solving a deficit in the Social Security system of 1.89 percent of taxable payroll taxes should be relatively easy. Without benefit cuts, Social Security would consume a greater proportion of GDP. But if GDP is twice as high, this does not require absolute retrenchment in other areas, just a slightly smaller share for these areas of a much larger pie.

Third, the New Economy has been raising the expected benefit of the average Social Security recipient. The real level of benefits is closely related to real wage growth, and real wage growth is closely related to productivity growth. Higher productivity growth has thereby been raising prospective benefits even with no explicit change in the benefit formula. This suggests a second mechanism that could be used to restore Social Security to solvency: loosen the linkage between real wage growth and promised benefits. If benefits were adjusted upward in real terms more slowly than real wage growth, then the actuarial payroll tax deficit would shrink over time, eventually restoring the Social Security system to solvency.

Fourth, the New Economy has whetted the appetite of reformers of the Social Security system to invest in the U.S. equity market. The performance of the U.S. stock market has been spectacular since 1982. Over that time period, the average annualized return of large capitalization stocks has been 14.2 percent. As a result, there have been proposals to invest a portion of the Social Security Trust Fund assets in equities or to privatize a portion of the Social Security system by allowing individual recipients to invest in equities as they manage their own individual retirement accounts.

This last consequence should be viewed with great caution:

—Equity investment is no panacea for the financial health of the Social Security Trust Fund.

—Privatizing Social Security undermines the social insurance function of Social Security.

—Privatizing Social Security increases the risk that individuals might not have sufficient resources to fund an adequate standard of living upon retirement.

Although the equity market has performed spectacularly over the past two decades, there is no guarantee that this will continue in the future. In fact, if one assumes that some of the spectacular performance of the equity market represents a narrowing of the equity risk premium due to the economy's reduced cyclicality, then the expected return on equities is now lower than it was before. In 1999 the Goldman Sachs Economic Research Group studied the issue of investing a portion of the Social Security Trust Fund into equities and concluded that the higher expected returns from equity investment would not be sufficient to forestall insolvency.[1]

With respect to privatization, three difficulties can be seen. First, the higher rate of return often cited by advocates of privatization is overstated. It is an apples-to-oranges comparison since the low returns calculated for Social Security as it now operates occur, in part, because existing contributions have to help pay for the past unfunded liabilities of the program. Privatization advocates often conveniently ignore that the cost of these liabilities would also have to be incurred under a privatized system. Moreover, it is important to recognize that the higher expected return would not be a free lunch. It would reflect the increased risk of investing in private-sector debt and equities compared to government securities.

Second, privatization proposals would typically undermine the social insurance role of Social Security because the private savings portion of the new system would not perform any income redistribution function. Social Security is the predominant source of income for many senior citizens, and it is the primary reason why the poverty rate for seniors has fallen sharply over time. For example, currently the poverty rate for those sixty-five years and over is virtually identical to those eighteen to sixty-four years old. In contrast, in 1960 the proportion of seniors below the poverty line was more than three times what it is now and was double the poverty rate for those in the eighteen- to sixty-four-year-old group. Currently, under the Social Security retirement plan, low-

1. William C. Dudley et al., "An Analysis of Social Security Trust Fund Investment into Equities." *Global Economics Paper* no. 18, June 11, 1999.

income beneficiaries receive a benefit that is significantly larger in proportion to their lifetime contributions compared to higher-income beneficiaries. If the Social Security system were partially replaced by personal retirement accounts (PRAs), this income redistribution element of the current system would presumably be weakened.

Third, privatization could result in lower benefits for some recipients. For low-income contributors in the Social Security system, their PRAs might not be able to accumulate sufficient assets to generate an annuity stream large enough to offset that portion of the benefit lost from the current system. For others who simply invested unwisely or were unlucky in terms of timing, the value of the PRAs might not be large enough to offset the value of the reduced benefits paid out of the Social Security system.

Some Potential Problems

Up to now, the focus here has been on the benefits of the New Economy for social insurance. It is also important to recognize that there also are some potential problems.

Income distribution has worsened in the New Economy. The returns to education and job training have increased. Those without have fallen further behind. This implies a greater need for social insurance to support those left behind.

The New Economy has also been accompanied by a switch from defined benefit to defined contribution retirement plans. While this has considerable advantages for the workers that switch employment several times during their career, it also means that the risk of bad investment performance falls mainly on the individual rather than on the corporate sector. This underscores the need for a social insurance safety net in which risk is pooled in the New Economy.

Finally, the possibility remains that the New Economy attributes that have been identified may not persist. In particular, the economy may again become more cyclical or productivity growth may falter in the months and years ahead.

On this score, although the risk of recession over the near term has clearly climbed, it is unlikely that the economy will revert to the degree of cyclicality it had prior to 1983. The structural changes that have made the economy less cyclical appear well entrenched. For example, there does not appear to be movement toward dismantling the just-in-time inventory management system, moving away from free trade and globalization, or reregulating large sectors of the U.S. economy. That does not mean that recession will be avoided, however. The good luck of recent years may not hold. Moreover, policy mistakes will still happen either because of recognition lags, political constraints, or bad decisionmaking.

A bigger risk is that the apparent productivity miracle of recent years could turn out to be a mirage. Historical experience shows that productivity growth has a cyclical component. When growth climbs, productivity growth rises. It is possible that, as the economy slows, the productivity performance will be disappointing. In this case, the New Economy idea could be called into question.

Another risk is that the investment boom will turn into a bust. If part of the investment boom was based on too optimistic earnings expectations, investment spending could fall sharply once those earnings expectations were disappointed.

PART II

Issues in Social Security Reform

THE FIRST SESSION OF THE National Academy of Social Insurance conference on which this book is based focused on issues in Social Security reform. John Palmer, dean of the Maxwell School of Citizenship and Public Affairs at Syracuse University, opened this session by stating that Social Security is one of our country's largest social programs and clearly among our most successful and popular ones. Its continued vitality is essential to our national welfare. It provides basic economic support and health care financing for the elderly, survivors of covered workers, and the disabled. It embodies a social compact across the generations and promotes our individual and collective well-being. Future forms of Social Security clearly will have broad impacts.

The chapters and commentaries in part two examine this important social institution and shed light on key issues in the Social Security reform debate. In chapter 3 Richard Berner examines the extent to which private equity returns can be expected to continue at the levels of the recent past and what this implies for both the general health of the economy and for financing social insurance programs. In chapter 4 Kilolo Kijakazi evaluates how various demographic groups are faring under present Social Security arrangements and the prospects for those groups under various reform plans. More specifically, Kijakazi examines whether Social Security or other programs and policies need to be shored up to provide additional support to low-wage earners. In chapter 5 Fay Lomax Cook and Lawrence Jacobs contrast survey data with three popular claims about public opinion on Social Security.

3

Future Investment Returns and Social Insurance

Richard Berner

THE DISAPPOINTING STOCK MARKET returns in 2000 have not dissuaded investors or policymakers that equities offer superior returns for retirement saving. Indeed, many believe that future returns may be closer to those of the past two decades than to those seen over the long-term history of the stock market. Even more optimistically, some believe that real equity returns will exceed real bond returns by a significant margin for the foreseeable future.

I believe these forecasts are too optimistic and should not be used to guide public policy. But that is not to say that no role exists for change or for new vehicles for retirement saving. It may be an old-fashioned notion, but I expect future returns to revert back toward—although perhaps not to—those seen over the long term. This chapter first examines the factors behind the superior returns of the recent past. It is important to assess why returns are likely to be lower in the future and what might be expected in terms of the overall need for social insurance in the United States. Next, the risk-reward tradeoff in stocks, which is still relatively unfavorable despite the aforementioned factors, is explored. Currently markets have more than adjusted to this backdrop, valuations are still high, and invested capital is not free. Finally, the implications of these factors on the future of social insurance are examined.

Bullish Factors Underpin Rational Exuberance

A quick tour of recent investment performance should help investors and policymakers appreciate how unique and special it was. Three factors help explain why in the past two decades real equity returns have been superior to those of the previous fifty years, and why they far exceeded forecasts. First,

Figure 3-1. *Lower Inflation, Higher Real Yields*

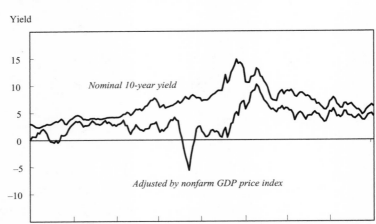

Apr. 1959 Feb. 1965 Dec. 1970 Oct. 1976 Aug. 1982 Jun. 1988 Apr. 1994

Source: Federal Reserve, Bureau of Economic Analysis.

better economic policies and a more flexible, open economy have reduced inflation and increased economic stability (see figures 3-1 and 3-2). The dramatic decline in inflation since 1980 reduced nominal interest rates and thus increased the valuation of future earnings and what investors were willing to pay for shares. Declining economic volatility also may have promoted a decline in the equity risk premium (ERP)—the real excess return over riskless assets that investors require to hold risky assets such as equities.

Those declines in inflation and economic volatility corrected an anomaly of the period between 1965 and 1980. In that high inflation period, investors accepted very low, or even negative, real returns on Treasury notes and correctly regarded stocks as highly risky assets. Subsequently, scarred by years of high inflation, they were reluctant to regard the initial decline in inflation as permanent, and inflation plunged by more than nominal yields. As a result, in the 1980s real risk-free yields rose back to levels not seen since the early part of the century. Since the yield on stocks is equal to the real risk-free yield plus the risk premium, this rise in real bond yields was consistent with a declining risk premium as part of the expansion in multiples.

Lower economic volatility also encouraged business investment by raising expected returns. In turn, investment in new technology increased the economy's sustainable rate of productivity and earnings growth (see figure 3-3). The

Figure 3-2. *More Stable Growth*

Standard deviation[a]

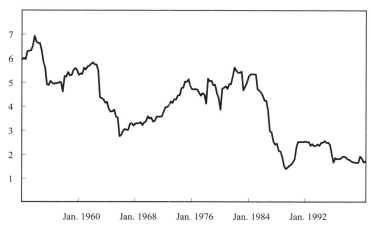

Jan. 1960   Jan. 1968   Jan. 1976   Jan. 1984   Jan. 1992

Source: Bureau of Economic Analysis.
a. Rolling 20-quarter standard deviation of growth in real GDP.

investment surge turned expectations into reality, as real returns on equity and assets for U.S. companies also increased.

The resulting virtuous circle produced spectacular results. Over the past ten years, real operating earnings per share for the Standard & Poor (S&P) 500 have grown at a 7.5 percent compound annual rate. In the previous fifteen years, real earnings grew at a 1.8 percent annual rate—or about at the long-term growth of real per share dividends since 1871. In addition, the advent of mutual funds and lower transactions costs has enabled investors to create diversified equity portfolios to capture the returns in indexes such as the S&P 500. These innovations may have reduced the gross equity risk premium by anywhere from 100 to 200 basis points.

Figure 3-4 sheds light on the equity risk premium. Using either the inverse of a modified Sharpe ratio or solving for the ERP on the assumption that stocks are fairly valued—two related, but far from identical metrics—calculations show that the ERP has steadily declined over the past two decades.

These factors together contributed to rational exuberance—investors bid up stock prices in anticipation of a permanently improved future as the more favorable and less risky economic and market backdrop became a more persistent phenomenon.

Figure 3-3. *Higher Growth in Both Productivity and Earnings*

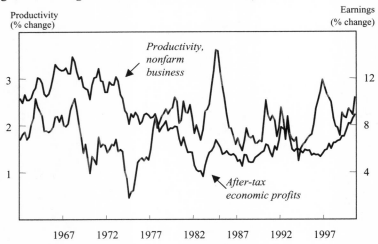

Source: Bureau of Labor Statistics; Bureau of Economic Analysis.

It Is More Than in the Price . . . Especially Risk-Adjusted

However past performance is no guarantee of future returns. Three considerations suggest that future returns are unlikely to match those of the past twenty years. Indeed, they are more likely to revert back toward historical levels, adjusted for transactions costs.

The first factor is that the upward valuation in equity prices of the past twenty years is not a sustainable trend. Rather, it has been a one-time adjustment to all the favorable fundamentals just discussed. During this period, equity returns have been much higher than the long-term average, thereby increasing the historical measured returns in the stock market and reinforcing the perception that higher returns could persist. Therefore, future returns likely will be lower—not higher—than in the recent past.

The good news is that stocks today are not significantly overvalued; in fact, many dividend-discount models suggest that they are somewhat undervalued. The price-earning (P/E) ratio for the S&P 500 has come down significantly from its peak as stock prices declined in 2000 and earnings growth continued; currently it stands at 22.3 on consensus operating earnings estimates, down from 26.0 in the early part of 2001. The bad news is that to return the S&P 500 P/E to 20.0—consistent with a 5 percent earnings yield or a 5 percent real return—per share operating earnings would have to grow by 18 percent from 2000 levels. (The 5 percent level is arbitrary, reflecting the 7 percent long-term historical

Figure 3-4.   *The Risk Premium: Two Calculations, One Answer*

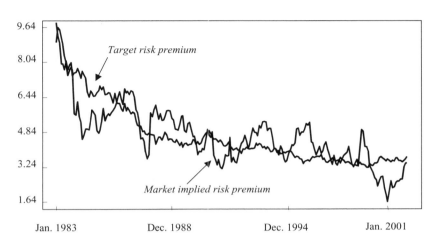

Source: Morgan Stanley Research Estimates.

return less 200 basis points to adjust for transactions costs.) Regardless of one's economic forecast, achieving that growth could take two years or more.

The second consideration pointing to lower future equity returns is that they will reflect the long-term *net* return—not the *gross* return—on investment. Optimists will ask: Doesn't sustainably higher growth in output and productivity argue for higher real returns? After all, today's real risk-free yields of 3–4 percent seem to suggest that all returns in today's economy should be higher than in the past.

In my view, faster productivity growth implies sustainably higher future gross returns. But permanently faster productivity growth also means that firms' cost of capital will also remain sustainably higher than in the past. As Jeremy Siegel of the Wharton School has noted on numerous occasions, per share earnings growth is determined by the reinvestment rate of the firm or the earnings yield less the dividend yield—*not* the rate of output growth. *Per share* earnings growth is unlikely to match the historical growth in earnings that investors are extrapolating from the current favorable economic backdrop.

Output growth cannot translate permanently into higher per share earnings growth because firms must raise capital through issuing more shares or debt to fund the investment in new technology that fuels the improvement in productivity and, thus, sustainable output growth. Higher real output growth would spur higher growth in earnings per share if it were associated with an increase

Figure 3-5. *Capital Deepening Fuels Productivity; Cost of Funding Growth Critical*

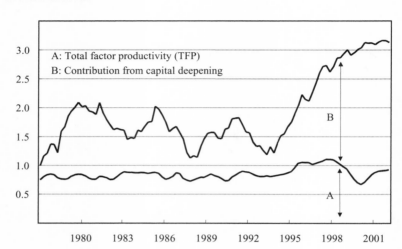

A: Total factor productivity (TFP)
B: Contribution from capital deepening

Source: Macroeconomic Advisers, LLC.

in total factor productivity (TFP) growth, but so far there is little evidence of such an increase.

Virtually all the research that explains the recent surge in labor productivity growth attributes it to capital deepening—in other words, firms are using more capital per worker and per unit of output (see figure 3-5). Technical innovations have continuously lowered the relative price of capital goods to promote this shift into labor-saving technology, but those innovations are merely maintaining, not increasing, the pace of TFP growth. Unless TFP growth increases and boosts the productivity of—and the net returns to—capital, growth in the economy will limit sustainable future earnings growth. Otherwise, profits as a share of gross domestic product would rise without limit. And sustaining high productivity growth rates requires continuous investment in new capital—*capital that must be financed.*

While all this sounds very much like Finance 101 laced with a course in graduate macroeconomics, these fundamental principles are of more than academic interest. According to my colleague Steve Galbraith, "The heady environment of the last few years led to a number of anomalies and excesses, but perhaps none more pronounced than investors' single-minded focus on growth—irrespective of cost."[1]

1. Steve Galbraith, "No More Free Lunches—Life After IPO à Go Go," *U.S. Investment Perspectives,* February 7, 2001.

From my vantage point, the recent experience of many telecommunications companies underscores the point. When investors were enamored of the growth potential in broadband and other revolutionary communications technologies, they focused only on long-term gross returns. But when the massive short-term funding needs of such companies became clearer, the calculus of net returns suddenly changed for investors. It is fair to say that the cost of capital for many such companies went effectively from zero to prohibitive in the space of six months. Put differently, we have been in a period of record high returns on capital combined with record low costs of capital—and assuming no tendency to revert to any mean seems ambitious to say the least.

The final reason to expect lower future equity returns is that even if the ERP has declined permanently, the recent increase in equity market volatility may appear to investors to represent an increase in the risk of owning stocks following two decades of declining risk. Just as investors bid up share prices in response to improving fundamentals over the past two decades, so may they now require higher yields to compensate them for the perceived higher risk of owning stocks. Indeed, my colleague Joe Mezrich notes that "the downward trend of the risk premium over the past 20 years or so was probably an important source of the great bull market of the end of the twentieth century. A declining risk premium as a source of bull-market fuel has been proposed by some as an empirical truth guiding stocks ever higher, as investors learn to grasp its significance for valuation. But the lesson [from figure 3-6] is that the U.S. stock market has been here before. Mean reversion is a market axiom that probably applies to the market risk premium as well."

Implication for Social Insurance: No Free Lunch

These considerations are highly relevant for considering the future of social insurance. If future returns are unlikely to match those of the recent past, investing a portion of the Social Security Trust Funds or a portion of the current flow of Social Security tax receipts in equities may not provide the hoped-for benefits that such investment aims at capturing. Eighteen months ago, three other analysts and I concluded that investing a major portion of the likely future flow of Social Security receipts in equities would not ensure the solvency of the trust funds through 2075. That is partly because achieving solvency would require assuming unreasonably high equity returns.[2]

2. Committee on Investment of Employee Benefit Assets, "Implications of Investing Social Security Funds in Financial Markets," June 25, 1999.

Figure 3-6.   *Risk-Adjusted Returns Still Unsustainably High*

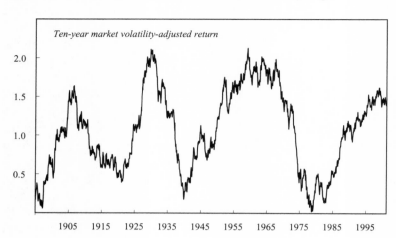

Source: MSDW Quantitative Strategies Group.

The fundamental macro point is that—as Federal Reserve chairman Alan Greenspan, Leah Modigliani, and I have each argued elsewhere—the process must create new national, and not just personal, savings.[3] Otherwise, the equities that displace Treasury securities in the Social Security Trust Funds would offset one-for-one the substitution in private portfolios of corporate securities by Treasuries. Such a shift would raise the amount of debt the Treasury must issue relative to demand and increase bond yields. Thus, ultimately, the crucial issue for Social Security's viability is how to increase national saving and allocate it between workers and retirees.

3. Leah Modigliani, "Social Security—$1 Trillion Is No Bonanza for Stocks," Morgan Stanley, November 20, 2000. Alan Greenspan, "Social Security," testimony before the Committee on the Budget, U.S. Senate, January 28, 1999.

4

Low-Wage Earners: Options for Improving Their Retirement Income

Kilolo Kijakazi

U NTIL RECENTLY, the Social Security reform debate has focused primarily on restoring long-term solvency to the program. The development of a non–Social Security surplus in the federal budget has made room in the debate for a discussion of initiatives to reduce poverty among elderly individuals, including low-wage earners, their spouses, and survivors. In December 2000 the White House estimated that the non–Social Security surplus would be approximately $2.4 trillion over a ten-year period; in January 2001 the Congressional Budget Office projected a non–Social Security surplus of $3.1 trillion. In reality, the amount of the surplus that will be available for new initiatives is significantly lower and closer to $2 trillion.[1] This lower level of available funds makes clear the need to set priorities for the use of the surplus and make hard choices about which initiatives should be funded. One of these priorities should be the reduction of poverty among elderly people.

Social Security has been accurately credited with being highly effective in reducing poverty among the elderly. The program is responsible for removing more people from poverty than all other government programs combined. Yet the labor experiences of some individuals place them at risk of being poor when they grow old, even after receiving Social Security. People of color, women, and other low-wage earners are among those at risk.

I wish to thank Wendell Primus, director of the Income Security Division at the Center on Budget and Policy Priorities, for his ideas and insights in developing this chapter and Bob Greenstein, executive director, for his thoughtful review and comments. I greatly appreciate the work of Lynette Rawlings and Allen Dupree, who provided extensive assistance in analyzing the data. This paper was written and presented prior to the enactment of the Economic Growth and Tax Relief Reconciliation Act of 2001 that costs more than $1.7 trillion from 2001 to 2011, including interest payments, and consumes the majority of the eleven-year non–Social Security surplus.

1. Greenstein (January 4, 2001, pp. 1, 2).

In 1998 the poverty rate for individuals age sixty-five and older declined from approximately 46 percent before Social Security to 12 percent after the receipt of Social Security (and other social insurance benefits).[2] About 3.8 million seniors were poor after receiving Social Security.[3] Those at greatest risk of experiencing poverty during their old age include unmarried women, African Americans, and Latinos. Twenty percent of elderly unmarried women were in poverty in 1998. This rate equals the poverty level for children in this country. The proportions of Latino and African American elders who were impoverished were even greater, at 24 percent and 30 percent, respectively.

Improvements can be made within Social Security to reduce poverty further among elderly individuals in these and other communities. Social Security alone, however, cannot compensate completely for the labor-market factors that result in lower retirement income for people of color and women. A three-pronged approach is needed to raise the income levels of low-income seniors. In addition to improvements in Social Security, changes also are needed in the Supplemental Security Income (SSI) program—a means-tested program that serves the elderly, blind, and disabled. An initiative also is needed to help low-wage workers accumulate retirement savings on top of Social Security.

At Risk: African Americans, Latinos, and Women— Their Working and Senior Years

Social Security benefits are driven by a worker's earnings history. A worker's level of attachment to the labor market and the wages earned each year will determine whether the worker will be eligible for Social Security and the amount of benefits the worker will receive. On average, people of color and women have had different work experiences than white men. In comparison to white workers and men as groups, African American, Latino, and female

2. It is important to note that the measure of poverty used throughout this report, unless otherwise specified, differs from the official poverty measure. In this report, the phrase "before (or without) Social Security" means the poverty rate was determined by counting only income from social insurance such as federal pensions and unemployment insurance benefits, not Social Security or any means-tested benefits. The phrase "after Social Security" means income from social insurance and Social Security was counted; benefits from means-tested programs were not. By contrast, the official poverty measure counts all cash income, including all government cash benefits. Benefits not in the form of cash (for example, food stamps) are not counted.

3. Using the official poverty measure, about 3.4 million elderly individuals were poor in 1998. Eighteen percent of elderly, unmarried women, 26 percent of elderly African Americans, and 21 percent of elderly Latinos were poor compared to 8 percent of white elderly.

Figure 4-1.   *Unemployment by Race, Ethnicity, and Gender, 1999*

Percent

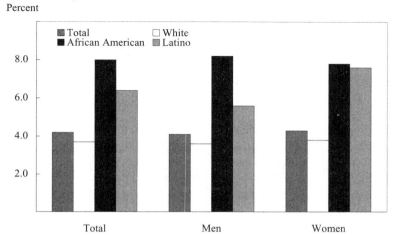

Source: U.S. Department of Labor, Bureau of Labor Statistics, *Employment and Earnings*, January 2000, table 5, p. 172.

workers are more likely to experience unemployment, hold part-time positions because they are unable to find full-time jobs, and work in relatively low-paid occupations.

Unemployment and Involuntary Part-Time Employment

The unemployment rate for the overall civilian noninstitutionalized population was lower in 2000 than it had been in thirty years.[4] Unemployment rates for African American workers were the lowest since 1969. These lower rates are good news and, if sustained, will contribute to higher retirement incomes for workers, especially younger workers, who are able to reap the benefits of reduced joblessness.

Individuals for whom a substantial proportion of their employable years has already passed, however, will have their retirement income determined primarily by past employment experiences. Moreover, even with today's low unemployment rates, unemployment is more widespread among people of color than among non-Latino whites (hereafter referred to as whites). The unemployment rate for non-Latino African Americans (hereafter referred to as African Americans) in 1999 was nearly two times greater than that of white workers (see figure 4-1). The jobless rate for Latino workers, although substantially lower

4. *Budget of the United States Government, Fiscal Year 2001* (2000, p. 23).

Figure 4-2. *Involuntary Part-Time Workers as a Percentage of Employed Persons, by Race, Ethnicity, and Gender, 1999*

Percent

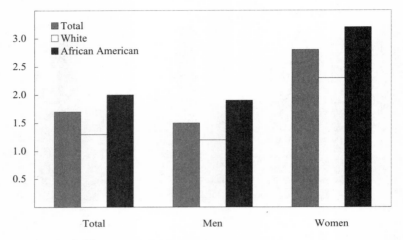

Source: U.S. Department of Labor, Bureau of Labor Statistics, *Employment and Earnings*, January 2000, table 5, p. 172 and table 8, p. 175.

than that of African Americans, was more than one and one half times higher than the rate for white workers. White and African American women experienced unemployment at rates similar to their male counterparts, while Latinas were more likely to experience unemployment than Latino men.

Workers who are looking for employment and are unable to find full-time positions may be forced to settle for part-time jobs. Such positions are sometimes referred to as *involuntary part-time jobs*. Figure 4-2 indicates that African Americans, both men and women, are more likely to be employed as involuntary part-time workers than whites. Some 2.3 percent of employed African American men are involuntary part-time workers compared to 1.2 percent of employed white men. Similarly, 3.2 percent of employed African American women are involuntary part-time workers compared to 1.9 percent of employed white women. Unfortunately, these data are not available for Latino workers.

Occupations and Earnings

The occupations in which people of color and women are overrepresented tend to be less well paid in comparison to other occupations. African American and Latino workers made up 11.3 percent and 10.3 percent, respectively, of people employed in 1999.[5] African Americans made up a disproportionate share of people employed in service occupations (18.3 percent) and of operators, fabricators, and laborers (15.7 percent). By contrast, African Americans accounted for only 8 percent of managerial and professional occupations. (It should be noted that there are exceptions, such as social work. African Americans made up 24.2 percent of the workers in this profession.)

Latino workers constituted 15.2 percent of those employed in service occupations and 16.6 percent of operators, fabricators, and laborers. Latinos also were disproportionately represented in the farming, forestry, and fishing occupations (23.1 percent). Latinos made up 12.8 percent of workers in the overall category of precision production, craft, and repair occupations, but some of the specific occupations within this category had a much larger share of Latino workers. For example, Latino workers accounted for 32.2 percent of the drywall installers and 20.4 percent of the concrete finishers (African Americans represented 25.2 percent of the concrete finishers). Conversely, Latino workers made up only 5 percent of managerial and professional occupations.

Women accounted for 46.5 percent of people employed in 1999. However, they made up the majority of workers in the technical, sales, administrative, and support occupations (63.8 percent) and service occupations (60.4 percent).

The median weekly earnings for service occupations, in which people of color and women were overrepresented, was $336 in 1999, compared to $797 for managerial and professional jobs (see table 4-1). The lowest paid field was farming, forestry, and fishing, in which Latino workers have a disproportionately high representation.

Given this distribution of workers across occupations, it is not surprising that the median earnings for people of color were lower than those of white workers. In 1999 median weekly earnings were $573 for white full-time workers, $445 for African American full-time workers, and $385 for full-time Latino workers (see table 4-2).

For each group, the wages of full-time women workers were substantially less than the wages their male counterparts received. Women of color had the lowest earnings. Latinas earned 55 percent of the wages earned by white men, and African American women earned 64 percent. By comparison, white women earned 76 percent, African American men earned 77 percent, and Latino men earned 64 percent. The wages of women of color represented a

---

5. U.S. Department of Labor, Bureau of Labor Statistics (2000, tables 10 and 11, pp. 177–83).

Table 4-1. *Earnings by Occupation*

U.S. dollars

Occupation	Median weekly earnings
Total	549
Managerial and professional speciality	797
Technical, sales, and administrative support	488
Service occupations	336
Precision production, craft, and repair	594
Operators, fabricators, and laborers	429
Farming, forestry, and fishing	331

Source: U.S. Department of Labor, Bureau of Labor Statistics, *Employment and Earnings*, January 2000, table 39, pp. 213–18.

larger share of their male counterparts' wages than the wages for white women represented of white men's wages. African American women and Latinas received median earnings equal to 84 percent and 86 percent of median earnings for African American and Latino men, respectively. These figures reflect the higher earnings of white men compared to the earnings of people of color, for both men and women, and also compared to the earnings of white women.

Impact of Employment Experience on Retirement Income for People of Color

One cumulative effect for people of color of higher unemployment and heavier concentration in lower-paying jobs is lower retirement income. African Americans and Latinos who are age sixty-five and older are much less likely to have income from pensions and investments than white elders. Social Security, consequently, is a key source of retirement income for African Americans and Latinos. The program is particularly beneficial to these com-

Table 4-2. *Median Weekly Earnings for Full-Time Workers, by Race, Ethnicity, and Gender, 1999*

U.S. dollars

Workers	Total	White	African American	Latino
Total	549	673	445	385
Men	618	638	488	406
Women	473	483	409	348

Source: U.S. Department of Labor, Bureau of Labor Statistics, *Employment and Earnings*, January 2000, table 37, p. 212.

Figure 4-3.   *Percentage of Elderly and Their Spouses with Income from Specified Sources, by Race and Ethnicity, 1994–98*

Percent

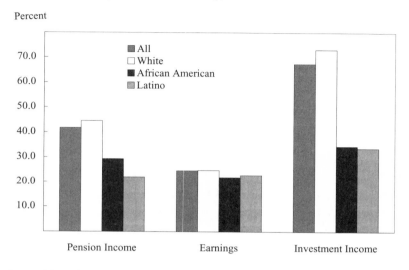

Source: These data are the result of analyses by the Center on Budget and Policy Priorities using 1994–98 Current Population Survey data collected by the Bureau of the Census.

munities because it is designed to ameliorate some of the negative effects of the labor market for low-wage workers.

Low-wage and part-time workers are less likely to have pension coverage, and when they retire they are less likely to have pension income. Given the higher concentration of people of color in low-wage and part-time jobs, the probability that these workers will have pension income when they grow old is lower than that of elderly white people. A recent study by the General Accounting Office found that employees with lower wages are much less likely to have pension coverage than those who are more highly paid.[6] The findings showed that in 1998 some 81 percent of employees earning less than $20,000 lacked pension coverage, more than twice the rate for employees with incomes of $20,000 or more (34 percent). The study also found that 79 percent of part-time workers and workers who were employed for part of the year lacked pension coverage, nearly double the proportion of full-time employees without coverage (40 percent). Figure 4-3 indicates that, upon reaching age sixty-five or older, only 29.3 percent of African Americans and 22 percent of Latinos received pension income during 1994–98 compared to 41.7 percent of white elders.

6. General Accounting Office (2000, pp. 13, 14).

The modest average wage levels offered by the occupations in which African American and Latino workers are overrepresented make it harder for these low-wage earners to set aside savings and investments for retirement. As shown in figure 4-3, the proportion of white elders who receive income from investments (including interest, dividends, and rent) during the 1994–98 period was more than twice as great as the proportion of elderly people of color.

Some elderly also have income from earnings. The average share of elderly with earnings is approximately the same across racial and ethnic groups.

The lower probability that elderly people of color will receive pension or investment income relative to elderly white people places greater importance on Social Security as a foundation for retirement income. Not surprisingly, Social Security made up a larger share of income for elderly people of color than for elderly white people. From 1994 to 1998 both African American and Latino seniors relied on Social Security for approximately 44 percent of their total income, while white elders and their spouses received about 37 percent of their total income from Social Security (see figure 4-4).

Unlike other sources of retirement income, Social Security is designed to help compensate for some of the employment experiences that impact low-wage workers. It does this through a progressive benefit formula that helps low-wage workers in two ways. First, the benefit formula provides low-wage workers with Social Security benefits that equal a substantially higher percentage of their preretirement earnings than is the case for high-wage workers. Social Security replaces 56 percent of the average lifetime earnings for low-wage workers, compared to 28 percent for workers with earnings equal to at least the maximum wage subject to payroll tax.[7] The second way the benefit formula is made progressive is through the determination of a worker's average lifetime wage. (The average lifetime wage is the amount of earnings to which the progressive formula is applied.) In determining the average lifetime wage, the forty years in which workers had their highest earnings are reviewed and the five lowest years of earnings (including years with no earnings) are eliminated. Since people of color are more likely to experience unemployment and involuntary part-time employment, the elimination of the five lowest years helps to raise the average earnings figure used to compute their Social Security benefits.

The employment experiences of people of color and the consequent impact of these experiences on retirement income result in a substantially higher probability of poverty for elderly African Americans and Latinos compared to

---

7. *The 2000 Annual Report of the Board of Trustees of the Federal Old-Age and Survivors Insurance and Disability Insurance Trust Funds* (2000, table III.B.5, p. 185).

Figure 4-4.　*Share of Income from Specific Sources, by Race and Ethnicity, 1994–98*

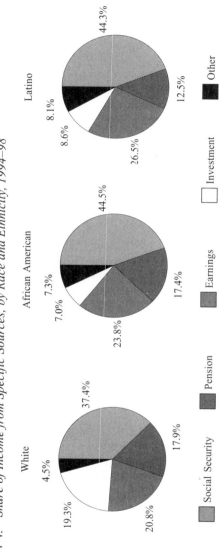

White

4.5%
37.4%
19.3%
20.8%
17.9%

African American

7.3%
44.5%
7.0%
23.8%
17.4%

Latino

8.1%
44.3%
8.6%
26.5%
12.5%

Social Security　Pension　Earnings　Investment　Other

Source: These data are the result of analyses by the Center on Budget and Policy Priorities using 1994–98 Current Population Survey data collected by the Bureau of the Census.

Table 4-3. *Poverty Rates among the Elderly before and after Social Security, 1998*

Percent

	White	African American	Latino
Before Social Security	44.6	63.2	54.9
After Social Security	8.9	29.9	23.9
Reduction in poverty	35.7	33.3	31.0

Source: These data are the result of analyses by the Center on Budget and Policy Priorities using 1998 Current Population Survey data collected by the Bureau of the Census.

Note: The measures of poverty in this figure differ from the official poverty measure, which lists rates as 8.2 percent for elderly whites, 26.1 percent for elderly African Americans, and 21 percent for elderly Latinos after Social Security. Reduction in poverty is the difference between the before and after entries.

the white elderly. Social Security, and its progressive benefit formula in particular, ameliorate the adverse effects of higher unemployment, lower wages, greater susceptibility to unreported earnings, lower rates of pension coverage, and lower levels of savings and investments. However, Social Security alone cannot fully offset the combination of these factors.

Table 4-3 illustrates that, before Social Security is counted, some 44.6 percent of white elderly individuals had income below the poverty line in 1998, as compared to 63.2 percent of African American elderly people and 54.9 percent of the Latino elderly. Social Security greatly reduces poverty for all three groups, cutting the proportion of elderly people who are poor by more than half for each group. A large proportion of each group is lifted out of poverty by Social Security, but approximately 30 percent of elderly African Americans and 24 percent of Latino elders remain poor.

Impact of Employment Experience on Retirement Income of Women

Women are more likely than men to be poor as they grow older. Without Social Security, 51.4 percent of women age sixty-five and older would have been poor in 1998, compared to 39.7 percent of elderly men.[8] As a result of receiving Social Security benefits, the proportion of the elderly living in poverty was reduced to 14 percent for women and approximately 8.4 percent for men. Social Security greatly reduced poverty for both genders, but the percentage of women remaining in poverty was nearly twice the percentage of elderly men.

8. These data are the result of analyses by the Center on Budget and Policy Priorities using 1999 Current Population Survey data collected by the Bureau of the Census.

Figure 4-5. *Percentage of Elderly Women and Their Spouses with Income Specified Sources, by Marital Status, 1994–98*

Percent

Source: These data are the result of analyses by the Center on Budget and Policy Priorities using 1994–98 Current Population Survey data collected by the Bureau of the Census.

Not only does financial well-being vary by gender, but the financial well-being of women also differs markedly by marital status, race, and ethnicity. Among elderly women, unmarried women are at greater risk financially largely because they are less likely to receive income from pensions, earnings, or investments than married women. Married women have access to their husbands' income from pensions, earnings, and investments in addition to their own income from these sources.[9] Figure 4-5 shows the percentage of elderly women who received retirement income from each of these sources during the period from 1994 to 1998. Some 51.6 percent of married women and their spouses had pension income, while only 21.4 percent of widows, 27.1 percent of divorced or separated women, and 38.9 percent of never married women had pension income.

The receipt of earnings and investment income by elderly women also varies by marital status. Figure 4-5 shows that elderly married women were

9. For the purposes of this chapter, the income of individuals age sixty-five and older and the income of their spouses (where relevant) are included, whether or not the spouse also is sixty-five or older. Counting the income of non-elderly spouses better captures the total cash income available to the elderly. See also Butrica, Iams, and Sandell (1999, p. 21).

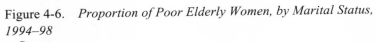

Figure 4-6.   *Proportion of Poor Elderly Women, by Marital Status, 1994–98*

Percent

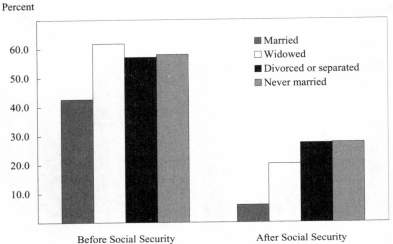

Before Social Security   After Social Security

Source: These data are the result of analyses by the Center on Budget and Policy Priorities using 1994–98 Current Population Survey data collected by the Bureau of the Census.

Note: The measures of poverty in this figure differ from the official poverty measure. The poverty rates "before Social Security" were determined by counting only income from social insurance, such as federal pensions and unemployment insurance benefits, but not Social Security or any means-tested benefits. The poverty rates "after Social Security" were determined by counting income from social insurance and Social Security; benefits from means-tested programs were not counted. By contrast, the official poverty measure counts all cash benefits. Benefits not in the form of cash (for example, food stamps) are not counted.

more likely to have income from earnings than elderly women who were widowed, divorced or separated, or never married. Elderly married women were much more likely to have investment income than any other group. Women of every marital status were more likely to have investment income than earnings or pensions.

Given the lower rate of receipt of income from pensions, earnings, and investments by elderly unmarried women compared to elderly married women, one might expect unmarried women to have a higher incidence of poverty than married women. Figure 4-6 illustrates that this is the case. Before counting Social Security, 61.8 percent of elderly widows were poor during the period from 1994 to 1998, as were 57.1 percent of divorced and separated women, and 58 percent of women who never married. By comparison, 42.7 percent of married women were poor before receiving Social Security.

Social Security reduced poverty substantially for women of every marital status. Figure 4-6 shows that the program lowered poverty rates for married women to just 6 percent and cut the percentage of women in poverty by more than half for each unmarried category. (Using the official poverty measure, poverty rates were 18.6 percent for elderly widows, 23.9 percent for divorced and separated women, 24.7 percent for never-married women, and 5.1 percent for married women.)

Several components of the Social Security system help to remove women from poverty. The progressive benefit formula favors women because they have lower lifetime earnings than men, on average, due to a combination of labor-market factors. Women are disproportionately represented among low-wage workers. While women accounted for about 48 percent of all workers in 1996, they made up 58 percent of minimum-wage workers.[10] Women also were more likely to be part-time workers. In 1999 some 62 percent of all part-time workers were women.[11] Women also spent twelve fewer years in the labor market than men, on average. This absence from the labor market often reflects time spent caring for family members.[12] The progressive benefit formula helps to counteract the effect of these employment experiences by replacing a larger share of preretirement earnings for women than men, on average. In December 1997 women received 53 percent of all Social Security retirement and survivors benefits but paid only 38 percent of payroll taxes.[13]

Women also are assisted more than men by the annual cost-of-living adjustment (COLA). Social Security benefits are increased each year to keep pace with inflation. The COLA is particularly important for women because they have a longer average life span than men. A sixty-five-year-old woman is expected to live to eighty-four, while a sixty-five-year-old man's anticipated life span is eighty.[14] Unlike most other sources of income for women, which dwindle as they grow older, Social Security benefits rise each year to maintain their purchasing power.

Auxiliary Social Security benefits, including spouse and survivors benefits, provide another fundamental source of protection for many married and widowed individuals, typically women. An elderly married woman can receive either a benefit based on her own earnings history or a spouse benefit equal to 50 percent of her husband's benefit, whichever is larger. (If the husband were the lower-wage earner, he would qualify for the spouse benefit instead of the

10. Mishell, Bernstein, and Schmitt (2000, table 2.41, p. 189).
11. U.S. Department of Labor, Bureau of Labor Statistics (2000, table 22, p. 198).
12. National Economic Council Interagency Working Group on Social Security (1998).
13. Porter, Larin, and Primus (1999, p. 25).
14. Centers for Disease Control (1997, table 6-1, p. 7).

Figure 4-7.   *Percentage of Elderly Women and Their Spouses Receiving Pension Income, by Race, Ethnicity, and Marital Status, 1994–98*

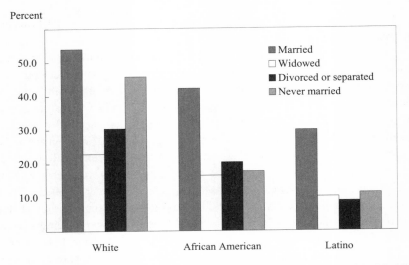

Source: These data are the result of analyses by the Center on Budget and Policy Priorities using 1994–98 Current Population Survey data collected by the Bureau of the Census.

wife.) An elderly woman who outlives her husband can receive a survivors benefit that is based on her own earnings history or she can receive an amount equal to 100 percent of her deceased husband's benefit, if that is greater than the benefit based on her own earnings.

Social Security is favorable to women across marital categories, but it is most advantageous to married women. The Social Security income a married couple receives is at least 150 percent of the benefit for the higher earner.

ELDERLY WOMEN OF COLOR

In addition to examining the financial well-being of elderly women by marital status, it is important to examine this population by race and ethnicity. When this is done, it becomes clear that women of color are some of the elderly individuals at greatest risk of having insufficient retirement income.

The proportion of women with pension income varies by race, ethnicity, and marital status within each racial or ethnic group (see figure 4-7). Elderly white women were the most likely to receive pension income in 1994–98, followed by African American women and Latinas. Married women had the highest rate of pension income regardless of race or ethnicity. (If a married

Figure 4-8. *Percentage of Elderly Women and Their Spouses Receiving Income from Earnings, by Race, Ethnicity, and Marital Status, 1994–98*

Percent

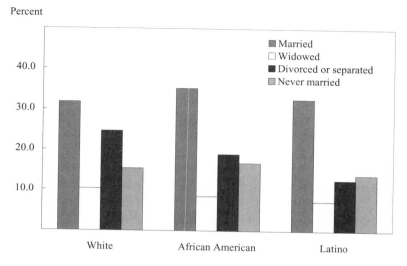

Source: These data are the result of analyses by the Center on Budget and Policy Priorities using 1994–98 Current Population Survey data collected by the Bureau of the Census.

woman does not have pension income, but her husband does, his pension income counts as income for her.) Among elderly white women, widows lagged behind women in all other marital categories in receipt of pension income. For African Americans and Latinas, the percentages of widows, divorced or separated women, and never-married women who received pension income were about the same.

Income from earnings was received by a comparable proportion of white, African American, and Latina women within most marital categories (see figure 4-8). That is, the percentage of married women with income from earnings was similar for whites, African Americans, and Latinas. (Income from earnings for married women includes their husbands' earnings. Women who do not work will have earnings income counted if their husbands have earnings.) The same was true for widows and never-married women. There was greater variation among divorced or separated women; the percentage of such women with income from earnings was only about half as high among elderly Latinas as among elderly white women.

Receipt of income from investments—income from interest, dividends, and rent—varied markedly by race and ethnicity, as well as marital status (see

Figure 4-9.   *Percentage of Elderly Women and Their Spouses Receiving*
Investment Income, by Race, Ethnicity, and Marital Status, 1994–98

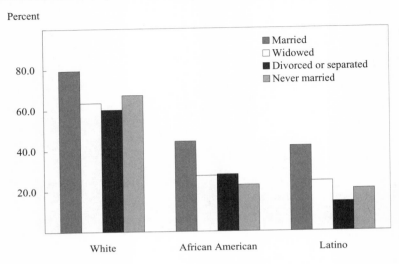

Source: These data are the result of analyses by the Center on Budget and Policy Priorities
using 1994–98 Current Population Survey data collected by the Bureau of the Census.

figure 4-9). Elderly white women were much more likely to have investment income than African Americans or Latinas. In addition, the proportion of elderly married women who had investment income was notably higher than the proportion of unmarried or separated women. (If a married woman does not have investment income of her own, but her husband has investment income, then her husband's income is counted as her investment income.) The likelihood of having investment income ranged from nearly 80 percent for elderly, married, white women to less than 20 percent for divorced or separated Latinas.

Social Security is by far the most prevalent source of income for women compared to other sources of funds. Figure 4-10 shows that from 1994 to 1998 Social Security accounted for an average of 42.6 percent of the income for elderly white women and their spouses, 52.5 percent of the income of African American women and their spouses, and 48 percent of the income of Latinas and their spouses. For each of these groups, the share of income received from Social Security was almost twice as great as the share of income from any other source.

The relatively lower rates and levels of income received from pensions, earnings, and investments by elderly women of color coincide with higher

Figure 4-10. *Average Share of Elderly Women's Income from Specific Sources, by Race and Ethnicity, 1994–98*

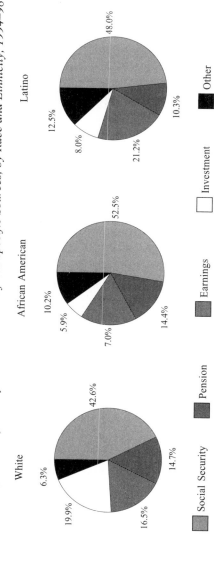

Source: These data are the result of analyses by the Center on Budget and Policy Priorities using 1994–98 Current Population Survey data collected by the Bureau of the Census.

Figure 4-11.   *Percentage of Poor Elderly Women, by Race and Ethnicity, 1994–98*

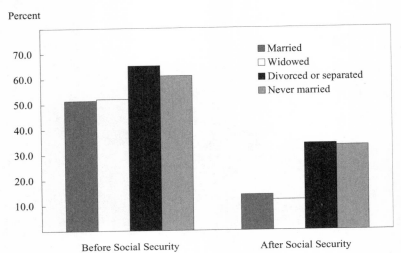

Percent

Before Social Security   After Social Security

Source: These data are the result of analyses by the Center on Budget and Policy Priorities using 1994–98 Current Population Survey data collected by the Bureau of the Census.

Note: The measures of poverty in this figure differ from the official poverty measure. The poverty rates "before Social Security" were determined by counting only income from social insurance, such as federal pensions and unemployment insurance benefits, but not Social Security or any means-tested benefits. The poverty rates "after Social Security" were determined by counting income from social insurance and Social Security; benefits from means-tested programs were not counted. By contrast, the official poverty measure counts all cash benefits. Benefits not in the form of cash (for example, food stamps) are not counted.

rates of poverty compared to elderly white women. Before receiving Social Security, 52 percent of elderly white women were poor during the period from 1994 to 1998, compared to 65.1 percent of African American women and 61.1 percent of elderly Latinas (see figure 4-11).[15] Social Security benefits reduce poverty by nearly 50 percent for African American women and Latinas and by substantially more than that for white women. However, the proportion of elderly women remaining in poverty was nearly three times greater for African Americans (34.1 percent) and Latinos (33.3 percent) than for whites (12.1 percent). (Using the official poverty measure, poverty rates were 30.3 percent, 27.2 percent, and 11.1 percent for elderly African American women, Latinas, and white women, respectively.)

15. These data are the result of analyses by the Center on Budget and Policy Priorities using 1994–98 CPS data collected by the Bureau of the Census.

Need for Improvement in Retirement Income for Low-Wage Earners

The previous sections illustrate that poverty among the elderly may be related to a number of employment experiences and to an individual's gender and marital status. The varied paths that may lead workers or spouses to poverty in the later years of their life suggest that several improvements are needed to enhance the economic status of the aged poor. Several proposals to reduce elderly poverty by improving Social Security and SSI and by facilitating the accumulation of retirement savings by low- and moderate-wage earners are examined in the remainder of this chapter.

Improvements in Social Security should be made within the larger context of extending the solvency of the program. Otherwise, program improvements would exacerbate the program's long-term financing problems. The existence of a non-Social Security budget surplus can help in this regard if a portion of that surplus is transferred to Social Security, but there is a finite amount of resources available to enhance the financial well-being of the elderly. Thus improvements in one aspect of Social Security may require trade-offs in another area. Hard choices are likely to be required in determining how best to make changes in Social Security.

Options for Improving Social Security

A number of proposals have been advanced for improving the Social Security program to enhance the financial well-being of elderly individuals who are susceptible to poverty. The first proposal would assist elderly widows (or widowers) by increasing the survivors benefit they receive. While this has been a popular proposal, it does not affect the financial circumstances of individuals who have never married or were married for less than ten years. Other methods of reducing poverty through Social Security also are needed. One approach is to design an effective minimum benefit. A well-designed minimum benefit has the potential to reach a sizeable proportion of workers who would otherwise be poor, regardless of their marital status.

Increase the Survivors Benefit for Elderly Widows

One of the points in a woman's life when she may become more susceptible to poverty is upon the death of her husband, because her income is likely to decline. Under current law, a married couple may receive 100 percent of the higher earner's benefits plus a spouse benefit equal to 50 percent of the higher earner's benefit. Alternatively, the spouse may receive benefits based on his or her own earnings history if this would result in benefits higher than the spouse benefit.[16] Under current law, a woman whose husband dies receives 100 percent of her own benefit or 100 percent of the deceased spouse's benefit, whichever is higher.

The decline in Social Security benefits after the death of a spouse can be substantial. For example, Mr. and Mrs. Jones both worked and had earnings histories that were comparable in terms of years worked and wages received. When they retired, they received 100 percent of Mr. Jones's benefit plus 100 percent of Mrs. Jones's benefit, based on her own earnings record. Mr. Jones received a Social Security benefit of $1,000 per month, and Mrs. Jones received $950 per month. Upon Mr. Jones's death, Mrs. Jones began receiving 100 percent of Mr. Jones's benefit, or $1,000, since it was higher than her own benefit. But she no longer received her previous benefit of $950. Social Security income to her household was reduced 49 percent.

On first glance, one might conclude that a reduction of almost 50 percent is appropriate since these benefits would provide for the needs of only one person rather than two. But this is not the case. Although some of Mrs. Jones's household expenditures will decline, such as food and clothing, others may not. Housing and utility expenses would not necessarily change much after her husband died, unless she moved to accommodations with a lower cost. Similarly, other expenses (for example, property taxes) are fixed regardless of the number of people living in the household.

A goal of strengthening the Social Security system should be to limit the reduction in benefits to a percentage comparable to the percentage that living expenses decline when a spouse dies. One method of approximating the change in the cost of living between a one-person elderly household and a two-person elderly household is to use the difference in the amount of income needed by each type of household to reach the official poverty line. The poverty line for an elderly one-person household equals 79 percent of the poverty level for an elderly two-person household.[17] Richard Burkhauser and Timothy Smeeding examined survivors benefits and recommended that these benefits should equal 75 percent of the poverty line for a two-person elderly household.[18]

16. The calculation of the spouse benefit also takes into account a woman's earnings history. If a spouse has an earnings history, his or her benefits are calculated based on this history and if the resulting amount is less than 50 percent of the primary worker's benefit, the spouse's benefit is "topped up" to an amount equal to 50 percent of the primary worker's benefit.
17. Dalaker and Naifeh (1998).
18. Burkhauser and Smeeding (1994, p. 12).

Based on this research, a majority of members of the 1994–96 Advisory Council on Social Security recommended that the elderly survivors benefit be raised to an amount equaling 75 percent of the *combined* benefits received by the couple prior to the death of one spouse.[19] Another way of saying this is that the surviving spouse's benefit should not be reduced by more than 25 percent of the couple's combined benefit. Following the preceding example, when Mr. Jones dies, Mrs. Jones would receive 75 percent of the combined benefit of the couple, or $1,463—that is, $0.75 \times (\$1,000 + \$950)$—rather than the $1,000 she would receive under present law. In this case the benefit is 46 percent larger than it would be under current law.

Increasing the Social Security benefit for widows, while helpful, would not be sufficient by itself to adequately reduce poverty among the elderly. Receipt by a surviving widow of 75 percent of the Social Security benefit that the couple was receiving will remove some widows from poverty but leave many other low-income beneficiaries below the poverty line. Women who never marry or were married for less than ten years, as well as various other low-wage earners—including many African American and Latino men—would not be assisted by this change.

Moreover, raising the survivors benefit without making additional improvements for other beneficiaries would create inequities.[20] Benefits would rise for surviving spouses who may not have worked or may have had brief work histories. For instance, an affluent married woman who did not work outside the home would receive an increased survivors benefit when her husband died. By contrast, a never-married woman or a woman married less than ten years who worked outside the home for low wages all her adult life would not gain from an improvement in the survivors benefit. Unless the increased survivors benefits are restricted to low- and moderate-wage earners, fairly well-to-do spouses who have not worked outside the home would receive an increase in benefits while low-wage workers who never married or were married less than ten years would not be aided.

Additional steps are needed to raise the income of poor, single elderly women and other low-wage earners. The long-term fiscal imbalance in Social Security places constraints, however, on the number and magnitude of the enhancements that can be made. If additional steps are to be taken to raise the benefit levels of other elderly individuals who are at risk of poverty, the

19. *Report of the 1994–1996 Advisory Council on Social Security, Volume I: Findings and Recommendations* (1997).
20. Urban Institute (2000, p. 14).

improvements in survivors benefits should be targeted to those who are financially vulnerable.

Design an Effective Social Security Minimum Benefit

One method of improving benefits for low-wage earners that is not dependent on a worker's marital status is the addition of an effective minimum benefit. Prior to 1982, a minimum benefit was paid to workers with low-earnings histories. This minimum exceeded what they would have received under the regular benefit formula.

Not all workers who have low earnings records are low-wage earners, however. There are many reasons workers may have low earnings records. Some types of workers who may have low earnings records include:

—workers who held minimum-wage jobs their entire careers

—domestic workers, farm workers, and other workers who have not received credit for all their earnings because employers (or the workers, if self-employed) failed to report them

—state and local workers who received most of their earnings in non-Social Security-covered employment but also were employed for a modest number of years in the private sector

—individuals who did not work much but are well off, such as spouses of high-wage earners

Although the minimum benefit was intended for workers who had low wages, it did not distinguish well between low-wage earners and individuals who were relatively well off and had low earnings records due to other factors. For this reason, and to reduce program costs, the minimum benefit was eliminated in January 1982 for workers who initially became eligible for Social Security after December 1981.[21] What remains is a small special minimum benefit.

The special minimum benefit was designed for low-wage workers with steady work histories.[22] The special minimum is intended to provide these workers with a higher monthly benefit than they would receive under the regular benefit formula. The regular benefit formula is computed by selecting the thirty-five years in which workers had their highest earnings, adjusting the wages in previous years for increases in average wages in the U.S. economy in subsequent years, and determining the average annual wage over these thirty-five years. (Workers who had fewer than thirty-five years of earnings covered by Social Security will have zeros added for the years in which they were not

---

21. Social Security Administration (1997, § 716).

22. For a more extensive discussion of the special minimum benefit, see Olsen and Hoffmeyer (forthcoming).

covered.) This annual average wage then is divided by 12 (for the twelve months in the year) to get the worker's average indexed monthly earnings (AIME). The Social Security benefit formula is applied to the AIME to determine the monthly Social Security benefit that workers will receive if they begin to draw benefits at the full benefit age, now sixty-five years and four months. This monthly benefit amount is known as the worker's primary insurance amount (PIA). In 2000 the PIA was determined by taking 90 percent of the first $531 a month of the AIME, 32 percent of the AIME between $532 and $3,202 (if the worker's AIME exceeds $531), and 15 percent of any amount above $3,202 in the worker's AIME.[23]

The special minimum benefit calculation can result in a higher benefit level for low-wage earners than the workers would receive under the formula just described. To qualify for the special minimum benefit, workers must meet certain criteria. They must have earned an annual amount equal to at least 15 percent of the "adjusted maximum taxable wage" in at least ten years;[24] in 2000 workers had to earn $8,055 to pass this threshold.[25] If this requirement is met, workers would receive about $29 per month for each year they worked (and earned at least the required amount) above the ten-year minimum, up to a maximum of $580 per month.[26] (Those who worked twenty or more years beyond the ten-year threshold would qualify for a special minimum benefit of $580 a month, which is the sum of $29 per year paid for each of the twenty years exceeding the ten-year threshold.) This maximum amount is lower than the 1998 poverty threshold for individuals age sixty-five and older. The annualized benefit amount is $6,960, which was substantially lower than the 1998 poverty line of $7,818.

Relatively few workers qualify for the special minimum benefit. In 1998 only 154,043 people—or 0.35 percent of all Social Security beneficiaries—received the special minimum benefit.[27] This provision is not making a substantial contribution to reducing poverty among the elderly. A number of proposals have been offered to improve or replace the special minimum benefit.

---

23. These dollar amounts are indexed to the Consumer Price Index and are increased annually. See *The 2000 Annual Report of the Board of Trustees* (2000, p. 204).

24. The adjusted maximum taxable wage is what the annual maximum wage subject to the payroll tax would have been in the absence of statutory increases in the maximum under amendments enacted in 1977. See Social Security Administration (1999, table 2.A12, p. 48).

25. *The 2000 Annual Report of the Board of Trustees* (2000, p. 205).

26. *The 2000 Annual Report of the Board of Trustees* (2000, p. 205).

27. Social Security Administration (1999, table 5A8, p. 197; table 5A1, p. 181).

Wendell Primus of the Center on Budget and Policy Priorities has developed an alternative minimum benefit proposal designed to improve benefits for steady minimum-wage earners without paying an unintended bonus to individuals who are not low income but have low levels of Social Security–covered earnings.

The calculation for the Primus minimum benefit proposal would substitute the benefit formula's multiple replacement rates of 90 percent, 32 percent, and 15 percent with a single replacement rate of 75 percent. (The regular benefit formula would not change for workers who do not qualify for the minimum benefit.) The 75 percent rate would be applied to a special AIME calculated solely for the purposes of determining the minimum benefit. Under the alternate AIME, the amount of earnings that would be counted for any month would be capped at an amount equal to 45 percent of the AIME for a worker who earned the average wage throughout his or her work life. In 1998 this amount was $973 per month. Regardless of how much a worker earned in a month, only up to $973 would be counted when calculating the alternative AIME. Thus the largest amount that could be paid through the minimum benefit formula would be $730 a month, or 75 percent of $973. If the minimum benefit formula results in a higher benefit than the regular formula, the worker would receive the minimum benefit amount. If the minimum benefit formula led to a lower benefit than the regular benefit formula yields, the worker would receive the regular benefit.

The Primus proposal can best be understood by comparing the work histories and benefits of two types of workers. (See box 4-1.) Ms. Hudson worked for thirty-five years at minimum-wage jobs and earned a total of $374,500 over this period. Under current law, her benefit would be $562 per month. By contrast, she would receive $669—or a 19 percent increase—under the Primus proposal. Mrs. Cleary worked for ten years and received above-average wages. Her total earnings also were $374,500. But the amount that she earned each month—$3,121—exceeded the cap on earnings that qualify for inclusion in the minimum benefit formula. Only $973 per month (45 percent of the average wage worker's AIME) would be counted when computing her special AIME. This would yield a minimum benefit of $209 per month. Since this amount is lower than the benefit of $562 per month that Ms. Cleary would receive using the regular benefit formula, her benefits would be calculated under the regular benefit formula. (See box 4-1.)

This approach should reduce poverty without undermining the link between work history and benefit levels. The PIA for workers who earned the minimum

28. Social Security Administration (1999, table 2.A26, p. 71).

Box 4-1.   *Primus Proposal Is Targeted to Low-Wage Steady Workers*

—Ms. Hudson: Steady Minimum-Wage Worker

—Ms. Hudson earned $10,700 per year for 35 years, or $374,500.

—Her average indexed monthly earnings (AIME) would be $892 per month [($374,500 / 35 years) / 12 months].

—Her 1998 primary insurance amount under the regular formula would be $562 per month (90 percent of the first $477 per month and 32 percent of the remaining $415 per month).

—Under this minimum benefit proposal, she would receive $669 per month (75 percent of $892). This is a 19 percent increase over the current formula.

Ms. Cleary: Above-Average-Income Worker with Few Years of Employment

—Ms. Cleary earned $37,450 per year for 10 years, or $374,500.

—The amount of earnings used in the formula to get the special AIME for minimum benefit purposes is capped at 45 percent of the AIME of the average wage earner. The AIME of the average wage earner was $2,163 in 1998. The cap is $973 per month (45 percent of $2,163).

—Only $973 would be counted for each month worked. The rest of the earnings are above the threshold and are not counted for purposes of this minimum benefit.

—Her total countable earnings over her 10 years of work would be $116,676.

—Her special AIME for minimum benefit purposes would be $278 per month [($116,676 / 35 years) / 12 months].

—Her benefit calculated under the minimum benefit proposal would be $209 (75 percent of $278). Since this amount would be less than her benefit amount based on the current formula, she would get the current benefit, or $562.

---

wage throughout their work lives was $623 in 1998.[28] This equals $7,476 per year, or 4 percent less than the poverty line of $7,818 for a person sixty-five or older in 1998. The largest minimum benefit for a worker under this proposal would be $8,760, which exceeds the poverty line by 12 percent. At the same time, this amount is well below the average wage earner's PIA of $11,772 per year.[29] It is likely that many low-wage earners receiving the minimum benefit would get less than $8,760, since low-wage earners are more likely to experi-

29. Social Security Administration (1999, table 2.A26, p. 71).

ence bouts of unemployment and may have fewer than thirty-five years of employment. Workers who have worked more or earned higher wages and paid more in payroll taxes would still receive substantially higher benefits than those receiving the minimum benefit.

The proposal also channels the increased benefits to steady low-wage earners by capping the level of earnings a worker can have and still qualify for this minimum benefit. A worker with an earnings record equal to that of a minimum-wage worker, but with substantially fewer years of work, would not get an increased benefit under this proposal.

This proposed minimum benefit formula is a substantial improvement over the current special minimum benefit. Furthermore, it targets limited resources to steady-wage earners most likely to be in poverty by directing the increased benefits to low-wage earners and disqualifying workers who have low levels of earnings covered by Social Security but are not really low-wage workers. At the same time, the design of the proposal maintains the link between work history and benefits.

The drawback of this proposal is that workers with the lowest earnings would not be affected. That is, workers with AIMEs that do not exceed the threshold for the 90 percent replacement rate would continue to get the regular benefit. These workers could include individuals with several bouts of unemployment and domestic workers or farm workers with unreported earnings.

Additional Changes Needed

Increasing the elderly survivors benefit and establishing an effective minimum benefit should improve the economic status of a sizeable number of impoverished African American and Latino seniors, as well as unmarried women of all racial and ethnic backgrounds. Even with such changes, however, a considerable number of the elderly—especially elderly people of color, women, and other low-wage earners—will remain poor. Additional changes within the Social Security program may not prove feasible, given the long-term fiscal imbalance the program faces. Fortunately, Social Security is not the only program upon which seniors can rely. The SSI program also is available to low-income elders. The next section presents proposals that would further reduce elderly poverty by making improvements in that program.

Improvements Needed in the Supplemental Security Income Program

In addition to enhancing Social Security benefits to improve the economic status of elderly people of color and women with low incomes, there are other steps that can be taken that will not cause Social Security costs to rise. Rather than relying solely on Social Security to improve the financial well-being of elderly people who remain in poverty, adjustments can be made in the SSI program. Established through legislation proposed by President Richard Nixon and enacted in 1972, the SSI program is a means-tested, federally administered program that provides cash benefits for low-income aged, blind, and disabled individuals. Certain changes in SSI could improve the income of elderly individuals with very low incomes without exacerbating the long-term financial imbalance in Social Security.

There is a second reason to modify the SSI program. If surviving spouse benefits are improved and minimum benefits are established in Social Security, as recommended earlier, some widows who would have been eligible for SSI under the current Social Security rules would be made ineligible as a result of their increased Social Security income. Each additional dollar of Social Security income received by SSI participants results in a dollar reduction in their SSI benefits. For some SSI participants, the increased Social Security benefit would push their income over the SSI income eligibility limit. This is of particular importance because Medicaid eligibility for the elderly is tied to receipt of SSI in most states. (In some states, Medicaid eligibility criteria are more restrictive than SSI eligibility rules. States also have the option of setting eligibility criteria that are more liberal than SSI eligibility rules.) Thus a widow whose Social Security benefit rises as a result of an increase in the surviving spouse benefit might lose SSI eligibility and, as a result, also lose her Medicaid coverage. Adjustments should be made in the SSI program to address unintended interactions resulting from improvements in Social Security.

Finally, changes in SSI are needed in the rules governing the type and amount of assets that an individual may own and still be eligible for the program. There is a need to both modernize the requirements for the assets that individuals may own and adjust the asset limits for inflation.

Fortunately, the Social Security Administration (SSA) released a report in 2000 that does an excellent job of describing the components of SSI that are used to determine program eligibility and benefit levels.[30] The report demonstrates that several components of the SSI eligibility and benefit structure have eroded because they have not adequately kept pace with inflation. The SSA report presents options for modernizing the program in these areas along with cost estimates. Some of the information in the SSA report is incorporated in this section.

30. Social Security Administration (2000, p. 9).

SSI's General Income Exclusion

While some elderly women become poor as the result of an event such as the death of their husbands, a study by Sharmila Choudhury and Michael Leonesio of the Social Security Administration showed that the most important determinant of poverty among elderly women is their poverty status *prior to reaching old age*.[31] Women who experience spells of poverty at younger ages are more likely to be poor when they get older. Women who did not experience poverty are not likely to become poor when they are elderly, even after a catastrophic event. This research suggests that women who have been in the labor market but earned low wages and were poor prior to retirement are more likely to be in poverty when they are elderly. Similarly, women who were married to men with low wages may be at greater risk of poverty when they grow old.

The SSI program assists elderly and disabled men, women, and children who are susceptible to poverty. To be eligible for the program, an individual must be at least sixty-five years old, blind, or disabled. Nearly one-third of SSI beneficiaries were sixty-five or older in 1998.[32] Program eligibility is also based on income and asset limits. SSI is intended to be a "program of last resort," and nearly all other income that an applicant receives is considered before SSI eligibility is determined.[33] Under the rules governing the federal SSI program, individuals and couples are eligible for federal SSI benefits if their countable incomes fall below the maximum monthly federal SSI benefit, which is $530 for individuals and $798 for couples in 2001.

Not all income is counted in determining SSI eligibility. Twenty dollars per month of income is excluded.[34] This is called the general income exclusion (GIE) and was originally intended to reward *past* work by ensuring that beneficiaries receiving Social Security income would have a higher total income than beneficiaries without income from Social Security.[35] An additional $65 of *earned* income plus 50 percent of any remaining earnings also are excluded. This is called the earned income exclusion and is intended to encourage *current* work by providing a higher total income to low-income beneficiaries with earnings.

By way of example, an elderly individual whose only source of income is a Social Security benefit of $450 a month would be eligible for an SSI benefit of

---

31. Choudhury and Leonesio (1997).

32. Social Security Administration (1999, table 7.E4, p. 303).

33. Committee on Ways and Means (1998).

34. Income from other federally funded means-tested programs is not excluded. See Social Security Administration, *Income and Resource Exclusions, op. cit.,* p. 8.

35. Social Security Administration (2000, p. 9).

$100. (The Social Security benefit of $450 minus the $20 GIE equals $430. When the $430 is subtracted from the SSI maximum benefit of $530, the remaining $100 is the SSI benefit amount.) In 1998 some 61 percent of elderly SSI beneficiaries received Social Security retirement benefits and, consequently, received the $20-a-month general income exclusion.[36]

The SSI program is an important source of income for the elderly, but the program can be made more effective in reducing poverty by increasing this GIE. The $20 GIE was established when the original SSI law was enacted in 1972. It has not been adjusted since then to keep pace with inflation. The SSA's recent report states:

> The $20 GIE amount as enacted in 1972, is now worth $5 [in 2000 dollars]. Therefore its significance as recognition of past work is substantially reduced. As a result, the value of SSI benefits has declined for many beneficiaries. In 1974, the $20 exclusion represented over 14 percent of the $140 Federal benefit rate (FBR) for an individuals. The Federal benefit rate is the maximum SSI benefit level. By contrast the $20 exclusion is less than 4 percent of the current $512 FBR for an individual.[37]

The consequence of maintaining such a low GIE is that retirees who worked steadily but earned low wages could have a combined Social Security and SSI benefit that is only slightly larger than the SSI benefit they would have received if they had not worked at all. For example, Ms. Harris worked hard all her adult life but earned the minimum wage throughout her work life (see box 4-2). The jobs she held were physically arduous, and she retired at age sixty-two in 1998. Ms. Harris's only source of income was Social Security until she turned sixty-five and became eligible for SSI benefits. Her Social Security benefit is $539 in 2001.[38] Therefore, she receives an SSI benefit of $11 per month, making her total income $550. Had Ms. Harris not worked at all and had no Social Security income, she would have received an SSI benefit of $530. Her hard work reaped *only $20 more per month* than not working, and her income level fell well below the poverty threshold. This is inconsistent with the bipartisan goals of encouraging and rewarding work.

36. Social Security Administration (2000, p. 8).
37. Social Security Administration (2000, p. 8).
38. In 1998 Ms. Harris would have received a Social Security benefit of $498. Her benefit would increase annually as a result of the cost of living adjustment and would be approximately $539 in 2001. See Social Security Administration (1999, table 2.A.26, p. 71).

Box 4-2. *Effect of the Low Supplemental Security Income General Income Exclusion on Total Income*

Ms. Harris, a minimum-wage worker, retired at sixty-two and began to receive Social Security benefits. At age sixty-five, she became eligible for SSI.

Social Security benefit	$539
SSI general income exclusion	− 20
Adjusted gross income	$519
Maximum SSI benefit	$530
Adjusted gross income	−519
SSI benefit	$ 11
Social Security benefit	$539
SSI benefit	+ 11
Total income	$550

If Ms. Harris had not worked at all, she would have received a benefit of $530 from SSI.

A principle that has enjoyed bipartisan support is that individuals who work should not be poor and those who work should be significantly better off than those who do not. Toward that end, Presidents Reagan, Bush, and Clinton and members of Congress have successfully pursued the development and improvement of programs such as the earned income tax credit to increase the income of the working poor. In that same vein, individuals who have worked hard but received low wages for the better part of their working lives—and individuals (typically women) who have taken time out of the labor market or worked part time to raise children or care for an infirm elderly relative—should not be consigned to a life of poverty in their later years.

One means of raising the level of income for individuals with a history of low wages is to increase the GIE.[39] Raising the GIE would reduce the amount of Social Security income counted in determining SSI eligibility and benefits. Consequently, SSI benefits for poor Social Security beneficiaries would rise. If the GIE were adjusted to account for inflation since 1972, the updated amount would be approximately $80.[40] A GIE of this level would substantially improve

39. Social Security benefits make up 91 percent of the unearned income received by SSI participants to which the general income exclusion is applied. Other sources of unearned income include veterans benefits, railroad retirement, black lung benefits, employment pensions, workers' compensation, and support from absent parents. See Committee on Ways and Means (1998, p. 300).

40. Congress passed legislation in 1972 that established the SSI program and designated 1974 as the initial year of benefit payments. Congress also established a cost-

the financial well-being of low-income elderly individuals. According to the SSA report:

> Such an increase would enable those SSI beneficiaries who are also receiving Social Security benefits and other unearned income to retain more of their SSI benefit, and would restore the exclusion to its original congressional intent by more tangibly rewarding past work.[41]

The $80 general income exclusion also would preserve SSI eligibility and, therefore, Medicaid coverage for some elderly women if the Social Security survivors benefit were increased (see box 4-3).

Beyond raising the GIE from $20 to $80 per month, the GIE should be automatically indexed to the Consumer Price Index (CPI) to prevent future erosion of the exclusion by inflation. Adjusting the GIE for inflation each year would make the treatment of the exclusion consistent with the treatment of the SSI maximum benefit.

The SSA report estimates that the cost of increasing the $20 GIE to $80 to compensate for erosion of the exclusion since 1972 would be $1.9 billion in 2001 and $20.7 billion over a ten-year period (see table 4-4). The cost of both increasing the exclusion to $80 and indexing it for inflation would be $24 billion over the next ten years. These costs will be reduced considerably if an increase in the GIE is coupled with an improvement in the Social Security survivors benefit. Improvement of the survivors benefit, by itself, will reduce the SSI costs.

In addition to this cost, Medicaid costs will rise as the number of newly eligible SSI participants rises, since SSI participants are categorically eligible for Medicaid in most states. No official cost estimates are currently available, but for the purpose of this analysis, estimates have been generated based on Medicaid costs for aged, blind, and disabled enrollees.[42] The federal share of the Medicaid cost for acute care would be approximately $1.75 billion per year if the SSI improvement were made by itself without an accompanying im-

---

of-living adjustment for SSI benefits, so that maximum benefit levels rise each year in tandem with the Consumer Price Index. No similar adjustments were made for the general income exclusion. Comparable treatment of benefit levels and the general income exclusion would require an adjustment in the GIE to reflect inflation since 1972. See Social Security Administration (1999, table 2.B1, p. 90). See also Social Security Administration (2000, pp. 4, 8–9).

41. Social Security Administration (2000, p. 9).

42. Estimates were derived using data provided by the Urban Institute on 1997 Medicaid costs for aged, blind, and disabled enrollees who were receiving cash assistance.

Box 4-3.   *Example of Social Security's Impact on Supplemental Security Income and Medicaid Eligibility*

Mrs. Carver is the widow of a minimum-wage worker who retired at age sixty-two. When the Carvers turned sixty-five, they became eligible for SSI and had the following income:

Social Security benefit	$791
SSI benefit	+ 25
Total income	$816

When Mr. Carver died, the following adjustments were made to Mrs. Carver's income:

Social Security benefit	$539
SSI benefit	+ 11
Total income	$550

If Mrs. Carver received a Social Security survivors benefit equal to 75 percent of what the couple would have received, she would receive a $593 Social Security benefit, but she would become ineligible for SSI and consequently could lose Medicaid coverage. By contrast, if the SSI general income exclusion were raised to $80, Mrs. Carver would maintain her eligibility for SSI and Medicaid, and she would have a larger total income bringing her closer to the poverty line (although she still would be below it).

Social Security benefit	$593
SSI general income exclusion	− 80
Adjusted gross income	$513
Maximum SSI benefit	$530
Adjusted gross income	−513
SSI benefit	$ 17
Social Security benefit	$593
SSI benefit	+ 17
Total income	$610

provement in Social Security benefits.[43] (The Medicaid cost estimate provided here is intended only to give a sense of the magnitude of the costs and should not be interpreted as an exact cost level.) The Medicaid cost would be lower if improvements in the Social Security survivors benefits also were made.

43. Acute care includes costs for inpatient and outpatient care, physicians, lab work, x-rays, prescriptions, and payments to managed care providers. Medicaid also covers long-term care, but these costs are not included in this estimate.

Table 4-4. *The Supplemental Security Income Cost of Increasing the General Income Exclusion*
Billions of U.S. dollars

Options	2001	2001–05	2001–10
Increase the GIE to $80	1.9	10.4	20.7
Increase the GIE to $80 and index to CPI	1.9	11.2	24.0

Source: Social Security Administration, *Report on Supplemental Security Income: Income and Resource Exclusions and Disability Insurance Earnings-Related Provisions*, March 2000, p. 60.

The cost of raising the GIE would need to be weighed against other demands on the budget. (As noted, the cost of improvements to the SSI program will not impact the solvency of Social Security. SSI is funded through general revenue.) If cost proves to be a barrier, the GIE could be raised from its current level of $20 to a level of less than $80.

Raise the Asset Limit for SSI

In general, eligibility for the SSI program is limited to individuals with no more than $2,000 in assets and couples with no more than $3,000. Some assets—such as the beneficiary's home, reasonably valued household goods and personal items, a car used for employment or to obtain medical care or transport a disabled individual, and life insurance with a face value of less than $1,500—are not counted.

The limits for countable resources for SSI have eroded since the program's inception because they have not kept pace with inflation. The limits were set at $1,500 for individuals and $2,250 for couples in 1972, when legislation establishing the program was passed. These limits took effect in 1974, when the program was implemented. In 1984 Congress enacted legislation that raised the thresholds, based on the schedule shown in table 4-5.

There has not been an increase in the SSI resource limits in more than a decade, although the cost of living climbed approximately 38 percent between 1989 and 2000. An adjustment could be made in one of two ways. The resource limit could be increased by a flat amount, as was done in the past. Alternatively, the asset limit could be increased each year based on the change in the CPI. This would be consistent with the treatment of SSI benefits, which are updated using the CPI. If these thresholds were adjusted to reflect inflation since 1989, the resource limit for individuals would rise to $2,845 in 2001, and the limit for couples would be $4,268. Adjusting for inflation since 1989 would not entirely correct for inflation that occurred since the asset limits were first established in 1972. If the thresholds were adjusted for inflation since 1972, the asset limit for

Table 4-5.   *Schedule of Increases in the Supplemental Security Income Asset Limits Enacted in 1984*

Effective Date	Individual	Couple
January 1, 1987	$1,800	$2,700
January 1, 1988	1,900	2,850
January 1, 1989, and thereafter	2,000	3,000

Source: Social Security Administration, *1997 Social Security Handbook* (U.S. Government Printing Office, 1997), § 2167.

individuals would be $5,959 in 2001, and the limit for couples would be $8,939.[44]

The Social Security Administration's report on income and resource exclusions shows that increasing the resource limits to $3,000 for individuals and $4,500 for couples would cost only a relatively small amount—$7 million in 2001, $65 million over the next five years, and $152 million over the next ten years (see table 4-6). Increasing the resource limit to $6,000 for individuals and $9,000 for couples would cost $89 million in 2001, $814 million over the next five years, and $1.8 billion over the next ten years. (This does not include increased costs in Medicaid.)

Excluding Defined Contribution Plan Balances from the SSI Asset Test

Defined contribution plans, or retirement plans that are based on contributions of workers and employers to individual accounts, represent a rapidly growing share of employer-sponsored pension plans. These accounts also may be part of forthcoming Social Security and pension reform legislation. Such legislation could take the form of retirement savings accounts (RSAs) outside the Social Security system, as proposed by the Clinton administration, or individual accounts that replace a portion of Social Security, as proposed by several members of Congress and President George Bush.[45] If such accounts are created, Congress and the president should exempt balances in individual accounts from counting as assets in SSI and other means-tested programs.[46]

44. These estimates are based on the CPI-U-XI (Consumer Price Index experimental series created by the Bureau of Labor Statistics, U. S. Department of Labor) rather than the CPI. The CPI-U-X1 more accurately captures changes in living costs and mortgage rates prior to 1983. See U.S. Census Bureau (1999, Appendix D).

45. Retirement savings plans and individual accounts are discussed in more detail in the next section.

46. See also Greenstein (2000). Larin and Primus (1999).

Table 4-6. *Supplemental Social Income Asset Limit Options*
Millions of U.S. dollars

Limit Options	2001	2001–05	2001–10
$3000/$4,500	7	65	152
$6,000/$9,000	89	814	1,800

Source: Social Security Administration, *Report on Supplemental Security Income: Income and Resource Exclusions and Disability Insurance Earnings-Related Provisions*, March 2000, p. 60.

Otherwise such accounts can have the perverse effect of making low-income workers and retirees ineligible for SSI, Medicaid, and food stamps.

This is not simply a problem that would arise if the federal government established new forms of individual retirement accounts and failed to exempt them from asset tests. The problem already exists with regard to employer-provided, defined contribution pension plans such as 401(k) plans. Assets in these plans are counted as assets in SSI in most states, in Medicaid. Low-income individuals with such accounts generally are ineligible for means-tested benefits unless they deplete their accounts prematurely. This problem has its origins in the 1970s, when the primary asset limits in the major means-tested benefit programs were developed. At that time, employer-sponsored, defined contribution plans were rare, especially for low-wage workers. (Most workers with pension coverage participated in defined benefit plans.) The asset tests in most means-tested benefit programs were designed to exclude "inaccessible" resources and count "accessible" resources. Pension benefits that workers have accrued in defined benefit plans are considered "inaccessible," but amounts in defined contribution plans—which feature individual accounts—are generally considered accessible even if there is a penalty for early withdrawal.

In recent years, an increasing number of employers either replaced defined benefit plans with defined contribution plans or established defined contribution plans where they previously had no plan. Women have been expanding their participation in the labor market at the same time that employers have been instituting defined contribution plans. As the number of low-income workers with defined contribution plans grows, an increasing number of workers may lose eligibility for means-tested benefits if account balances are counted as assets.

Because defined benefit pension funds are not accessible, while withdrawals generally can be made from defined contribution plans, current law discriminates against low-income workers whose employers participate in a defined contribution retirement plan, as compared to workers whose employers provide a defined benefit plan. It also discriminates against retirees whose employers offered defined contribution rather than defined benefit plans. Low-income workers with defined contribution accounts generally must withdraw most or all of their accounts and spend those assets down, regardless of any early withdrawal penalty or tax consequences, before they can qualify for means-tested programs such as SSI and Medicaid.

Failure to exclude amounts in such accounts from asset tests in means-tested programs would create a perverse incentive for poor elderly individuals to withdraw funds from their retirement accounts prematurely and spend them; only then would they be eligible for SSI and Medicaid. Moreover, nonelderly workers who experienced temporary periods of need, such as during a recession, would be forced to liquidate and spend the retirement savings they had managed to accumulate—and often to pay substantial early withdrawal and often tax penalties—to be eligible for Medicaid during the economic downturn. Some workers who were hard-pressed during a downturn—and withdrew most of the funds in their retirement accounts because they could not receive means-tested assistance until the accounts were spent down and consequently could not meet current needs without drawing on their retirement funds—can reach retirement with little left in their accounts.

Forcing low-income workers and retirees to deplete their savings before they can access means-tested benefits runs counter to efforts to encourage low-income workers to save for retirement and does not represent sound policy. Federal policy ought to encourage low-income workers to build retirement savings. It should encourage low-income retirees to withdraw funds from their retirement accounts gradually over their remaining years (rather than in a lump sum) so that sufficient funds remain to avert severe poverty when they become old. This is particularly important for reducing high rates of poverty among elderly women, since women have longer life expectancies than men.

There still is a small enough number of low-wage workers with defined-contribution plans that these aspects of the asset rules of means-tested programs are not invoked much. Not many people lose mean-tested benefits for this reason. As a result, making this change should have little cost in the next five or ten years.

Congress and the Bush administration could address these problems through changes in asset rules in means-tested programs to treat defined-contribution accounts in the same manner as defined-benefit plans. If an individual (whether a retiree or a younger household) withdraws funds from a tax-deferred retirement account, the amounts withdrawn should be counted as income. But amounts not withdrawn should not be considered an asset for means-tested program eligibility purposes. Such an approach is important if new forms of individual accounts (whether in the form of RSAs or other individual accounts within Social Security) and employer-sponsored, defined contribution plans are to help low-income workers save for retirement and to enable low-income retirees to have adequate income that lasts into very old age.

Facilitate Savings for Retirement by
Low- and Moderate-Wage Workers

In examining the economic status of low-wage earners—especially elderly people of color and women—one might be misled to a conclusion that these communities would fare better under a system of partially or fully privatized individual accounts in lieu of a portion or all of Social Security. Under such a system, some or all of a worker's payroll tax contributions would be diverted from the Social Security Trust Funds, where they currently flow, into a private retirement account that may be invested in stocks or bonds. Such a conclusion would be faulty, however, and would place elderly African Americans, Latinos, and women in more precarious financial circumstances by undermining the valuable protections that Social Security accords them. Under an individual account system, workers would get back the retirement savings they contribute plus earnings *or losses*. These accounts would not have the internal redistribution provided by Social Security's progressive benefit formula that helps to compensate for the labor market experiences of people of color and women.

Rather than weakening or withdrawing resources from the Social Security program, reform proposals should build on the existing program by creating vehicles outside the Social Security system that would facilitate additional retirement savings for low- and moderate-wage workers. One possible alternative is something like the retirement savings accounts plan proposed by President Clinton in his fiscal year 2001 budget. This proposal was targeted to low- and middle-income workers who might otherwise have insufficient retirement savings of their own.

The "three-legged stool" is an often-cited metaphor for the type of retirement package that individuals should have. Social Security, pension income, and personal savings are the three legs of the stool that would provide the elderly with a reliable stream of income upon which they could depend. Earlier sections of this chapter showed that people of color and unmarried women are less likely to have sufficient savings than white elderly individuals and married women. In 1999 President Clinton proposed the creation of universal savings accounts (USAs) to promote personal savings by workers, in addition to Social Security. Congress did not act on the USA proposal, and Clinton introduced a revised version of this plan—the retirement savings accounts—in his 2001 budget.[47]

---

47. White House, Office of the Press Secretary (2000). See also *Budget of the United States Government* (2000); Orszag and Orszag (2000).

Under the RSA plan, a worker between the ages of twenty-five and sixty who earns at least $5,000 a year could contribute up to $1,000 per year into an RSA account. Contributions by workers would be matched by the federal government on a progressive basis. Individuals (as distinguished from couples) with annual earnings of $12,500 or less would receive a $2 federal match for each $1 of the first $100 they save. These matching amounts would phase out for individuals with incomes between $12,500 and $40,000. In addition, workers would receive a $1 match for every $1 of the next $900 they contribute. This match also would phase out for individuals earning between $12,500 and $40,000. Couples earning $25,000 or less could contribute up to $2,000 a year. They would receive a $2 match for each $1 of the first $200 they save, and a $1 match for the next $1,800. The match for couples would be phased out for those with earnings between $25,000 and $80,000.

Workers would be given the option of having their accounts maintained by their employers—like 401(k)s—or placed in private financial institutions—like IRAs. Similar to IRAs and 401(k)s, RSAs could be invested in a broad range of investment vehicles, with the contributions being tax deductible. Withdrawals from these accounts could be made only after five years and only to pay for medical care, to purchase a home, to pay for college, or for retirement purposes.

Most current federal incentives to save are linked to the income tax system, but low-wage earners are less likely to benefit from those saving incentives. Treasury data show that two-thirds of existing pension tax subsidies go to families in the top 20 percent of the income distribution, while just 12 percent go to families with incomes in the bottom 60 percent of the distribution.[48] RSAs would help address this imbalance.

The argument could be made that low-wage earners have the least ability to put aside money and therefore would be the least able to take advantage of the RSA plan, despite the progressive match. However, data on participation rates in 401(k) plans among low- and moderate-wage workers show that a relatively large share of these workers participate in the plans if offered the chance.[49] The data indicate that 44 percent of workers earning $10,000 to $15,000 in 1993 who were offered the opportunity to participate in a 401(k) plan chose to participate. Only 21 percent of these workers were offered 401(k) plans, however, so the overall participation rate was only 9 percent.

The Clinton administration estimated the RSA plan could benefit 76 million individuals.[50] Twenty-five-year-old workers who contributed the maximum of

48. White House (2000, p. 5).
49. Orszag and Greenstein (2000). See also U.S. Department of Labor (1994, table C7).
50. White House (2000, p. 1).

$1,000 per year and received the maximum federal match each year for forty years could accumulate $266,000 by age sixty-five. With these savings workers could purchase an annuity upon retirement that would provide them with $24,000 in retirement income each year. The administration estimated in 2000 that the RSA plan would cost $54 billion over ten years.

Unlike the individual accounts under many Social Security privatization proposals, the RSA plan would supplement Social Security. None of the payroll tax reserves going to the trust funds would be diverted, and transition costs would not be created. Therefore, guaranteed Social Security benefits would not need to be reduced (or payroll taxes increased) more than would otherwise be necessary in order to shift resources from Social Security to private accounts. Instead, the RSA plan would leave the Social Security system intact and build on it.

Conclusion

The Social Security program has been a constant upon which most workers have been able to depend to receive income for themselves and their families when they retire, become disabled, or die. The program has been one of the nation's most effective defenses against poverty. As the country moves forward toward reforming Social Security, it is important that solutions be adopted to reduce poverty further among those who still are vulnerable in their old age.

There are limits to what Social Security can and should be expected to do to reduce poverty. There is a role for programs such as SSI and a need to find ways to facilitate savings among low- and moderate-wage earners. There also are steps that should be taken early in individuals' lives to assist them in obtaining better-paying jobs. These improvements are beyond the scope of this discussion.

This chapter considers steps to alleviate poverty among seniors who remain at risk. Increasing the elderly survivors benefit would reduce the number of widows who fall into poverty. Implementing an effective minimum benefit also would help aid other low-income elderly unmarried women (and men).

Improvements in the SSI program would target elderly individuals and couples with the lowest incomes. Adjusting the GIE and asset limits for inflation and excluding defined contribution plan balances from the asset test would modernize the SSI program and increase the number of poor elderly who benefit from the program.

Finally, a federally matched retirement savings plan targeted to low- and moderate-wage earners has the potential to place many such workers in better financial positions as they grow old.

There is a price tag for these proposals. A short time ago, the solutions proposed here would not have been fiscally viable. The emergence of budget surpluses has given policymakers the financial wherewithal to move from discussing poverty among the elderly to taking greater action to reduce it.[51]

Priorities for the budget surplus must be set, and tough choices must be made about uses of the surplus. The options within this chapter must compete with an array of other proposals, including large tax cuts that disproportionately accrue to those on the high end of the income spectrum. These tax cuts could consume most or all of the available non-Social Security, non-Medicare surpluses. There is also a need to balance funding for program initiatives intended to address the needs of the nonelderly population with money spent on the elderly. Within that balance, there should be room to make more secure those low-income individuals who face poverty in their old age.

References

Burkhauser, Richard V., and Timothy M. Smeeding, 1994. *Social Security Reform: A Budget Neutral Approach to Reducing Older Women's Disproportionate Risk of Poverty*. Syracuse, N.Y.: Maxwell School of Citizenship and Public Affairs/Center for Policy Research.

Butrica, Barbara A., Howard Iams, and Steven H. Sandell. 1999. "Using Data for Couples to Project the Distributional Effects of Changes in Social Security Policy." *Social Security Bulletin* 62, no. 3 (1999): 20–27.

Budget of the United States Government, Fiscal Year 2001. 2000. Government Printing Office.

Centers for Disease Control. 1997. *Vital Statistics of the United States, 1993: Life Tables*. U.S. Government Printing Office.

Choudhury, Sharmila, and Michael Leonesio. 1997. "Life-Cycle Aspects of Poverty among Older Women." *Social Security Bulletin* 60 (2): 17–36.

Committee on Ways and Means, U.S. House of Representatives. 1998. *The Green Book*. Government Printing Office (May).

Dalaker, Joseph, and Mary Naifeh. 1998. *Poverty in the United States: 1997*. U.S. Department of Commerce, Bureau of the Census.

General Accounting Office. 2000. *Pension Plans: Characteristics of Persons in the Labor Force without Pension Coverage*. Government Printing Office (August).

Greenstein, Robert. 2000. *Building Retirement Savings Can Cause Low- and Moderate-Income Working Families to Lose Means-Tested Assistance in Times of Need*. Washington: Center on Budget and Policy Priorities (September 20).

51. The need for improvements in SSI, initiatives to enhance retirement savings outside Social Security, and additional resources to fund a long-term solvency package for Social Security that includes program improvements, underscores the problem with the magnitude of the tax cut enacted this year. The need for such improvements also indicates the importance of scaling back elements of the tax cut that were disproportionately targeted to the wealthy and that have not yet taken effect, in order to free up funds for other national priorities, including reducing elderly poverty.

————. 2001. *Can the New Surplus Projections Accommodate a Large Tax Cut?* Washington: Center on Budget and Policy Priorities (January 4).

Larin, Kathy, and Wendell Primus. 1999. *Individual Accounts, Defined-Contribution Plans, and Assets Tests in Means-Tested Programs.* Washington: Center on Budget and Policy Priorities (March 29).

Mishell, Lawrence, Jared Bernstein, and John Schmitt. 2000. *The State of Working America 2000–01.* Washington: Economic Policy Institute.

National Economic Council Interagency Working Group on Social Security. 1998. *Women and Retirement Income.* (October). Washington.

Olsen, Kelly, and Don Hoffmeyer. Forthcoming. *Social Security's Special Minimum Benefit: A Description and Analysis of Current Law.* Washington: Social Security Administration.

Orszag, Peter, and Robert Greenstein. 2000. "Toward Progressive Pensions: A Summary of the U.S. Pension System and Proposals for Reform." Paper prepared for the conference on "Inclusion in Asset Building: Research and Policy Symposium." Washington University, St. Louis, September 21–23.

Orszag, Peter, and Jonathan Orszag. 2000. *Would Raising IRA Contribution Limits Bolster Retirement Security for Lower- and Middle-Income Families or Is There a Better Way?"* Washington: Center on Budget and Policy Priorities (April).

Porter, Kathryn H., Kathy Larin, and Wendell Primus. 1999. *Social Security and Poverty among the Elderly: A National and State Perspective.* Washington: Center on Budget and Policy Priorities (April).

Report of the 1994–1996 Advisory Council on Social Security, Volume I: Findings and Recommendations. 1997. Washington.

Social Security Administration. 1997. *Social Security Handbook, 1997.* Washington.

————. 1999. *Annual Statistical Supplement to the Social Security Bulletin, 1999.* Government Printing Office.

————. 2000. *Report on Supplemental Security Income: Income and Resource Exclusions and Disability Insurance Earnings-Related Provisions.* Washington (March).

Urban Institute. 2000. *Social Security: Out of Step with the Modern Family.* Washington.

U.S. Census Bureau. 1999, September. *Money and Income in the United States: Current Population Reports, Consumer Income, 1998.* Government Printing Office.

U.S. Department of Labor, Social Security Administration, Small Business Administration, and Pension Benefit Guaranty Corporation. 1994. *Pension and Health Benefits of American Workers.* Washington.

U.S. Department of Labor, Bureau of Labor Statistics. 2000. *Employment and Earnings.* Government Printing Office (February).

White House, Office of the Press Secretary. 2000. *President Clinton's Tax Agenda for Community, Opportunity, and Responsibility* (January 27).

The 2000 Annual Report of the Board of Trustees of the Federal Old-Age and Survivors Insurance and Disability Insurance Trust Funds. 2000. Government Printing Office.

5

Assessing Assumptions about Attitudes toward Social Security: Popular Claims Meet Hard Data

Fay Lomax Cook and Lawrence R. Jacobs

THE HISTORY OF THE DEVELOPMENT of Social Security has been one of incremental action. Since 1935, when Old Age Insurance was passed as a part of the Social Security Act, the program has expanded, but there have been no major departures from the original purposes of the Social Security system as reflected in the 1935 legislation and the 1939 amendments.[1] However, in the past few years, proposals have been made that would change the character of Social Security. Most recently, the 2000 election debate offered very different visions for the future of Social Security—one incremental, the other a fundamental change in the structure of the program. The question today is not whether to reform the program but in what ways.

Proponents of divergent proposals for reforming Social Security often rest their claims on a set of working hypotheses about the public's confidence in the program and support for current arrangements and reforms. In particular, reform proposals tend to rest on three interrelated claims about public opinion. First, proponents of reform often build their case for change on claims about low and precipitously declining public confidence in the future of Social Security; the implication is that the public is losing faith in the program and dramatic steps are necessary to avoid a complete collapse. Second, the low and rapidly eroding confidence in Social Security will produce, reform proponents often claim, a decline in public support for Social Security; reform is necessary to protect public support for Social Security. Third, the toxic mixture of low and declining confidence in Social Security is creating a new openness among

For expert research assistance on table and figure preparation and for useful advice, we are grateful to Jason Barabas and Dukhong Kim.

1. Ball (2000, p. 275).

Americans for incremental reforms and for privatization—the option for individuals to invest some portion of their Social Security contributions in the stock and bond markets.

Proponents of reforming Social Security tend to work one or more of these working hypotheses about public opinion into their arguments for their desired change. The motivation is clear: Wrapping reform proposals in favorable public opinion reassures politicians worried about voter retribution and greases the legislative skids for passage. Just as serious reform proposals are vetted by experts on program financing, proposals that rest on claims about political feasibility also require vetting by experts on public opinion. Unfortunately, working hypotheses that suggest likely public support for reforms have generally not been carefully examined despite a large and swelling warehouse of public opinion data. In the absence of this kind of independent and careful analysis of public opinion, reform proponents are given a veritable free pass to make assertions without the kind of careful scrutiny that would accompany claims about finance and program design. The result is a kind of wild west in which dueling sets of reformers selectively pick poll questions that mesh with their own views, take findings out of context, and repeat claims about public opinion that are inaccurate.[2]

Claims about public opinion toward Social Security require careful and independent evaluation. Particular attention should be paid to survey items that were worded in an identical or similar manner over a long period of time. As survey researchers know, poll results are very sensitive to the question wording; the way a question is formulated can affect how people respond to it. Examining identically or similarly worded questions from several surveys over time allows real trends and patterns in public opinion to be identified. By following these practices, excessive generalizing from any one survey's results can be avoided.

The results of an exhaustive review of hundreds of separate public opinion survey items are presented in this chapter. This review demonstrates that the three working hypotheses of policymakers are either false or substantially overstated. These findings should elicit the same disquiet that greets evidence that reform proposals contain significantly flawed financial or program assumptions. The consequence of policymakers taking actions on the basis of inaccurate assumptions about public opinion could undermine (rather than bolster) public confidence and support for the Social Security system.

---

2. Cook, Barabas, and Page (2000); Jacobs and Shapiro (1998a, 1998b, and 2000).

Working Hypothesis #1: Confidence in Social Security Is Low and Declining

The first working hypothesis that reformers often insert into their case for altering the Social Security program is that the public's confidence in the future of the program is low and precipitously declining; the public is losing faith in the program, they assert, and dramatic steps are necessary to avoid a crisis of confidence in the program. The poster-child for this claim is a Third Millennium poll (conducted by the Luntz Research Company) that purports to show that young people are more likely to believe in unidentified flying objects (UFOs) than to believe that Social Security will be there for them when they retire. For example, in a hearing on reform options for Social Security, Senator Charles Grassley (R-Iowa) said, "I have heard it said that young people think that they are more likely to see a UFO in their lifetime than be able to retire on Social Security."[3] Senator Ron Wyden (D-Ore.) told the story with even more dramatic flair: "We all know we have a demographic tsunami coming, 75 million baby boomers. At home, I can tell you, more of the young people think they are going to have a date with an extraterrestrial than to get a Social Security check."[4] Some members of Congress have generalized the finding from young people to baby boomers. According to Senator John Breaux (D-La.), "There are 77 million baby boomers waiting to become retirees, beginning in the year 2010. Many of those baby boomers believe more in UFOs than they believe in the fact that Social Security will be there when they are ready to retire."[5]

The claims about the UFO poll are misleading, illustrating some of the more general limitations with the first working hypotheses. In 1994 the Luntz Research Company conducted a survey of 5,000 eighteen- to thirty-four-year-olds to get the "Generation X" perspective on Social Security. Respondents were asked, "Do you think Social Security will still exist by the time you retire?" Sixty-three percent said no. Eight questions later, interviewers asked, "And one final question, and I ask you to take this seriously—Do you think UFOs exist?" Forty-six percent said yes. The results show that two questions at nearly opposite ends of a survey indicate that a larger proportion of young adults aged eighteen to thirty-four thought UFOs exist than thought Social Security would exist when they retire. However, this is not what was reported: contrary to the claims about the survey, respondents did not directly compare their belief in UFOs to their belief in Social Security and conclude that the

3. Grassley (1997).
4. Wyden (1998).
5. Breaux (1998).

Table 5-1.   *Measuring Confidence: UFOs versus Social Security*
Percent

	All respondents	18- to 34- year-olds
1994 Luntz/Siegel and Third Millennium[a]		
Social Security will exist in retirement?		
Yes	. . .	28
No	. . .	63
Don't know/refused	. . .	9
Do UFOs exist?		
Yes	. . .	46
No	. . .	43
Don't know/refused	. . .	11
1997 Employee Benefit Research Institute[b]		
Greater confidence?		
Receive social security	71	63
Alien life exists	26	33
Don't know/refused	3	4

a. The Third Millennium survey was conducted September 8–10, 1994, by Luntz Research Company and Mark A. Siegel and Associates. A total of 500 eighteen- to thirty-four-year-olds were interviewed to get the "Generation X" perspective on Social Security. The Social Security question was the sixth item and the UFO question was asked as the fourteenth item. The question for the Social Security was, "Do you think Social Security will still exist by the time you retire?" The question for the UFO item was, "And one final question, and I ask you to take this seriously—Do you think UFOs exist?"

b. In July 1997 Matthew Greenwald and Associates conducted the Retirement Confidence Survey for the Employee Benefit Research Institute and American Savings Education to compare beliefs about the existence of Social Security and UFOs in the same question. In their survey of eighteen- to thirty-four-year-olds (*N* unavailable) the question asked, "Which do you have greater confidence in . . . receiving Social Security benefits after retirement or that alien life from outer space exists?"

former was more likely than the latter (as members of Congress mistakenly presumed).[6]

The misleading conclusion from the survey by Luntz Research (which has been censured by the American Association of Public Opinion Research for inappropriate professional conduct) was directly tested by the Employee Benefit Research Institute (EBRI). EBRI asked young adults aged eighteen to thirty-four in a 1997 survey to compare beliefs about the existence of Social Security and UFOs in the same question: "Which do you have greater confidence in—receiving Social Security benefits after retirement or that alien life from outer space exists?" Asked this way, as table 5-1 shows, 63 percent have greater confidence in Social Security, while 33 percent have greater confidence in the existence of alien life.

The UFO poll illustrates the danger of presumptive claims about public opinion that are not carefully scrutinized. It is hard to imagine that a false claim

6. Jacobs and Shapiro (1998a, 1998b).

Figure 5-1.   *Confidence in Social Security, 1975–2000*

Percent

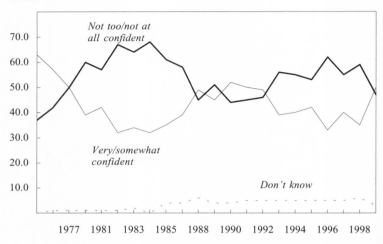

Source: A "Monitoring Attitudes of the Public" survey sponsored by the American Council of
Life Insurance and conducted by Yankelovich, Skelly, and White (1975–82) and the Roper
Organization/Roper Starch Worldwide (1983–2000). More than 1,000 respondents participated
in each survey. The question was, "How confident are you, yourself, in the future of the Social
Security system? Would you say you are very confident, somewhat confident, not too confident,
or not at all confident?"
Note: The question was not asked in 1999.

about Social Security finances would have been as widely circulated by the press
and touted by leading policymakers of both political parties as this claim about
public opinion. As Jacobs and Shapiro note, "the true state of public opinion on
Social Security turns out to be more complicated than this popular sound bite
suggests—a lot more complicated. . . . It has as much to do with leading (or
misleading) poll questions as it does with the merits of the actual plan."[7]

Careful analysis of public confidence in the future of Social Security
indicates that the working hypothesis of low and declining confidence is also
overstated. Figure 5-1 displays responses to an identically worded question
about confidence in the future of the Social Security system that has been
fielded from 1975 to 2000.

Two points are especially important with regard to the first working hypothesis. First, in 2000 more Americans were confident in the future of Social
Security than not, and they were more confident than they have been in nearly a
decade. Second, instead of declining (as policymakers presume), confidence
rose by 15 percentage points in 2000 from its level in 1998 at the time of the
previous survey. This may in part be due to the attention given to Social Security

7. Jacobs and Shapiro (1998a).

in the presidential election campaign, in which both candidates devoted considerable attention to Social Security and both made it clear that they wanted to strengthen the program, even though their solutions were different.

Although confidence in the future of Social Security has recently risen and is not low in historical perspective, it is nonetheless true that only half the public is confident. No responsible policymakers can be fully satisfied with only half of Americans expressing confidence in the country's largest social welfare program. Indeed, surveys suggest that caution is not unwarranted. Table 5-2 shows that in four surveys from 1998 to 1999 fairly stable majorities of between 49 and 57 percent believed that Social Security was heading for "major trouble," and between 57 and 61 percent believed it needed "big changes" to "keep the Social Security program out of trouble in the future." Although the working hypothesis about historically low and declining confidence is overstated, responsible policymakers should nonetheless be concerned about the public's faith in the program.

The data suggest four reasons why responsible policymakers should not overreact with outsized reform proposals to evidence that half of the public has low confidence, perceives "major trouble," and supports "big changes. First, "big changes" is an ambiguous term and is open to divergent interpretations by policymakers and the public. By way of comparison, President Bill Clinton attempted his overhaul of the health care system in the first half of the 1990s when nine of ten Americans favored "major changes" or a "complete rebuilding" of the health care system.[8] The proportion of Americans in favor of "big changes" for Social Security is substantially lower. Policymakers would be well advised not to overinterpret the public appetite for changing the structure of the program.

Second, table 5-2 also shows that the public sees "major trouble" but has not panicked into the conclusion that the system is collapsing. Only 32 percent believe that the if no changes occur, Social Security will "run out of money altogether." In a separate May 1999 survey by Peter Hart Research Associates, only 31 percent of young adults eighteen to thirty-four thought that Social Security would "not be paying benefits at all" when they reached retirement age (45 percent thought the program would pay benefits but "less than now" and 15 percent believe it would pay the same level of benefits).[9] Third, the public's concerns tend to mirror the information and arguments made by elites: the reasons that the public offers for upcoming trouble reflect the divergence of

8. Jacobs and Shapiro (2000).

9. The survey was conducted for the 2030 Center and interviewed 403 18-34 year olds May 17-24, 1999. Respondents were asked: "When you reach retirement age, do you think that Social Security will be paying the same level of benefits as it pays now, paying less than now, or will it not be paying benefits at all?"

Table 5-2. *Perceptions of Problems with Social Security*

Percent

Perceptions of problems	*March 1998*	*August 1998*	*February 1999*	*May 1999*
Degree of trouble with system[a]				
Major trouble	55	49	53	57
Minor trouble	29	31	31	29
Secure and solid (no trouble)	10	12	10	9
Don't know/refused	6	8	6	5
Size of changes needed[b]				
No changes	7	5	3	5
Small changes	30	30	30	32
Big changes	57	58	61	58
Don't know/refused	6	7	6	5
If no changes, what happens[c]				
Run out of money	32	34	34	32
Pay less than half benefits	37	32	32	36
Pay three-quarters benefits	12	11	10	12
Pay full benefits	9	13	13	10
Don't know/refused	10	10	11	10
Reason for upcoming trouble[d]				
Government spent SS reserves	45	47	41	43
More retirees than workers	26	26	32	26
Cost-of-living too high	12	10	10	11
Wealthy get benefits	6	6	7	8
Retirees get too much	5	5	6	6
Don't know/refused	6	6	4	6

Source: Princeton Survey Research Associates.

Note: Percentages do not always sum to 100 percent due to rounding. $N = 1,200$ for March 1998 and July 1998; $N = 1,000$ for February 1999; $N = 1,001$ for June 1999.

a. The question was, "Some people now think Social Security is heading for financial trouble in the future, while other people think the program is basically secure and solid. What is your view? Do you think Social Security is headed for major trouble, minor trouble, or do you think the program is secure and solid?"

b. The question was, "Which of the following comes closest to describing what you think is needed to keep the Social Security program out of trouble in the future? Do you think this program needs no changes, small changes, or big changes?"

c. The question was, "If no changes are made to the Social Security program over the next twenty years, what do you think will happen? Will Social Security. . . ." The N for this question was 628 in July 1998, 502 in February 1999, and 508 in June 1999.

d. The question was, "And, which of these do you think is the main reason the Social Security program might be headed for financial trouble? [The choice categories were as follows:] The government has spent the Social Security reserves for other programs; the number of older people is growing faster than the number of workers; the cost-of-living increases are too high; even people who could afford to live comfortably on their own get benefits; most older people get more money than they paid in; none of these [volunteered]; don't know/refused."

debate among policymakers over whether Social Security's financial troubles principally stem from government expenditure of its reserves (that is, the public's top choice is in line with charges that the program represents a "ponzi scheme" or that it would be better served with a "fully funded" system without the burden of large liability) or from more retirees than workers (although demographers emphasize that the dependency ratio of workers to all dependents—children as well as retirees—was higher in the 1960s than in the coming decades).[10] The public's concern is, in part, the creation of a divided elite.

Fourth, confidence in Social Security is a function of confidence in government in general and press reporting. Changes in Social Security confidence broadly parallel fluctuations in public confidence toward the government as a whole, which fell during the second half of the 1970s, rose in the early 1980s, and declined in the mid-1980s before rising again during the late 1990s. Moreover, Social Security confidence is also influenced by fluctuations in press coverage, which tends to highlight problems with the program.[11] For instance, the dip in 1998 corresponds with the increased attention that policymakers and journalists devoted to reforming the program.[12] When the press increases its coverage, the flow of negative information about Social Security that reaches the public also rises. The point, then, is that confidence in Social Security may, in part, reflect influences on the public that are not directly related to the program itself.

In short, the first working hypothesis—that confidence is low and rapidly eroding and requires dramatic steps to reverse—is not supported by public opinion data. Instead, more Americans are confident in the system than not in 2000, confidence is rising, and the public—while clearly concerned about the program—has not panicked.

Working Hypothesis #2: Support for Social Security Is Weakening

The second working hypothesis that figures prominently in arguments for reforming Social Security is that low and rapidly declining confidence in Social Security will produce a decrease in public support for Social Security: As confidence declines, support is also expected to drop. Reformers then don

10. A *ponzi scheme* is named after Charles Ponzi, who ran an investment program in Boston in 1919–20, in which he promised 50 percent returns on investments in forty-five days or 100 percent in ninety days. Although he was able to pay initial investors in full, he eventually was not able to deliver when he had $7 million in claims and only $2 million to pay them.

11. Jacobs and Shapiro (1995); Jacobs, Watts, and Shapiro (1995).

12. Cook and Jacobs (1998).

Figure 5-2. *Support for Social Security Spending, 1984–2000*

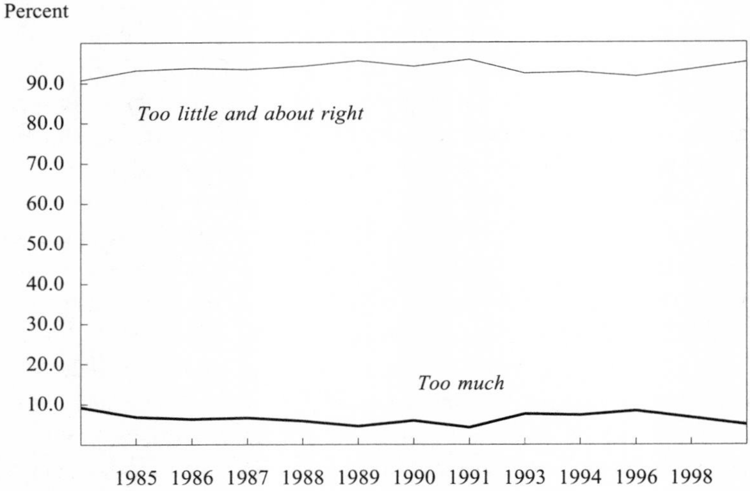

Percent

Source: General Social Survey (GSS) data from the National Opinion Center (NORC). The question asked was, "Are we spending too much, too little, or about the right amount on Social Security?"

the mantle of Social Security protector by claiming that reform is necessary to protect and rebuild what had been strong public support for the program.

This popular hypothesis is utterly lacking evidence. This is *not* a case of competing sets of evidence, with contending sets of reformers choosing among them; the evidence is uniform, clear, and not disputed.

The public opinion data demonstrate two points. First, a large and somewhat diverse body of data indicates unusually strong and stable public support for Social Security. Figure 5-2 shows the results of surveys conducted by the National Opinion Research Center (NORC) from 1984 to 2000 that asked large nationally representative samples of respondents if we are "spending too much, too little, or about the right amount on Social Security?" Public support—defined as those who say we are spending too little or about the right amount—is remarkably high and unchanging. For thirteen years 90 percent or more of the general public supported Social Security, and the trend hardly varied.

The University of Michigan's National Election Studies (NES) asked a similar question about whether spending on Social Security should be increased, decreased, or kept the same in each year of a national election between 1984 and 1996. Defining support as saying spending should be increased or kept the same, the findings from the NES surveys tell the same story as the NORC data in figure 5-2: the public is overwhelmingly supportive with more than 90 percent favoring maintaining or increasing spending.

The Gallup Organization conducted the final series of surveys that examined support for Social Security over time for the Chicago Council of Foreign Relations.[13] Every four years between 1982 and 1998, Gallup has asked respondents whether the Social Security program should be "cut back," "expanded," or "kept about the same." The results are remarkably consistent with the results from NORC and NES: once again, a consistent nine in ten Americans believed that Social Security should be "expanded" or "kept about the same."

Large and diverse bodies of data show that public support for the present Social Security program is strong and has been stable across many years. Public support is sufficiently unambiguous that both Social Security critics and supporters readily acknowledge it. A spokesman from the Cato Institute, an organization that is highly critical of Social Security, acknowledged, "No one should doubt the continued popularity of Social Security. Our poll results clearly showed that Social Security remains one of the most popular of all government programs, with two-thirds of those polled holding a favorable view of the program."[14] From a diametrically opposite end of the spectrum, Bob Ball (a former Social Security commissioner and a strong supporter of the program) also highlighted public support: "Whenever Social Security's long term stability has been threatened by circumstances warranting a legislative response, strong public support has encouraged political leaders to seek bipartisan solutions that build on Social Security's inherent strengths."[15]

The second point is that public support is not related to public confidence; the presumption that low confidence in Social Security's future erodes support for Social Security lacks support. Comparing figure 5-1 (confidence) and figure 5-2 (public support) shows that neither low confidence nor downward shifts in confidence consistently coincide with declining support. Confidence rose from 1984 to 1988 with no appreciable change in support for the program; the decline in confidence from 1992 to 1996 was correlated with no statistically significant drop in support.

The working hypothesis that the public's backing for Social Security is eroding under the strain of low and declining confidence is simply not

13. Rielly (1999).
14. Tanner (1996).
15. Ball (1997).

supported by available evidence. In the language of social science, confidence and support do not seem to co-vary.

Working Hypothesis #3: Growing Public Support for Privatization and Incremental Reform

The third working hypothesis that creeps into claims about Social Security is that low and declining levels of confidence in Social Security are creating a groundswell among Americans for incremental reforms and for privatization. The evidence once again provides little corroboration for what policymakers assume about public opinion.

Public Ambivalence and Opposition toward Privatization

Policymakers regularly invoke public opinion to substantiate their case for privatization. Between January 1993 and December 1999 Congress held forty hearings that focused at least in part on the privatization of Social Security. At these hearings, a number of commentators claimed that the public supports privatization or partial privatization of Social Security. Senator Chuck Hagel (R-Neb.) argued, "Personal retirement accounts would harness the power of private markets and compound interest, giving individuals ownership of their retirement savings. *Americans want more power, more choice, more responsibility in deciding their own future and economic well-being.* It's their money."[16] When one think tank expert was asked if the public was really "ready" for privatization, he answered enthusiastically, "Absolutely! There's not the slightest doubt in my mind that they are."[17] Public opinion data do not concur.

The public is, at best, ambivalent toward Social Security privatization; survey data based on balanced questions find solid opposition. This is evident in two patterns. First, when not reminded of the risks associated with equity investments or with the costs of transitioning to a privatized system, the public supports partial privatization (namely, being able to invest a portion of their Social Security taxes into a personal retirement account) and opposes both full privatization and government investment of contributions in equities.

Public support for partial privatization in the abstract is clear. Table 5-3 shows that public support emerges from nineteen separate poll items over the past five years. The wordings of the questions vary widely; they vary from

16. Hagel (1998).
17. Glassman (1998).

Table 5-3. *Support for Social Security Partial Privatization When No Risks Are Considered*

Percent

	Favor	Oppose	No opinion/ don't know
March 1996[a]	72	13	15
June 1996[b]	69	15	16
June 1996[c]	74	13	13
April 1998[d]	80	16	4
April 1998[e]	66	20	13
April 1998[f]	76	20	4
May 1998[g]	64	32	4
June 1998[h]	69	20	11
December 1998[i]	74	22	5
July–Sept. 1999[j]	70	22	8
January 2000[k]	62	33	5
May 2000[l]	64	31	5
May 2000[m]	53	38	9
June 2000[n]	65	30	5
June 2000[o]	51	36	13
Sept. 2000[p]	59	37	4
Sept. 2000[q]	53	39	8
Oct. 2000[r]	66	30	4
Oct. 2000[s]	58	35	8

a. Public Opinion Strategies (POS) for the Cato Institute, March 27–31, 1996, $N = 800$. National registered voters likely to vote only. The question was, "Now that you have heard all six parts of the new proposal to change the Social Security system, do you favor, oppose, or have no opinion of the entire plan, or would you like me to read the key points of the plan to you again before you make a decision? (Read plan only if respondent asks.) People would be allowed to keep and invest the amount they now pay in Social Security taxes to save for their own retirement. You would decide how to invest the money, with some restrictions to limit very risky investments. Money could not be drawn until retirement and any money left in your account when you die becomes part of your inheritance. There will be no reduction in benefits for current Social Security recipients. People under age sixty five years old but over age eighteen would have the choice of staying in the current Social Security system or moving to the new privatized system. Those choosing the new system will receive some partial benefits under the old system. (If favor/oppose, ask:) Would that be strongly (favor/oppose) or just somewhat (favor/oppose)? (If no opinion, ask:) Which way do you lean? Do you lean to favor the proposal or do you lean to oppose the proposal?"

b. POS for the Cato Institute, June 12–16, 1996, $N=800$. National registered voters likely to vote only. The question was, "Now that you have had an opportunity to hear more about Proposal B (to change the Social Security system), the proposal that would allow you to invest your Social Security taxes into your own personal retirement account like an IRA (Individual Retirement Account) or 401(k), do you favor, oppose, or have no opinion of the proposal? (If favor/oppose, ask:) Would that be strongly (favor/oppose) or just somewhat (favor/oppose)? (If no opinion, ask:) Which way do you lean? Do you lean to favor the proposal or do you lean to oppose the proposal?"

continues

Table 5-3.   *Continued*

c. POS for the Cato Institute, June 12–16, 1996, $N = 800$. National registered voters likely to vote only. The question was, "Now that you have heard all seven parts (people would be allowed to keep and invest the amount they now pay in Social Security taxes to save for their own personal retirement, you would decide how to invest the money with some restrictions to limit very risky investments, money could not be drawn until retirement, any money left in your account when you die becomes part of your inheritance, there will be no reduction in benefits for current Social Security recipients, people under age sixty five years old but over age eighteen would have the choice of staying in the current Social Security system or moving to the new privatized system, those choosing the new system will receive some partial benefits under the old system) of the Proposal B (to change the Social Security system), do you favor or oppose, or have no opinion of the entire plan, or would you like me to read the key points of the plan to you again before you make a decision? (If favor/oppose, ask:) Would that be strongly (favor/oppose) or just somewhat (favor/oppose)? (If no opinion, ask:) Which way do you lean? Do you lean to favor the proposal or do you lean to oppose the proposal?"

d. I.C.R. Survey Research Group for Associated Press, April 27–31, 1998, $N = 1,102$. The question was, "I'm going to read some proposals that have been made for changes in the Social Security system. For each proposal, tell me whether you favor or oppose it. . . . Letting workers shift some of their Social Security tax payments into personal retirement accounts that they would invest on their own."

e. American Viewpoint National Monitor Survey, April 1998, $N = 1,000$. The question was, "As you may know, each year there are more and more retirees collecting Social Security benefits and fewer workers whose payroll taxes fund the system. In fact, by the year 2012, the government will be paying out more Social Security benefits than it is collecting in payroll taxes and if nothing is changed, the system will go broke by the year 2029. As you may know, workers are now required to contribute 12.5 percent of their income to Social Security. Would you favor or oppose changing the formula so that they would continue to pay the same amount toward their retirement but just 10.5 percent would to go Social Security and the other 2 percent would be used by workers to invest their own private retirement accounts? (If favor or oppose, ask:) Is that strongly favor/oppose or somewhat?"

f. Yankelovich Partners Inc. survey for *Time*/CNN, April 8–9, 1988, $N = 1,011$. The question was, "Do you favor or oppose allowing Americans to put a portion of their Social Security taxes into a personal savings account to be used for retirement?"

g. Chilton Research Services/Harvard University, May 6–10, 1998, $N = 1,014$. The question was, "(I am going to read you a list of some ways that have been suggested to deal with the future financial problems of Social Security. For each one, please tell me if you would favor or oppose such a proposal.) How about . . . people having individual accounts and making their own investments with a portion of their Social Security payments?"

h. Princeton Survey Research Associates (PSRA), June 4–8, 1998, $N = 1,102$. The question was, "Generally, do you favor or oppose this proposal (which would allow Americans to put a portion of their Social Security taxes into a personal savings account to be used for retirement)?"

i. Associated Press, December 2–6, 1998, $N = 1,006$. The question was, "(I'm going to read some proposals that have been made for changes in the Social Security system. For each proposal, please tell me whether you favor it or oppose it.) . . . Letting workers shift some of their Social Security tax payments into personal retirement accounts that they would invest on their own."

j. PSRA, July 14–9, 1999, $N = 3,973$. The question was, "Generally, do you favor or oppose this proposal (which would allow Americans to put a portion of their Social Security taxes into a personal savings account to be used for retirement?"

k. Gallup Organization, January 13–16, 2000, $N = 1,027$. The question was, "A proposal has been made that would allow or require people to put a portion of their Social Security payroll taxes into personal retirement accounts that would be invested in private stocks and bonds. Do you favor or oppose this proposal?"

l. ABC News, *Washington Post*, May 7–10, 2000, $N = 1,068$. The question was, "Would you support or oppose a plan in which people who chose to do so could invest some of their Social Security contributions in the stock market?"

continues

Table 5-3. *Continued*

m. Opinion Dynamics, May 10–11, 2000, $N = 900$. The question was, "With regard to Social Security, do you believe it should continue working as it currently does, or do you think people should have the option to invest part of their Social Security contributions themselves?" (Choices were: continue, option to invest privately, and don't know.)

n. Gallup Organization, June 6–7, 2000, $N = 1,059$. The question was, "A proposal has been made that would allow people to put a portion of their Social Security payroll taxes into personal retirement accounts that would be invested in private stocks and bonds. Do you favor or oppose this proposal?"

o. PSRA, June 22–23, 2000, $N = 750$. The question was, "As you may know, the (2000) presidential candidates have made some proposals to change or supplement Social Security to help Americans save more money for their retirement. One of these proposals would change Social Security to allow workers to invest some of their Social Security payroll taxes in the stock market. In general, do you favor or oppose this proposal?"

p. ABC News, *Washington Post*, September 4–6, 2000, $N = 1,065$. The question was, "Would you support or oppose a plan in which people who chose to could invest some of their Social Security contributions in the stock market?" (Choices were support, oppose, or no opinion).

q. Yankelovich Partners Inc., September 6–7, 2000, $N = 1,278$. The question was, "Do you favor or oppose allowing individuals to invest a portion of their Social Security taxes in the U.S. (United States) stock market?"

r. Gallup Organization, October 25–28, 2000, $N = 1,004$. The question was, "Suppose that on election day this year (2000) you could vote on key issues as well as candidates. Please tell me whether you would vote for or against each one of the following propositions. Would you vote . . . for or against a law that would allow people to put a portion of their Social Security payroll taxes into personal retirement accounts that would be invested in private stocks or bonds?"

s. ABC News, October 28–30, 2000, $N = 1,020$. The question was the same as p.

Yankelovich's simple query ("Do you favor or oppose allowing Americans to put a portion of their Social Security taxes into a personal savings account to be used for retirement") to the long and multipart question posed by the Cato Institute. (The wordings are included in table 5-3.) These differences in question wording account for some of the variations in the results presented in table 5-3. But even allowing for variations owing to different wordings, a majority of Americans support the option of investing a portion of their Social Security taxes in stocks and bonds: from 51 to 80 percent of respondents backed partial privatization, with opposition never reaching 40 percent.

Table 5-4 offers more direct support that, in the abstract, Americans prefer partial privatization to government investment in equity markets or full privatization. Four surveys conducted between August 1998 and May 1999 showed that in response to separate questions Americans opposed government investment (opposition ranged from 48 to 61 percent) and favored partial privatization (support ranged from 52 to 65 percent). One survey in March 1999 found that full privatization was opposed by 57 percent of respondents (42 percent favored it).

The second pattern suggests that Americans' support for privatization fades and then turns to opposition when respondents are reminded of the "risks" of

Table 5-4. *Support for Social Security Privatization Options*
Percent

Social Security Policy Reform	August 1998[a]	February 1999[b]	March 1999[c]	June 1999[d]
Partial privatization				
Government invests SS[e]				
Favor	40	36	38	40
Oppose	48	53	61	52
Neither/don't know/refused	12	11	2	8
Individuals invest SS[f]				
Favor	52	55	65	58
Oppose	38	37	33	33
Neither/don't know/refused	10	8	3	9
Full privatization				
Full privatization option[g]				
Favor	. . .	. . .	42	. . .
Oppose	. . .	. . .	57	. . .
Neither/don't know/refused	. . .	. . .		. . .

Note: Figures do not always sum to 100 percent due to rounding.

a. Princeton Survey Research Associates (PSRA) data, August 6–27, 1998, $N = 2,008$.

b. PSRA data, February 2–14, 1999, $N = 1,000$.

c. National Public Radio (NPR)/Kaiser/Kennedy School Poll (NPR/Kaiser/JFK) data, March 4–24, 1999, $N = 1,203$.

d. PSRA data, May 3–17, 1999, $N = 1,001$. Question wording: All PSRA questions began with the following statement: "Now I'd like to get your opinion on some specific proposals for how Social Security might be changed in the future. If I ask you anything you feel you can't answer, just tell me. Do you favor or oppose the following proposals. . . . (insert—read and rotate) Do you strongly (favor/oppose) this proposal, or moderately (favor/oppose) it. The NPR/Kaiser/JFK questions began with the statement: "I am going to read you a list of some ways that have been suggested to deal with the future financial problems of Social Security. For each one, please tell me if you would favor or oppose such a proposal. How about (read items)? Do you (favor/ oppose) this proposal strongly, or not strongly?" See specific wording below.

e. PSRA: "Changing Social Security from a system where the money in the trust fund is invested in government bonds to a system where some of the money is invested in the stock market." NPR/Kaiser/JFK: "As a way of dealing with the future financial problems of Social Security, do you favor or oppose having the government invest in the private stock market a portion of Social Security reserve funds, which are currently invested in government bonds? (Get answer, then ask) Do you (favor/oppose) this proposal strongly, or not strongly."

f. PSRA: "Changing Social Security from a system where the government collects the taxes that workers and their employees contribute to a system where individuals invest some of their payroll tax contributions themselves." NPR/Kaiser/JFK: "People having individual accounts and making their own investments with a portion of their Social Security payments."

g. NPR/Kaiser/JFK: "Allowing workers to take all of their Social Security taxes out of the Social Security system and invest them on their own."

stock and bond markets and the costs of the transition to a privatized system—including increased taxes. A series of questions revealed that the majorities favoring privatization in table 5-3 narrow when respondents are informed of additional taxation to pay for the transition costs. For instance, a 1997 *Los Angeles Times* survey found that majority support for partial privatization dimmed to a narrow 49–44 margin when respondents were alerted that a "new 1.6% payroll tax would be imposed."[18] In a January 1997 survey conducted by NBC/*Wall Street Journal* 61 percent concluded that the costs of privatization outweighed its benefits when informed of the transitional costs of honoring the commitments to current retirees.[19]

The most accurate test of public sentiment toward privatization are "balanced frame" questions that offer respondents both a strong positive case for the reform (greater returns) and a strong negative case (greater risks of losing money). Table 5-5 presents six sets of results from surveys by Yankelovich Partners and Hart and Teeter (for the *Wall Street Journal* and NBC). The results present the most direct challenge to the presumption of public support for privatization in five of the six surveys: between 51 and 63 percent of Americans oppose privatization when offered a balanced choice.

The public's opposition to privatization (when offered fuller information) is confirmed by a series of queries in a June 2000 Princeton Survey Research Associates' poll, which is presented in table 5-6. The first item shows the majority support for partial privatization reported earlier in table 5-3: by a 51–36 margin, the public favors "allow[ing] workers to invest some of their Social Security payroll taxes in the stock market." The survey proceeded to test the reaction of privatization supporters when they were provided with additional information. When informed that privatization might reduce benefits, a majority of those who initially favored privatization now opposed it: 57 percent opposed versus 33 percent in favor. The third item found that a clear majority

18. The question was, "As you may know, government experts say that because the baby boom generation is so large, Social Security will begin to run out of money when those who are in their forties and fifties retire. To solve that problem a federal advisory committee has come up with three different proposals to keep the retirement fund solvent. Would you please tell me whether you favor or oppose each of those plans. Under a third plan, the current Social Security system would be kept intact, but in addition, there would be a compulsory individual savings account with funds that would be automatically deducted from workers' salaries. With these savings accounts, individuals could invest as they wish to supplement their retirement benefits. Under this plan, a new 1.6 percent payroll tax would be imposed. Do you favor or oppose this plan?"

19. The question was, "This proposal to allow people to invest Social Security contributions in the stock market also includes an increase in the payroll tax for current employees, as well as an increase in the federal deficit, so that benefits to current retirees also can be maintained. Do you think the benefits of allowing people to invest Social Security contributions in the stock market outweigh these costs of higher payroll taxes and deficits, or do you think the costs outweigh the benefits?" Only 22 percent believed that the benefits outweigh the cost.

Table 5-5.   *Support for Social Security Partial Privatization When Risks Are Considered*

Percent

	Favor	Oppose	No opinion/ don't know
December 1996[a]	36	56	8
January 1997[b]	22	61	17
March 1997[c]	35	63	2
April 1998[d]	52	41	7
October 1998[e]	43	52	5
March 1999[f]	44	51	5

a. Yankelovich Partners, December 11–12, 1996, N = 818. The question was, "Some people favor investing a portion of Social Security tax funds in the stock market because this might lead to higher investment returns. Other people oppose this because this is too risky. What is your opinion? Do you favor or oppose investing a portion of the tax money collected for Social Security in the stock market?"

b. Hart and Teeter Research Companies (HTRC), January 25–27, 1997, N = 1,002. The question was, "This proposal to allow people to invest Social Security contributions in the stock market also includes an increase in the payroll tax for current employees, as well as an increase in the federal deficit, so that benefits to current retirees also can be maintained. Do you think the benefits of allowing people to invest Social Security contributions in the stock market outweigh these costs of higher payroll taxes and deficits, or do you think the costs outweigh the benefits?"

c. *Washington Post*, March 13–23, 1997, N = 1,309. The question was, "Some people favor investing a portion of Social Security tax funds in the stock market because this might lead to higher investment returns. Other people oppose this idea because they say the stock market is too unpredictable. What is your opinion?" Do you favor or oppose investing a portion of the tax money collected for Social Security in the stock market?"

d. HTRC, April 18–20, 1998, N = 1,004. The question was, "One proposal has been made that would allow or require people to put a portion of their Social Security payroll taxes into personal retirement accounts that would be invested in private stocks and bonds. Some people think that individuals would have more money for retirement if they were allowed to invest and manage some of their Social Security payroll taxes themselves. Others think that it is too risky and could leave some people without adequate money for retirement if the stock market were to decline in value significantly. Do you favor or oppose this proposal?"

e. HTRC, October 24–28, 1998, N = 1,025. National registered voters only. The question was, "A proposal has been made that would allow or require people to put a portion of their Social Security payroll taxes into personal retirement accounts that would be invested in private stocks and bonds. Some people think that individuals would have more money for retirement if they were allowed to invest and manage some of their Social Security payroll taxes themselves. Others think that it is too risky and could leave some people without adequate money for retirement if the stock market were to decline in value significantly. Do you favor or oppose this proposal?"

f. HTCR, March 4–7, 1999, N = 2,012. The question was the same as e.

of 60 percent thought partial privatization was a "bad idea" when informed that it "might make more money for the fund but would involve greater risk."

Although the public seems opposed to privatization of the existing Social Security system, they appear quite supportive of creating a supplemental savings program outside of Social Security in which individuals could invest in the stock and bond markets. A June 2000 Princeton Survey Research Associ-

Table 5-6.   *Preferences Regarding Policy Options to Invest Social Security Funds in the Stock Market*

Percent

Policy Option	
Allow workers to invest Social Security payroll taxes in the stock market[a]	
Favor	51
Oppose	36
Don't know	13
(Of those who favor) Still favor if it reduces seniors' benefits[b]	
Yes, would still favor	33
Oppose	57
Don't know	10
Invest Social Security trust fund in stock market if risk is involved[c]	
Good idea	30
Bad idea	60
Don't know	10

a. Princeton Survey Research Associates (PSRA), June 22–23, 2000, $N = 750$. The question was, "As you may know, the (2000) presidential candidates have made some proposals to change or supplement Social Security to help Americans save more money for retirement. One of these proposals would change Social Security to allow workers to invest some of their Social Security payroll taxes in the stock market. In general, do you favor or oppose this proposal?"

b. PSRA, June 22–23, 2000, $N = 759$. Registered voters who said they favored the proposal (51 percent of registered voters). The question was, "You say you generally favor the proposal allowing workers to invest some Social Security payroll taxes in the stock market. Would you still favor this proposal if you heard it might require reducing the Social Security benefits that seniors have?"

c. PSRA, June 22–23, 2000, $N = 750$. The question was, "Some people have suggested investing some of the Social Security trust fund in the stock market, which might make more money for the fund, but would involve greater risk. Do you think some of the Social Security trust fund in the stock market is a good idea or bad idea?"

ates survey found that a striking two-thirds favored a "supplemental savings program that allow workers to put up to $2,000 a year of tax-deductible savings in retirement accounts outside the Social Security system . . . [with the government] offer[ing] matching funds based on income level."[20] The public, then, is not innately hostile to investing in equity markets; however, they remain reluctant to commit Social Security funds to it.

Overall, the public seems to favor some form of partial privatization of Social Security in the abstract, but their support is replaced by ambivalence and then opposition as they are informed of the costs and risks associated with it. Policymakers should not wade into the thicket of Social Security reform believing they are protected against the potential of a strong public backlash. The public is supportive, though, of a private investment program that is outside Social Security.

20. Princeton Survey Research Associates, June 22–23, 2000.

Tepid Support for Incremental Changes

A range of incremental changes has been recommended to strengthen Social Security's finances long term. Shifting the focus of reform from changing the structure of the Social Security system to making incremental adjustments in the existing system finds some but far from uniform support among Americans. Proposals for incremental changes fall into one of two categories—reducing benefits or raising taxes.

REDUCING BENEFITS

Three reforms are most often mentioned as means for reducing benefits. First, extending the age at which people are eligible for receiving full Social Security payments creates a reduction in benefits; a rough rule is that benefits are cut by 5 percent for each year added to the normal retirement age. Americans have consistently expressed opposition to raising the normal retirement age. Since 1977 at least nineteen surveys have asked Americans about their attitudes toward hiking the age of eligibility for Social Security; the consistent finding was that majorities opposed these changes.[21] The one exception occurred two decades ago in July 1981 when a CBS-*New York Times* poll asked: "To save money, would you favor or oppose increasing the age at which people were eligible to receive full Social Security from 65 to 68 if that change became effective 20 years from now?" By 50 to 42 percent, Americans favored raising the retirement age. Note the two conditions put in the question: the purpose was "to save money" and the changes would not be effective until "20 years from now." In fact, these conditions were very close to the 1983 Social Security Amendments that have been slowly raising the age of eligibility.

The consistent pattern since 1977 of public opposition to increasing the retirement age continues to hold today. Table 5-7 shows that in three surveys by Princeton Survey Research Associates 74 percent of Americans opposed gradually raising the retirement age to seventy. One wrinkle in this persistent pattern is that the public is divided on the issue of gradually raising the *early* retirement age from sixty-two to sixty-five for partial receipt of Social Security. In particular, the public was evenly split in its support for this option in two surveys and opposed to it by a 52-43 margin in a third poll.

The second reform to reduce benefits is to lower the cost-of-living adjustments (COLAs) for beneficiaries. Table 5-7 shows that the public opposes lowering COLAs in all three Princeton surveys, although the opposition

21. Jacobs and Shapiro (1998b).

Table 5-7. *Support for Incremental Changes in Social Security*
Percent

Policy option	August 1998	February 1999	May 1999
Reducing benefits			
Raise the retirement age to seventy years[a]			
Strongly or moderately favor	23	24	22
Strongly or moderately oppose	74	74	74
Neither/don't know	3	2	4
Gradually increase early retirement age from 62 to 65[b]			
Strongly or moderately favor	47	43	46
Strongly or moderately oppose	47	52	48
Neither/don't know	6	5	6
Lower cost-of-living adjustment[c]			
Strongly or moderately favor	34	37	40
Strongly or moderately oppose	61	56	53
Neither/don't know	5	7	7
Reduce benefits for the wealthy (over $60,000)[d]			
Strongly or moderately favor	54	54	58
Strongly or moderately oppose	40	40	37
Neither/don't know	6	6	5
Raising taxes			
Increase payroll tax from 6.2 to 6.7 percent[e]			
Strongly or moderately favor	40	44	44
Strongly or moderately oppose	54	50	50
Neither/don't know	6	6	6
Raise earnings ceiling from $68,000 to $100,000[f]			
Strongly or moderately favor	50	59	61
Strongly or moderately oppose	29	28	29
Neither/don't know	11	13	10
Trade-offs			
Raising taxes or reducing benefits[g]			
Avoiding any tax increases	33	32	34
Avoiding any future cuts	55	59	53
Neither/don't know	12	9	13

Source: Princeton Survey Research Associates.

Note: N = 2,008 for August 1998; N = 1,000 for February 1999; N = 1,001 for May 1999. The question was, "I'd like to get your opinion of some specific proposals of how Social Security might be changed in the future. If I ask you anything you feel you can't answer, just tell me. Do you favor or oppose the following proposals?"

a. ". . . Gradually raising the age when a person can collect Social Security benefits to age seventy. . . . Do you strongly favor/oppose this proposal, or moderately favor or oppose it?"

b. ". . . Gradually increasing the early retirement age for collecting reduced benefits from age sixty-two to sixty-five. . . . Do you strongly favor/oppose this proposal, or moderately favor or oppose it?"

c. ". . . Cutting the amount of Social Security benefits go up each year for changes in the cost of living. . . . Do you strongly favor/oppose this proposal, or moderately favor or oppose it?"

d. ". . . Reducing Social Security benefits for people who have retirement incomes over about $60,000 per year. . . . Do you strongly favor/oppose this proposal, or moderately favor or oppose it?"

continues

Table 5-7. *Continued*

e. ". . . Increasing the payroll tax that workers and employers each pay into the Social Security system from 6.2 percent to 6.7 percent. . . . Do you strongly favor/oppose this proposal, or moderately favor or oppose it?"

f. ". . . Collecting payroll taxes on earnings up to $100,000 per year, instead of the current cut-off of about $72,000. . . . Do you strongly favor/oppose this proposal, or moderately favor or oppose it?" (For the question of August 1998, the cut-off was $68,000).

g. "People have different opinions how the Social Security system might be changed for the future. We'd like your opinions on what policy makers' priorities should be when they are making decisions about Social Security's future. When decisions about Social Security's future are being made, which do you think is more important . . . avoiding any tax increases for workers and employers, or avoiding any future cuts in Social Security benefit amounts?"

weakened by 8 percentage points between August 1998 and May 1999 (from 61 percent to 53 percent).

The third reform is reducing the benefits for the affluent, defined as beneficiaries with retirement incomes over $60,000 per year. Table 5-7 indicates that solid majorities of between 54 and 58 percent favored reducing the benefits of the affluent.

RAISING TAXES

Policymakers and journalists often assume that the American public will not tolerate tax increases to bolster Social Security. However, survey data show that this generalization is overstated; Americans—by a narrow margin—oppose increased payroll taxes but back raising the payroll base and prefer tax increases to benefit cuts.

On the one hand, the conventional wisdom of opposition for taxes to fund Social Security is corroborated by some evidence in table 5-7. Majorities oppose increasing payroll taxes from 6.2 percent to 6.7 percent. The narrow (and shrinking) margins by which Americans oppose the tax hike, however, suggest that public opposition is certainly not lopsided or one-sided.

On the other hand, the conventional wisdom is wrong that tax hikes for the concrete purpose of strengthening Social Security are off the table in the public's mind. Social Security actuaries estimate that raising the ceiling on earnings subject to the payroll tax would bring in sufficient additional tax revenue to eliminate 68 percent of the anticipated Social Security revenue shortfall over the seventy-five-year forecasting period.[22] Table 5-7 shows that sizable majorities of approximately 60 percent favored "collecting taxes on earnings up to $100,000 per year, instead of the [then] current cut-off of about $72,000."

22. Advisory Council on Social Security (1997).

Reducing Benefits versus Raising Taxes

When the public is forced to wrestle with the trade-offs facing policymakers, tax hikes are preferred over benefit cuts. Princeton Survey Research Associates put respondents in the bind of choosing between "avoiding any tax increases for workers and employers, or avoiding any future cuts in Social Security benefit accounts." Table 5-7 shows that solid majorities of between 53 and 59 percent choose avoiding benefit cuts; only a distinct minority of 32 to 34 percent preferred to avoid any tax increases. When Americans are forced to make tradeoffs, there is little doubt that they prefer—by a substantial margin of 20 percentage points—to swallow tax hikes in order to avoid benefit cuts.

The Public's Signals to Policymakers Designing Reforms

The public's attitudes toward Social Security reforms provide a set of green, yellow, and red lights to policymakers. The public is sending red signals of opposition on what many policymakers consider to be starting points for reform—raising the normal retirement age and reducing COLAs. The history of public opinion suggests that this opposition has not been rigid; when presented with a clear rationale and payoffs, the public actually supported a gradual increase in the normal retirement age prior to the last major round of Social Security reform in 1983. The public's red lights defy simple partisan categories: Americans oppose proposals embraced most enthusiastically by Republicans to privatize Social Security fully or partially (when informed about financial costs and market risks) as well as the proposal preferred by many Democrats—increasing payroll taxes. The public is flashing a caution-ary yellow signal to policymakers on increasing the age of early retirement; this may be an area where broad agreement among policymakers and clear information could well influence public thinking.

It is wrong to assume that the public is opposed to all forms of reform. The public provides welcoming green lights to policymakers on reducing benefits to the affluent, and it accepts raising the base on which payroll taxes are paid, preferring tax increases over benefit reductions. The public also prefers by a wide margin supplemental savings accounts as a means for investing in stock and bond markets.

Responding to Public Opinion and Responsibly Making Social Security Policy

Policymakers often rest their proposals for reforming Social Security on a set of calculations or expectations about how Americans evaluate and think about the program. These expectations are often passed along—like a well-worn family antique—from one policymaker to another until they assume the mantle of accepted truth. Rarely, however, are these presumed truths compared to hard data on public opinion. We closely examined three working hypotheses that are often invoked by policymakers and found them to be contradicted by a large body of hard data. Some of the most widely cited claims about public opinion are wrong or distorted: public confidence is higher in 2000 than it had been in a decade and has risen by 15 percentage points from the time of the last survey in 1998; public support is extraordinarily high and unwavering; and the public supports a range of pragmatic incremental reforms aimed at strengthening the existing Social Security system rather than altering its basic structure. Claims that structural reforms involving the introduction of privatization are necessary to respond to low and declining confidence are wrong; an exhaustive analysis of hundreds of independent surveys finds no support for them.

If government officials repeatedly erred in their analysis of fundamental financial or program arrangements related to Social Security, they would be publicly challenged by colleagues and journalists and forced to correct their statements. It is high time for journalists and others to hold policymakers accountable: policymakers should be asked to offer evidence to support their claims about public opinion, and journalists and others should test these claims against independent evidence.

The implication that policymakers ought to listen to public preference on critical policy issues like Social Security is not widely accepted in Washington, although large majorities of Americans hold this view.[23] In particular, the public's policy preferences are often criticized by policymakers and pundits for irresponsibly favoring inaction in the face of pressing policy matters that demand remediation. On Social Security, however, the public supports a series of policy reforms that are often mentioned by experts as options on the policy menu—from a supplemental market approach outside Social Security to raising the base on which payroll taxes are paid. The challenge is whether policymakers are willing to respond to the public's preferences or whether Democrats and Republicans will substitute their own preferences and those of their supporters.

The fundamental question is: Will Social Security policymaking follow the direction seen in a number of policy areas of declining government responsiveness to public preferences? Fundamental changes in American politics over the past two decades or so have reversed the myth that politicians "pander" to public opinion by tailoring their decisions to polls. The influence of ideologi-

23. Jacobs and Shapiro (2000).

cally extreme party activists, campaign contributors, interest groups, and other forces have increased, raising the risks to policymakers who defy the preferences of these forces in an effort to respond to what majorities of Americans prefer. A quick list of policies on which government officials defied large majorities of Americans would include impeachment, tobacco legislation, and elimination of the marriage penalty. Two or three decades ago, when these new forces in American politics were less influential, policymakers were more responsive to public opinion. The situation is much different today than in the past: Instead of polls and public opinion driving many policy decisions, these decisions drive the public opinion research to identify the words, arguments, and symbols that seem most likely to manipulate public opinion to support what policymakers and their supporters most desire.[24]

Adding Social Security reform to the growing list of policies on which policymakers have defied public opinion has clear political risks. Republican insistence on privatization proposals in the face of harsh opposition by Democratic members of Congress, who will undoubtedly invoke citizens' genuine reservations about its costs and risks, could recreate the kind of devastating political backlash that Clinton suffered in the 1994 elections after his health care reform campaign failed (another policy proposal that defied important aspects of public thinking).

On the other hand, Democratic intransigence that repeatedly blocked Social Security reform in the face of Republican leadership that followed the broad contours of public opinion could well neutralize Social Security as a "Democratic issue" on which political party has traditionally been considered more trustworthy by Americans. One of the defining accomplishments of Bill Clinton was to neutralize what Americans had long considered "Republican issues," such as law-and-order issues and welfare reform.

Table 5-8 suggests a gradual narrowing of the Democratic Party's advantage over the Republican Party in the public's eye for its job of "protecting" or "dealing with" Social Security. Between fall 1986 and fall 2000 at least thirty-six separate surveys asked the public some variant of the question: "Which political party, the Democrats or the Republicans, do you trust to do a better job protecting the Social Security system." (Some of the questions during 2000 were posed only to likely voters rather than to all adults, but this did not seem to explain the variations in results.)

During the Reagan and Bush administrations, the Democratic Party's advantage was a glaring 21 to 34 percentage point gap. But the Democratic advantage shrank to fewer than ten points in the aftermath of Clinton's failure

---

24. Jacobs and Shapiro (2000).

Table 5-8.   *The Public's Assessment of Which Party Is More Likely to Make Right Decisions about Social Security*

Percent

Political period		Demo-crats	Repub-licans	Both equally	Neither	Don't know/ no opinion
Reagan/	9/86[a]	60	26	4	3	7
Bush	1/90[b]	52	31	3	9	4
	4/91[c]	52	29	7	8	4
Clinton/	11/94[d]	42	36	7	10	5
collapse	6/95[e]	35	26	16	15	8
	12/95[f]	44	22	14	14	6
	10/96[g]	36	24	17	15	8
	9/97[h]	33	19	18	22	8
	1/98[i]	26	15	34	18	7
	1/98[j]	48	38	3	7	5
	7/98[k]	51	35	3	6	6
	7/98[l]	43	37	3	9	9
	7/98[m]	28	19	34	14	5
	8/98[n]	46	30	4	9	11
After	9/98[o]	37	21	25	13	4
government	10/98[p]	44	21	25	6	4
shutdown	10/98[q]	52	29	4	4	11
	11/98[r]	49	27	6	12	6
	12/98[s]	48	33	3	9	9
	1/99[t]	51	30	2	4	13
	3/99[u]	39	21	23	11	6
	3/99[v]	52	29	3	8	7
	4/99[w]	35	23	24	12	6
	10/99[x]	56	33	3	4	3
	11/99[y]	49	33	2	3	13
	1/00[z]	49	33	2	7	10
	5/00[aa]	48	30	4	5	12
Bush	6/00[bb]	40	42	3	6	11
unveiling	6/00[cc]	38	34	4	13	11
of	7/00[dd]	43	35	3	5	14
proposals	8/00[ee]	35	37	4	5	19
	8/00[ff]	48	34	3	2	13
	9/00[gg]	48	36	3	3	10
	10/00[hh]	47	37	2	3	9
Fall	10/00[ii]	47	36	4	4	9
campaign	10/00[jj]	50	36	2	4	8
	10/00[kk]	46	38	3	2	10

a. ABC News/*Washington Post* (ABC/*WP*), September 18–28, 1996. Asked of registered voters. "I am going to mention a few national problems and issues. Regardless of how you feel about the two parties, I'd like you to tell me which one, the Republican Party or the Democratic Party, would do a better job of handling each particular problem or issue. How about . . . protecting the Social Security system. Would the Republican party or the Democratic party do a better job?"

Table 5-8. *Continued*

b. ABC/*WP*, January 11–16, 1990. "Which political party, the Democrats or the Republicans, do you trust to do a better job . . . protecting the Social Security system?"

c. ABC/*WP*, March 1–4, 1991. "Which political party, the Democrats or the Republicans, do you trust to do a better job . . . protecting the Social Security system?"

d. Wirthlin Group, November 9, 1994. "Now I am going to read you a list of issues. This time I want you to concentrate on the two major political parties, and as I read each one, please tell me whether you think the Republican party or the Democratic party can best handle that problem. Protecting Social Security."

e. Hart and Teeter Research Companies (HTRC), June 2–5, 1995. "When it comes to the following issues, which party do you think would do a better job—the Democratic party, the Republican party, both about the same, or neither? . . . Dealing with Social Security?"

f. HTRC, December 1–5, 1995. "When it comes to . . . dealing with Social Security . . . which party do you think would do a better job—the Democratic party, the Republican party, both about the same, or neither."

g. HTRC, October 19–22, 1996. "(Let me read you some specific issues.) When it comes to . . . dealing with Social Security . . . which party do you think would do a better job—the Democratic party, the Republican party, both about the same, or neither?"

h. Princeton Survey Research Associates, January 9–10, 1997. "Do you have more confidence in the Republican party or the Democratic party to deal with problems in the Social Security system?"

i. HTRC, September 11–15, 1997. "(Let me read you some specific issues.) When it comes to . . . dealing with Social Security . . . which party do you think would do a better job—the Democratic party, the Republican party, both about the same, or neither?"

j. Gallup Organization, October 27–28, 1997. "(Do you think the Republican party or the Democratic party would do a better job of dealing with each of the following issues and problems?) . . . Social Security."

k. HTRC, January, 1998. "When it comes to dealing with Social Security, which party do you think would do a better job—the Democratic party, the Republican party, both about the same, or neither?"

l. Gallup Organization, July 13–14, 1998. "In your view, which party would do a better job dealing with the issue of Social Security—the Republican party or the Democratic party?"

m. HTRC, July 25–27, 1998. "When it comes to dealing with Social Security, which party do you think would do a better job—the Democratic party, the Republican party, both about the same, or neither?"

n. The Tarrance Group and Lake, Snell, Perry (TGLSNP), August 24–26, 1998. Asked of national registered likely voters. "I would like to read you a list of issues that some people from this part of the country have said are important for government to deal with. Please tell me, for each one, whether you have more confidence in—the Democrats in Congress or the Republicans in Congress—to deal with this issue . . . Strengthening Social Security?"

o. HTRC, September 10–13, 1998. "(Let me read you some specific issues.) When it comes to . . . dealing with Social Security . . . which party do you think would do a better job—the Democratic party, the Republican party, both about the same, or neither?"

p. HTRC, October 24–27, 1998. "Of these specific issues, when it comes to the following issue, which party do you think would do a better job—the Democratic party, the Republican party, both about the same, or neither? . . . Dealing with Social Security?"

q. CBS News/*New York Times* (CBS/*NYT*), October 26–28, 1998. "Regardless of how you usually vote, do you think the Republican party or the Democratic party is more likely to make the right decisions about Social Security?"

r. Wirthlin Worldwide, November 6–8, 1998. "I am going to read you a list of statements and I want you to concentrate on the two major political parties. As I read each one, please tell me whether you think the Democratic party or Republican party is best described by that statement . . . Guaranteeing Social Security for existing and future recipients?"

s. Gallup Organization, December 4–6, 1998. "In your view, which party would do a better job dealing with the issue of Social Security—the Republican party or the Democratic party?"

continues

Table 5-8. *Continued*

t. CBS/*NYT*, January 1–February 1, 1999. "Regardless of how you usually vote, do you think the Republican party or the Democratic party is more likely to make the right decisions about Social Security?"

u. HTRC, March 4–7, 1999. "When it comes to . . . dealing with Social Security . . . which party do you think would do a better job—the Democratic party, the Republican party, both about the same, or neither?"

v. ABC/*WP*, March 11–14, 1999. "Which political party, the Democrats or the Republicans, do you trust to do a better job . . . protecting the Social Security system?"

w. HTRC, April 17–19, 1999. "When it comes to dealing with . . . Social Security . . . which party do you think would do a better job—the Democratic party, the Republican party, both about the same, or neither?"

x. ABC/*WP*, August 30–October 2, 1999. "And which political party, the Democrats or the Republicans, do you trust to do a better job . . . protecting the Social Security system?"

y. CBS/*NYT*, November 4–7, 1999. "Regardless of how you usually vote, do you think the Republican party or the Democratic party is more likely to make the right decisions about Social Security?"

z. TGLSNP, January 3–5, 2000. Asked of likely voters and registered voters who said they are somewhat/very/extremely likely to vote in the congressional and presidential elections in 2000. There was an oversample of 250 Hispanics, in addition to the national sample of 1,000. Results weighted to be representative of a national registered likely voters sample. "I would like to read you a list of issues that some people from this part of the country have said are important for government to deal with. Please tell me, for each one, whether you have confidence in—the Democrats in Congress or the Republicans in Congress to deal with this issue . . . Strengthening Social Security?"

aa. TGLSNP, May 1–3, 2000. $N = 1,000$, The question was the same as z.

bb. TGLSNP, June 11–13, 2000. $N = 1,000$. The question was the same as z.

cc. PSRA, June 22–23, 2000. $N = 750$. The question was, "Do you have more confidence in the Republican party or the Democratic party to deal with problems in the Social Security system?"

dd. CBS/*NYT*, July 20–23, 2000. $N = 953$. The question was the same as y.

ee. CBS/*NYT*, August 4–6, 2000. $N = 1,139$. The question was the same as y.

ff. CBS/*NYT*, August 18–20, 2000. $N = 1,254$. The question was the same as y.

gg. CBS/*NYT*, September 27–October 1, 2000. $N = 1,462$. The question was the same as y.

hh. Greenberg, Quinlan Research (GQR), October 9–10, 2000. $N = 1,027$. National registered likely voters. The question was, "(I am going to ask you something different. I am going to read a list of issues and I want you to tell me whether, overall, you think the Democrats or the Republicans would do a better job with this issue. If you do not know, just tell me and we will move on to the next item.) . . . *Retirement and Social Security*. Do you think the Democrats or Republicans would do a better job with that? (If Democrats/Republicans ask:) Would that be much better or somewhat better?" *Research notes*: National registered likely voters are registered voters who voted in the 1996 presidential election for president, were ineligible, or too young, and said they would probably vote or are almost certain to vote in the presidential election in 2000.

ii. GQR, October 18–20, 2000. $N = 1,009$. The question was the same as hh.

jj. GQR, October 24–25, 2000. $N = 998$. The question was the same as hh.

kk. GQR, October 30–31, 2000. $N = 1,016$. The question was the same as hh.

to pass health care reform in 1994 and the Republican landslide in the November 1994 election. The period that followed the congressional Republicans' efforts to shut down the government saw the Democrats regain some of the public's confidence as the protectors of Social Security but fail to reach the level of dominance during the Reagan and Bush eras. By the summer of 2000, however, Social Security was neutralized as Governor George W. Bush unveiled his proposals for reform during the presidential campaign. Although the Democrats once again regained some ground during the fall 2000 political campaign, their advantage was cut in half from its levels during the late 1980s and early 1990s. In short, Democrats no longer monopolize the public's trust as protectors of Social Security; the actions of both parties during the George W. Bush administration will determine whether the Republican president succeeds in stealing a previously "Democratic issue" or if it returns to the Democratic fold.

References

Advisory Council on Social Security. 1997. *Report of the 1994–1996 Advisory Council on Social Security: Volume I: Findings and Recommendations*. Government Printing Office.

Ball, Robert M. 1997. "Testimony." Congressional hearing on "The Future of Social Security for this Generation and the Next." U.S. House of Representatives, Committee on Ways and Means (September 24). Government Printing Office.

———. 2000. "A Program for the Future." In *Insuring the Essentials: A Selection of Articles and Essays from 1942 through 2000*, ed. Thomas N. Bethell, 273–292. New York: Century Foundation Press.

Breaux, John. 1998. "Comments." Congressional hearing, "The Stock Market and Social Security: The Risks and the Rewards." U.S. Senate, Special Committee on Aging (April 22).

Cook, Fay Lomax, Jason Barabas, and Benjamin Page. 2000. "Polls, Policy Debates, and the Future of Social Security." Paper presented at the conference on Polls, Policy and the Future of American Democracy. Evanston, Ill.: Northwestern University (May 13).

Cook, F. L., and L. Jacobs. 1998. "Deliberative Democracy in Action: Evaluation of *Americans Discuss Social Security*." Report to the Pew Charitable Trusts. Evanston, Ill.: Institute for Policy Research.

Glassman, James. 1998. "Testimony." Congressional hearing on "Enhancing Retirement through Individual Investment Choices." U.S. House of Representatives, Committee on Commerce (July 24). Government Printing Office.

Grassley, Charles. 1997. "Comments." Congressional hearing on "2010 and Beyond: Preparing Social Security for the Baby Boomers." U.S. Senate, Special Committee on Aging (August 26). Government Printing Office.

Hagel, Charles. 1998. "Testimony." Congressional hearing on "The Stock Market and Social Security: The Risks and the Rewards." U.S. Senate, Special Committee on Aging (April 22). Government Printing Office.

Jacobs, Lawrence R., and Robert Y. Shapiro. 1995. "The News Media's Coverage of Social Security." Report prepared for the National Academy of Social Insurance. Washington (March).

———. 1998a. "More Social Security Bunk: UFO Stories." *The New Republic* (August 10), 12–13.

————. 1998b. "Myths and Misunderstandings about Public Opinion toward Social Security." In *Framing the Social Security Debate: Values, Politics, and Economics,* edited by R. Douglas Arnold, Michael J. Graetz, and Alicia H. Munnell, 355–88. Brookings.

————. 2000. *Politicians Don't Pander: Political Manipulation and the Loss of Democratic Responsiveness.* University of Chicago Press.

Jacobs, Lawrence R., Mark Watts, and Robert Shapiro. 1995. "Media Coverage and Public Views of Social Security." *Public Perspective* (April/May): 9–10, 48–49.

Rielly, John E. 1999. *American Public Opinion and U.S. Foreign Policy.* Chicago Council on Foreign Relations.

Skidmore, Max J. 1999. *Social Security and Its Enemies: The Case for America's Most Efficient Insurance Program.* Boulder, Colo.: Westview Press.

Tanner, Michael. 1996. "Testimony." Congressional hearing on "Social Security Reform Options: Preparing for the 21st Century." U.S. Senate, Special Committee on Aging (September 24). Government Printing Office.

Wyden, Ron. 1998. "Comments." Congressional hearing on "The Stock Market and Social Security: The Risks and the Rewards." U.S. Senate, Special Committee on Aging (April 22). Government Printing Office.

Comment by Howard Fluhr

I am not a pollster, economist, or policy analyst. As I look at chapters 3–5, there are several key issues that need to be addressed concerning public policy and the Social Security system and its future.

First, the facts that are needed to produce sound public policy must be considered. John Ruskin said in *The Stones of Venice* that "the work of science is to substitute facts for appearances and demonstrations for appearances," and in these chapters facts are replacing impressions. To analogize with some economic theories, bad information drives out good. Therefore, it is important that policymakers hear and understand these analyses.

The fundamental purpose of Social Security, going back to its origins in the 1930s, has been to provide both some redistribution and a safety net. It goes back to the proverbial three-legged stool of retirement security for the American people. Discussions about individual accounts and privatization generally disregard these fundamentals. It was reassuring to read in more than one of these chapters a fundamental understanding of what Social Security is about.

When evaluating predictions about the economy, it is important to be very careful about making long-term bets on relatively short-term experience. If one harkens back to the hyperinflation days, one can find papers, articles, and books saying that this environment would continue indefinitely (including 15 percent interest rates and high inflation) and could effectively explain why that was the new state of the world. Something else has been heard since the late 1980s and early 1990s, and it is good to come back to the reality that if we are going to make a big bet like the Social Security system, we had better be sure that the future economic and market risks are understood.

In thinking about the survival of Social Security, you may be surprised to know that the eighteenth-century political philosopher Voltaire actually had some advice. He said, "I'd advise you to go on living solely to enrage those who are paying your annuities." Regarding the notion of the existence of UFOs, it is not reassuring that 30 percent of the people in any age range think that they exist, but it is reassuring to know there is confidence in the future of Social Security.

The safety net aspect of Social Security cannot be underscored enough in public policy discourse. It is somewhat reassuring that public debate is taking place and that the subject is in the public's awareness. That should give the policymakers—in addition to the analysts—the courage to face up to what has to be done. It is important for them to know that they have public support. They also have to understand it is their obligation to do the right thing. No doubt a survey of the American people would indicate that few want to delay the retirement age. No one wants to reduce the benefit. No one wants to raise taxes—except on other people, therefore the majority of people believe it is okay to raise the covered wage base to $100,000, since the majority of people do not earn at that level. It is not a popularity contest. It is a question of what combination of changes will allow the system to survive. Certainly, the change in life expectancy connects well to the idea of extending the retirement age. While both presidential candidates did not seem to know that had already been done, it is reassuring that the public has some understanding of what Social Security is about.

As in any debate, the advocates are choosing the "facts" that support their positions. If the policymakers understand and utilize research-based facts, they are more likely to come to sound solutions. We need to try to overcome the natural inclination to accept what supports our beliefs and to dismiss what does not.

While it is not clear how to resolve the issue of incremental change versus fundamental change, it is clear that we need change. The fact that the good economy of the last ten years has in some ways eased the need to change means that this is a good time, coupled with more public discourse, to make these fundamental changes. Even if their implementation is incremental, it is important that American citizens face up to the fact that these changes are necessary.

My unsolicited advice to the policymakers, and some of the survey information analyzed correctly reinforces the general population's understanding of the needs for reform of Social Security, is what Mahatma Gandhi said about leadership. He said that "leadership is finding out what the people want and getting in front of them." So this might be the right time.

The problem of people in poverty at advanced ages is a fundamental concern, and Social Security has historically been part of the solution. In fact, in many cases, it has been the only solution, since it provides a safety net and redistributes income. Much of this issue has to do with earnings histories for these unfortunate individuals, and that is a fundamental economic situation that cannot really be dealt with in addressing Social Security. However, approximately half of the private working population of the United States is covered by private pensions. Therefore, the other half is not. So, recalling the three-legged stool—personal savings, private pensions, and Social Security— attention must be paid to those who are not covered. Such ideas as a voluntary addition in the Social Security program, a mandatory addition in Social Security above the basic defined benefit portion, or even a mandated minimum benefit could be considered. But those at the lower end of the earnings scale cannot be ignored. The disparity between the wealthy and the poor is getting wider, making it even more appropriate to pay attention to this group. It makes good sense to deal with such situations when the economy is strong. On the other hand, many will remember that we tried to spend the peace dividend about five times. So when looking at this strong economy, we should not overspend.

One of the advantages that economists and actuaries have over weather forecasters is the time horizon. Although weather forecasters deserve our compassion, the issue of the Social Security system and its future is profound. In the public discussion and debate, a range of economists and actuaries should be included among the policymakers to help understand the consequences of the decisions.

The notion that we need to encourage ever-increasing investing in equities is troubling. The ultimate size of that market is a concern. A widely respected and knowledgeable economist, Leah Modigliani, who is with Morgan Stanley Dean Witter and is the granddaughter of Franco Modigliani—the Nobel Laureate in economics—raises that issue and says that it is, in a way, a fool's journey to think that further and further opportunities can be expanded for investing in equities without affecting the equities and fixed-income marketplace.

Comment by Cecilia Muñoz

Much of the focus in the first chapters has been on the 50 percent of Americans without access to pensions. My organization, the National Council of La Raza, is a Latino civil rights organization and, therefore, represents a large number of people without pensions. Much of our work focuses on the economic status of the Latino community, and that is the source of our interest in the Social Security debate.

Kilolo Kijakazi has discussed the importance of preserving the social insurance aspect and the impact of the Social Security program on poverty. This is an issue of critical importance to Latinos, who will largely be relying on Social Security as they retire. Their lack of pensions and the ability to save are the result of both low income and lack of information, access, and know-how with respect to the way that savings and investments work.

Kijakazi presented information that fuels an argument to expand this debate beyond examining the impact of the Social Security system on the low-wage work force as they retire to looking at the impact of the contribution of the low-wage work force into the Social Security system. This piece of the debate is in danger of being missed as the discussion about the health and future of the Social Security system is continued. To illustrate that, by 2030, a key date with respect to the fiscal health of this system, fully one in five Americans of working age will be Hispanic American. Furthermore, analysis of work force trends today shows that Latinos are heavily concentrated in the low-wage, low-skilled sector of the work force, while substantially underrepresented in the professional and managerial positions. The economic place of this sector of the work force, which is growing dramatically, has an impact on the solvency of the system and has an impact on the future of Social Security. It is absolutely critical that this debate be expanded beyond its current focus on the impact of the Social Security system on poverty among elders. We also need to discuss integrating people currently underrepresented into the new economy. This is a question of fundamental economic health, a question of ultimate contributions to the system, and a fundamental aspect of the future of the Social Security system. That means increasing access to technology and increasing skill levels. It means increasing the capacity to invest. This is a very basic issue for Latinos. There are still significant numbers of people who are not involved in the banking system, let alone in more sophisticated investments. In addition, retirement savings and pension coverage are extremely critical issues that are related to location in the work force and whether or not that changes over time.

The second point that I wanted to make has to do with the opinion survey data that Cook and Jacobs contributed. As a person involved in the policy process based in Washington, I am only too aware that the debate is focused on misuse of polling data to serve the various interest groups in this debate. Hopefully the kind of information that was presented in their chapter can help us get to a much better informed debate. If nothing else, it will have been an extraordinary service if this can put the "UFO standard" to rest.

Comment by Robert Rosenblatt

I started covering Social Security during the Greenspan Commission in 1983. In this short article I bring a political view and perspective to this topic.

First, Richard Berner warned us that future returns may not be as good as what has gone on over the long term in the stock market. I believe what is happening in the market is somewhat irrelevant to the debate unless the market crashes. If it crashes and is down for a prolonged period of time, then the talk about privatization fades away. But if the market stays level or goes up, it is a live issue. People who believe in privatization believe in it as a matter of faith. It does not matter how much economic analysis you produce. If you believe that privatization is a good idea, if you believe that it gives individuals more control over money and more control over the future of their retirement, then you believe in privatization. This is an article of faith with the Republican Party. It is an article of faith with President George Bush. Therefore, that is a key issue.

Second, Kilolo Kijakazi's chapter has given a lot of valuable information on improving the welfare of the poorest segment of society with new benefits. Adding a minimum benefit, having an upward adjustment in Supplemental Security Income, and improving the survivor benefit. All of those could add to the well-being of a lot of people. These ideas have been around for a long time. They have never been implemented because somehow there is not an interest in reforming Social Security broadly and bringing these things into it. These ideas are just out there. Commission after commission says it is a good idea, but nothing happens.

Let me suggest a possibly interesting scenario. Suppose the administration tells the liberals in Congress that it will provide an improved survivor benefit, an improved SSI, and a minimum benefit, but in return they have to have privatized accounts. What would happen? Would they be able to split the liberal wing of the Democratic Party? How would the AFL-CIO react to that?

This would be an interesting case because the people who are opposed to privatization regard it as the beginning of the end of Social Security. They feel that once you let in private accounts, you are taking a major step down the road to ruining the Social Security system. So what if the advocates of private accounts put together a package deal? It could create an interesting political opportunity for privatization.

Going against privatization, the Senate is much more liberal than it used to be. The key advocates on the Democratic side who have entertained privatization, Daniel Patrick Moynihan and Bob Kerry, are gone from the Senate. Moynihan was replaced by Hillary Rodham Clinton, who is much more in the traditional

Democratic mold of not entertaining any ideas at all about changing Social Security. The position of those to whom privatization is anathema is strengthened by the new composition of the Senate.

Third, I turn to polling and the public's confidence in Social Security. One of the conclusions Larry Jacobs offers is that when press coverage increases, there is a flow of negative information that misleads the public. That represents a basic misunderstanding of the First Amendment. The press is not supposed to report that the planes did not crash or that the electricity is still on. Those are common and expected events. When the plane crashes and the lights go out, that is big news.

With Social Security, there is a constant strong support for it. But when someone recommends a change in it, that becomes news. Whether you think it is based on sound economics or demographics is irrelevant. The president of the United States has a bully pulpit. In 1982 Ronald Reagan was talking about cutting early retirement benefits significantly, about 25 percent. Congress passed a sense of the Senate resolution that opposed that idea 93-0, and the Democrats picked up a lot of seats in the 1982 elections on the issue.

Whether you think news coverage is misleading or not, President George Bush believes in privatization. He will trumpet this under the reform banner. It then becomes an issue, and then people will have to decide if this is something that they like or not. I have worked in Washington for a long time and have been assigned to the White House. I knew the president could set the agenda, but it was amazing to me how much power the White House has to shape the debate that is going on. How they can influence everything. The talk about privatization will be a real issue. Whether it goes anywhere remains to be seen.

Watch closely what happens with the new Social Security commissioner— whether that person has any independence or, like the first two, is strictly towing the White House line. Moynihan pushed through independent agency legislation because of the importance of the agency and the Social Security program. But no tradition has yet been established. The commissioner has always strictly gone along with the White House program. It will be interesting to see what the new one does.

PART III

The Future of Retirement Income

THE TWO CHAPTERS and three commentaries in part three focus on the private retirement system and the major changes that have been taking place. The chapters in this section address those issues raised by session mediator Thomas Paine, who, from his fifty years as a consultant in employee benefits, observed that the trend away from defined benefit pension plans toward defined contribution pension plans underlies the promise of a secure retirement income that employers give employees. Paine noted that from the employer's perspective defined contributions are precisely the way that the Social Security system is formed. "[The employer] makes a contribution and that is his only obligation. He is not at risk for the investment; neither does he have any unfunded liabilities."

Paine further advised that administrative costs, and investment yield and risk, define the problems that we have to work on to make the retirement income system more reliable.

Chapter 6 by Jack VanDerhei and Craig Copeland provides new data and insights on the prospects for defined contribution retirement assets. Chapter 7 by Jeffrey R. Brown raises issues of how individuals and public policy can anticipate longevity risk to their retirement income stream.

6

The Changing Face of
Private Retirement Plans

Jack VanDerhei and Craig Copeland

A RAPIDLY GROWING public policy concern facing the United States is whether future generations of retired Americans, particularly those in the "baby boom" generation, will have adequate retirement incomes.[1] One reason is that Social Security's projected long-term financial shortfall could result in a reduction in the current-law benefit promises made to future generations of retirees.[2] Another reason is that many baby boomers will be retiring with employment-based defined contribution (DC) plans, as opposed to the "traditional" defined benefit (DB) plans that historically have been the predominant source of employer-provided retirement income. Both of these factors are likely to reduce the amount of life annuity benefits that future retirees will receive relative to current retirees, raising questions as to whether other sources of retirement income—such as individual account plans (DC plans and individual retirement accounts, or IRAs)—will make up the difference.[3]

This chapter was written before passage of the Economic Growth and Tax Relief Reconciliation Act of 2001. This legislation changes the requirements for qualified retirement plans, including the contribution limits imposed on participants in defined contribution plans. The chapter is derived from the April 2001 *EBRI Issue Brief*, published by the Employee Benefit Research Institute.

1. Baby boomers are the post–World War II demographic wave of children born between 1946 and 1964, consisting of about 77 million people.
2. Based on current intermediate projections, after the trust fund is depleted in 2038 current-law benefits would need to be reduced by more than 25 percent across the board.
3. Social Security pays life annuity benefits, and most traditional, employer-sponsored defined benefit plans pay benefits in the form of life annuities. In general, life annuity benefits are payments made on a periodic basis, often monthly, for the life of the beneficiary. In addition, life annuities frequently have additional provisions for benefit payments to the beneficiary's spouse or widow/widower.

This chapter highlights changes in private pension plan participation for DB and DC plans. Next, a description of and results from the Employee Benefit Research Institute's (EBRI) Retirement Income Projection Model are presented. This model is able to quantify how much the importance of individual account plans is expected to increase because of the change from DB to DC plan participation. Because individual account plans tend to pay lump-sum benefits at retirement rather than life annuities, this chapter concludes by discussing the risk of outliving one's assets.[4]

Defined Benefit versus Defined Contribution Plans

Although both qualified DC and DB plans are tax-favored vehicles for providing retirement income, they differ in a variety of important ways. One is how plan contributions are made. Under a DC plan, employer contributions are based on a predetermined formula, and, most frequently, all contributions (made by both employers and employees) are placed in individual accounts on behalf of each participant.[5] In comparison, DB plans are typically noncontributory, and plan contributions are held in one trust on behalf of all participants. Employers offering DB plans must make contributions based on federal funding rules and regulations in order to maintain the plan's qualified (tax-favored) status.

Another important way DC and DB plans differ is in which party directly assumes the investment risk on plan assets and whether that investment risk directly affects plan benefits. The overwhelming majority of DC plans offer participants a choice of account investment options, and plan participants directly assume all investment risk. DC plan benefits are determined by plan contributions, any plan forfeitures, and investment returns on account assets.[6]

---

4. Lump-sum benefits provide the beneficiaries with their total accrued plan benefit generally in a single payment.

5. Technically, most private, qualified defined contribution plans are either money purchase or profit sharing. Sec. 401(k) plans are of the latter type. Under the former, the plan sponsor typically commits to a fixed percentage of compensation each year. For a profit-sharing plan, plan contributions may be made on a discretionary basis by the plan sponsor, but how these contributions are allocated among individual employee accounts must be based on a specified, predetermined formula that meets certain requirements if the plan is to qualify for tax-favored status.

6. Employer contributions may be subject to vesting rules, such that participants do not have full legal right to employer contributions made on their behalf until they have reached a certain minimum number of years of service. Forfeitures arise when employers terminate employment and leave nonvested benefits in the plan. Nonvested portions of any terminating employees' accounts may be used to reduce employer contributions or may be reallocated among the remaining defined contribution plan participants.

That is, employers do not guarantee a specific benefit level to DC plan participants, and benefits are directly related to investment returns. In comparison, employers offering DB plans have fiduciary responsibilities for investing trust assets on behalf of plan participants, and employers directly assume all investment risk.[7] DB benefit formulas directly determine plan benefits owed to participants. That is, employers guarantee specific benefit levels to DB plan participants regardless of the plan assets' investment performance.

A third important way DB and DC plans differ is the form in which they generally pay plan benefits. As indicated above, DC plans usually offer lump-sum benefits. If retirees need this amount to ensure adequate retirement income over the course of their retirement, they must manage (for example, invest and spend) the amount in a manner that ensures that outcome. Otherwise retirees run the risk of outliving their lump-sum benefit and having an inadequate retirement income. Alternatively, DB plans tend to offer life annuities (a set amount paid out regularly over time, typically monthly, for as long as the beneficiary lives), which beneficiaries are not responsible for managing. (However, lump-sum distributions are increasingly available in DB plans.[8])

Participation Trends

According to estimates from the U.S. Department of Labor, the percentage of private wage and salary workers participating in a primary DB plan decreased from 38 percent in 1977 to 22 percent in 1996 (the most recent data available, figure 6-1). During that same period, the percentage of those participating in a primary DC plan increased from 7 to 23 percent, and the percentage of those participating in supplemental DC plans gradually increased from 10 to 16 percent.

Not surprisingly, higher DC plan participation rates have led to an increase in the percentage of households that likely will rely primarily on DC plans for

7. Investment risk affects defined benefit plan participants' benefits indirectly. Poor investment returns, for example, may affect the funding status of the plan itself. However, the Pension Benefit Guaranty Corporation insures defined benefit accruals up to a limit, thereby reducing the risk. Poor investment performance also may indirectly affect plan benefits if it results in a curtailment of future benefit accruals or affects the employer's ability to provide ad hoc benefit increases to retirees. Some employers offer ad hoc benefit increases to offset the effects of inflation on the value of DB plan benefits.

8. Seventy-six percent of full-time workers participating in a DB plan in a medium or large establishment were not offered a lump-sum distribution in 1997 (U.S. Department of Labor, 1999). This is down from 85 percent in 1995 (U.S. Department of Labor, 1998).

Figure 6-1. *Approximate Private Wage and Salary Worker Participation Rates under Primary and Supplemental Pension Plans, 1977–96*

Percent

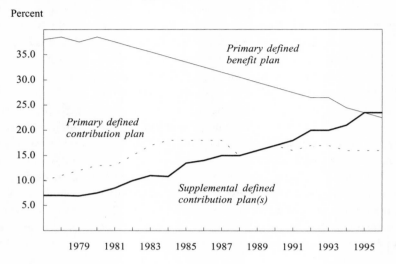

Source: Department of Labor, 1999–2000.

retirement income. But these higher DC participation rates are also accompanied by a dramatic increase in the percentage of households that may have DC plans as their *only* source of employment-based retirement income. In a recent EBRI study of households' pension participation rates from the Survey of Consumer Finances (SCF), the percentage of households with only a DB plan decreased from 39.6 percent in 1992 to 19.9 percent in 1998 (figure 6-2).[9] Meanwhile, the percentage of households with only a DC plan increased from 37.6 to 57.3 percent, and the percentage of households with both DB and DC plans remained steady at 22.8 percent. These findings are applied universally across household demographics.

In addition to the fact that DC plans are becoming an increasingly important source of future retirement income, DB plans increasingly are adopting DC-like features that may result in fewer life annuity payments for future retirees. Lump-sum payment options are becoming more frequent among DB plans. This is due in part to the conversion of traditional DB plans to cash balance

9. See Copeland and VanDerhei (2000). The Survey of Consumer Finances is a triennial survey, conducted by the Federal Reserve Board, that collects comprehensive, nationally representative data on the wealth of American households. It collects data on households' total liabilities and assets, including pension wealth.

Figure 6-2.   *Households by Pension Type, 1992–98*

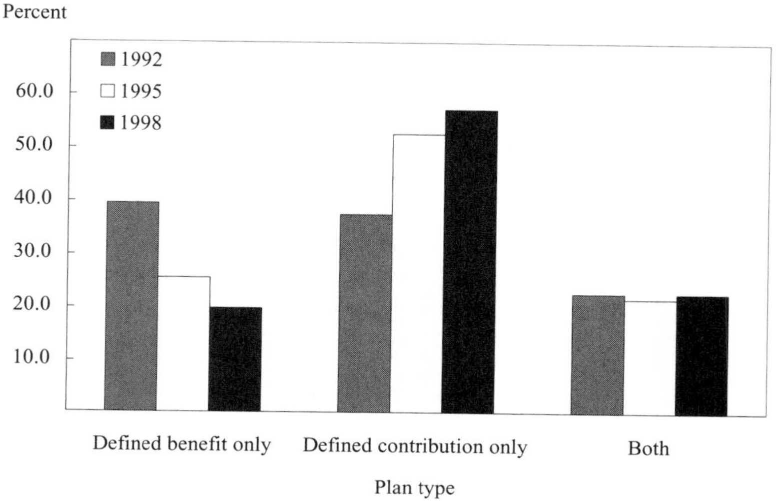

Percent

Source: Employee Benefit Research Institute estimates of the 1992, 1995, and 1998 Survey of Consumer Finances.

plans. Cash balance plans are DB plans under which employers usually communicate benefits as "account balances." Although cash balance plan "account balances" are notional only, cash balance plans generally offer benefits in the form of lump-sum distributions.[10]

Changes in Asset Holdings

The significant shift in participation rates from DB to DC plans and the rise in the number of households with DC plans only have been accompanied by an increase in DC plan assets. Private trusteed DC plan assets first surpassed private trusteed DB plan assets in 1997 and continued to grow steadily relative to DB plan assets through 1999 (figure 6-3). Furthermore, assets held in IRAs, which are also individual account plans, surpassed both DC and DB trusteed plan assets in 1999.[11] That year, IRA assets equaled $2.47 trillion, compared with $2.45 trillion and $2.21 trillion for trusteed DC and DB plans assets, respectively.

10. See Quick (1999).
11. Individual retirement accounts can be established by individual workers or can be offered as the funding vehicle under simplified employee pension plans.

Figure 6-3.   *Private Trusteed Pension Plan Assets versus IRA Assets, 1992–99*

Trillons of U.S. dollars

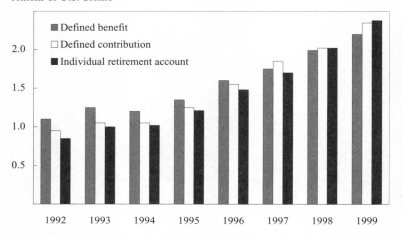

Source: Employee Benefit Research Institute, *Pension Investment Report*, 2d Quarter 2000 (Washington, December 2000); and Craig Copeland, Employee Benefit Research Institute, *EBRI Notes* 1 (January 2001):1–8.

The significant shift in participation rates from DB to DC plans and the rise in the number of households with DC plans exclusively have also been accompanied by an increase in IRA assets. That is because when qualified DC plan participants terminate employment with the sponsoring employer, they may avoid current taxation on their DC plan assets by rolling them over into IRAs. In fact, a 1997 estimate determined that 22 percent of additions to IRAs in that year were attributable to rollovers, whereas only 2 percent were attributable to direct IRA contributions (the remaining 76 percent resulted from investment gains).[12] Although individuals can purchase life annuities with their IRA assets (or choose annuities as their IRA investment selection), they may withdraw their IRA assets in essentially any manner they choose, including in the form of lump-sum or periodic distributions.[13]

Rollovers

Before retirees need to make decisions about how to spend their IRA assets, they need to make decisions in order to accumulate those assets in the first

12. See Sabelhaus (1999).

13. Such withdrawals are subject to penalties for early withdrawal and minimum distribution requirements that apply beginning at 70 years and six months of age.

place. Specifically, employees who leave a job must decide to roll over their assets into an IRA from a qualified plan or to leave their assets in their existing DC plan, as opposed to "cashing out" their benefits and spending them. In a study of Hewitt 401(k) data, 57 percent of participants who removed their assets from a previous employer's plan cashed out their assets, 6 percent rolled them into another qualified plan, and 37 percent rolled them into an IRA.[14] Participants who rolled over their DC plan assets typically rolled over larger amounts: The average account balance for those who rolled over their account balances to an IRA was $68,107, compared with $8,445 for those who cashed out. This finding suggests that perhaps participants with smaller account balances do not appreciate the considerable retirement income that can be amassed over time by preserving even small amounts of DC plan assets.

Model Description

The model used in this analysis is based on results from a four-year time series of administrative data from more than 10 million 401(k) participants and more than 30,000 plans, as well as a time series of several hundred plan descriptions used to provide a sample of the various DB and DC plan provisions applicable to plan participants. In addition, several public surveys based on participants' self-reported answers—SCF, the Current Population Survey, and the Survey of Income and Program Participation (SIPP)—were used to model participation, wages, and initial account balance information.[15]

The model attempts to estimate the balance of any defined contribution plan or IRA (whether funded through regular contributions or rollovers) of the individual at Social Security normal retirement age.[16] In addition, it estimates the accrued benefits earned and assumed to be retained by defined benefit plan participants; it then converts this amount to a present value at normal retire-

14. See McCarthy and McWhirter (2000). Rather than rolling over or cashing out defined contribution plan assets, participants may leave their assets in their previous employer's plan. While the assets or balances remain in the plan, they are still accumulating investment gains (or losses). Participants who choose this option may withdraw those assets at a later date by taking periodic installments, receiving a lump-sum cashout, or rolling them over to another qualified plan or an IRA.

15. The Survey of Income and Program Participation is a longitudinal survey conducted by the U.S. Census Bureau to collect data on income sources and amounts, labor force participation, program eligibility and participation, and general demographic characteristics. Previously, households were followed for two and one-half years, but starting in 1996 households were followed for four years.

16. Future versions of the model will include a subroutine for early retirement behavior.

ment age for comparison of relative magnitudes of those benefits that are typically thought of as "guaranteed" (usually by an implicit employer annuity) versus those that are typically perceived as a lump sum by the employee (although the employee may have the option of converting the distributions to an annuity).[17]

The notion of cash balance plans presents at least a conceptual difficulty for purposes of this distinction, since they are legally DB plans but are often perceived by employees to be DC plans in the way that they accrue benefits. Since many of the cash balance benefits appear to be taken as lump sums, the projected "balances" from these plans are added to DC plans for purposes of presenting the results in this report.

Estimating Current and Future Accrued Benefits and Account Balances

In general, the model in this analysis uses a combination of Form 5500 data from the Department of Labor and self-reported responses to public survey instruments to model coverage, participation, and initial account balance information for all DC participants, as well as contribution behavior for non-401(k) defined contribution plans.[18] Asset allocation information is based on previously published results of the EBRI/Investment Company Institute 401(k) database, and employee contribution behavior to 401(k) plans is provided by an expansion of a method based on both employee demographic information and plan-matching provisions.[19]

A combination of Form 5500 data and self-reported results was also used to estimate defined benefit participation models; however, it appears that information in the latter is rather unreliable with respect to estimating current and future accrued benefits. Therefore, a database of DB plan provisions for salary-related plans was constructed to estimate benefit accruals.

Self-reported results were used to initialize IRA accounts. Future IRA contributions were modeled from SIPP data, while future rollover activity was assumed to flow from future separation from employment in those cases in

---

17. An alternative method of comparison would leave the defined benefit accruals as annual benefits and "annuitize" the defined contribution and IRA balances. However, this presents additional complications in modeling employee purchasing behavior.

18. The Employee Retirement Income Security Act requires that pension plan sponsors file with the Internal Revenue Service an annual financial report on Form 5500 containing financial, participant, and actuarial data about the pension plan. The IRS keys the data and forwards it to the Department of Labor.

19. See Holden and VanDerhei (2001) on the EBRI/ICI Participant-Directed Retirement Plan Data Collection Project.

which the employee was participating in a DC plan sponsored by the previous employer. A component was also included in the model to estimate withdrawals from IRAs.[20]

Defined Benefit Plans

A stochastic job duration model was estimated and applied to each individual in the model to predict the number of jobs held and the age of each job change. Each time the individual starts a new job, the model simulates whether or not it will result in coverage in a DB plan, a DC plan, both, or neither.[21] If coverage in a DB plan is predicted, time series information from the Bureau of Labor Statistics (BLS) is used to predict whether it will be:

—a nonintegrated (with Social Security) career-average plan

—an integrated career-average plan

—a five-year final-average plan without integration

—a three-year final-average plan without integration

—a five-year final-average plan with covered compensation as the integration level

—a three-year final-average plan with covered compensation as the integration level

—a five-year final-average plan with a primary insurance amount (PIA) offset[22]

—a three-year final-average plan with a PIA offset

—a cash balance plan

—a flat-benefit plan

While the BLS information provides significant detail on the generosity parameters for DB plans, preliminary analysis indicated that several of these provisions were likely to be highly correlated (especially for integrated plans). Therefore, a time series of several hundred DB plans per year was coded to allow for assignment to the individuals in the model.[23]

---

20. This component was based on results reported in Sabelhaus (2000), which combined survey data on IRA balances with individual tax return data on IRA flows to study IRA accumulation and withdrawal patterns across cohorts.

21. Thus the current version of the model ignores the possibility that an employer will adopt a new retirement plan—or change an existing plan—prior to the employee's job separation or retirement.

22. For additional detail on integrated defined benefit plans, see chapter 4 of Allen, Melone, Rosenbloom, and VanDerhei (1997).

23. BLS information was utilized to code the distribution of generosity parameters for flat-benefit plans.

Figure 6-4.   *Average 401(k) Account Balance by Age and Tenure, 1999*

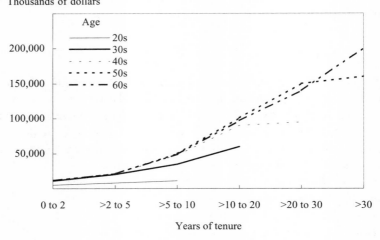

Thousands of dollars

Years of tenure

Source: Tabulations from EBRI/ICI Participant-Directed Retirement Plan Data Collection Project

Although the Tax Reform Act of 1986 at least partially modified the constraints on integrated pension plans by adding Sec. 401(l) to the Internal Revenue Code (IRC), it would appear that a significant percentage of DB sponsors have retained PIA-offset plans. In order to estimate the offset provided under the plan formulas, the model computes the employee's average indexed monthly earnings, primary insurance amount, and covered compensation values for the birth cohort.

Defined Contribution Plans

INITIAL ACCOUNT BALANCES

Previous studies on the EBRI/ICI 401(k) database have analyzed the average account balances for 401(k) participants by age and tenure (see figure 6-4).[24] The most recently published results show that the year-end 1999 average balance ranged from $4,479 for participants in their twenties with less than three years of tenure with their current employer to $198,595 for participants in their sixties who have been with the current employer for at least thirty years (thereby effectively eliminating any capability for IRA rollovers).

24. See Holden and VanDerhei (2001) and cites therein.

Unfortunately, this database does not currently provide detailed information on other types of DC plans, nor does it allow analysis of DC balances that may have been left with previous employers. The model used in this report uses self-reported responses for whether an individual has a DC balance to estimate a participation model, and the reported value is modeled as a function of age and tenure similar to figure 6-4.

CONTRIBUTION BEHAVIOR

Previous research on employee contribution behavior to 401(k) plans has often been limited by lack of adequate data. This is primarily due to the types of matching formulas utilized by sponsors. These formulas are often complicated due to the desire of sponsors to provide sufficient incentives to non-highly compensated employees to contribute in order to comply with technical nondiscrimination testing. This complexity makes it virtually impossible to appropriately analyze the employee's behavior if one is forced to observe either aggregate plan data or use information on the plan contribution formulas provided by the participant.

With the exception of studies based on administrative data, employee contribution behavior is typically assumed to be a function of employee demographic data and perhaps an employee's estimate of the employer-matching rate or a proxy based on Form 5500 data.[25] However, as shown by Kusko, Poterba, and Wilcox, a significant percentage of the employee contribution behavior appears to be determined by plan-specific provisions.[26] For example, in figure 6-5, the percentage of employees contributing up to either the maximum amount of compensation matched, the plan maximum, or the IRC Sec. 402(g) limit is shown as a function of age for one of the plans studied by Yakoboski and VanDerhei.[27] Figure 6-6 shows similar information as a function of salary. It would appear from this limited sample that significantly more than 50 percent of the employee contributions occur at "corner points" that would not be identified in the data described above.[28]

VanDerhei and Copeland provide preliminary findings that introduce new methodology to expand the usefulness of modeling these data, as well as a

25. Bassett et al. (1998); Papke (1995).

26. Kusko, Poterba, and Wilcox (1994).

27. Yakoboski and VanDerhei (1996). 402(g) denotes the IRC section that limits employee deferrals to a specific amount per year. Unlike the other two variables, this value is constant across all plans for any particular year.

28. Clark, Goodfellow, Schieber and Warwick (2000) also use administrative data but only investigate the match rate, not the maximum amount of compensation matched or the maximum amount of compensation allowed by the plan.

Figure 6-5.   *Company A Contribution Rates by Age*

Percent of participants

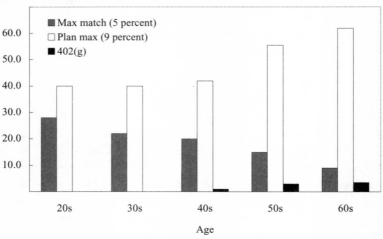

Source: Yakoboski and VanDerhei (1996).

better understanding of contribution behavior by 401(k) plan participants.[29] A sequential response regression model was used to allow for the differing incentives faced by the employees at various levels of contributions. Based on findings from 137 distinct matching formulas, a behavioral model was estimated that is able to control for the tendency of employers to substitute between the amount they match per dollar of employee contribution and the maximum percentage of compensation they are willing to match. Employee contribution behavior is decomposed into a series of 1 percent of compensation intervals, which therefore permits modeling not only the marginal incentives to contribute at that interval but also the "option value" that making the contribution at that interval provides for the employee. Figure 6-7 illustrates the predicted employee contributions from the model as a function of employee demographics and the employer's matching formulas.

While the 401(k) plans used by VanDerhei and Copeland, as described above, provided the exact matching formulas adopted by the plan sponsor, the vast majority of the 30,000 plans in the EBRI/ICI Participant-Directed Retirement Plan Data Collection Project do not contain that information, and due to strict confidentiality standards no information on the plan sponsor's identity

29. VanDerhei and Copeland (2001).

Figure 6-6. *Company A Contribution Rates by Salary*

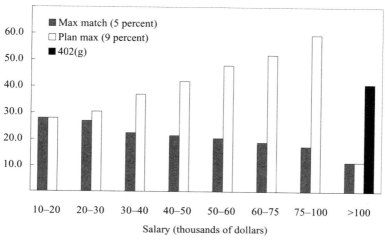

Percent of participants

Max match (5 percent)
Plan max (9 percent)
402(g)

Salary (thousands of dollars)

Source: Yakoboski and VanDerhei (1996).

was included. However, the database does break out the source of contributions (for example, employee before-tax, employee after-tax, employer matching, qualified nonelective contributions, and others), and a series of computer algorithms has been developed to classify additional plans by the types of incentives provided to employees at various contribution levels (for example, a 50 percent match for the first 6 percent of compensation). This information has been used to expand the previous sample and provides the predicted employee contributions for 401(k) plans in this chapter.

Contribution behavior for DC plans other than 401(k) plans is estimated from self-reported responses to public survey data.

INVESTMENT RETURNS

Although the model has been designed to generate investment rates of return on a stochastic basis, for purposes of this chapter the results are obtained from running it in a deterministic mode.[30]

30. The model assumed a Consumer Price Index growth rate of 3.50 percent, a real rate of return for stocks of 6.98 percent, and a real rate of return for bonds of 3.00 percent. In addition, 1 percent is subtracted from each of the stock and bond real rates of return to reflect administrative costs.

Figure 6-7. *Predicted Contributions for Selected Persons and Plans*

Percent of compensation

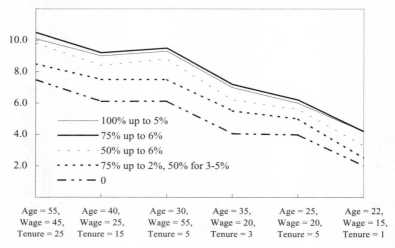

Age = 55,	Age = 40,	Age = 30,	Age = 35,	Age = 25,	Age = 22,
Wage = 45,	Wage = 25,	Wage = 55,	Wage = 20,	Wage = 20,	Wage = 15,
Tenure = 25	Tenure = 15	Tenure = 5	Tenure = 3	Tenure = 5	Tenure = 1

Source: VanDerhei and Copeland (2001).

Results

Panel A in table 6-1 provides the composition of estimated retirement wealth for males at Social Security normal retirement age under the baseline assumptions, by birth cohort.[31] Similar figures for females are provided in panel A of table 6-2. The same information is presented graphically in figures 6-8 (males) and 6-9 (females). It is readily apparent from these graphs that both genders have an appreciable drop in the percentage of private retirement income that is attributable to DB plans (other than cash balance). Females start with a slightly higher defined benefit concentration than men (49.7 percent versus 39.0 percent for the 1936 cohort), and the difference remains fairly constant over time (37.2 percent versus 26.4 percent for the 1964 cohort).

The baseline results are based on several assumptions that may prove to be biased when additional information becomes available. Therefore, this analysis explores how sensitive the results are with respect to:

—trends in cash balance plans

—long-term asset allocation for defined contribution plans

—cash-out behavior for defined benefit terminated vested participants

31. *Estimated retirement wealth* is defined as the value of account balances from defined contribution plans, IRAs, and cash balance plans and the present value of accruals from other defined benefit plans.

Table 6-1. Composition of Estimated Retirement Wealth for Males at Social Security Normal Retirement Age

Percent

Type of plan	1936	1938	1940	1942	1944	1946	1948	1950	1952	1954	1956	1958	1960	1962	1964
Panel A: Baseline assumptions															
Defined benefit	39.0	38.5	38.4	38.2	37.3	36.2	34.1	32.7	32.7	32.8	31.3	30.3	28.6	27.0	26.4
Defined contribution + cash balance	33.2	32.3	32.3	32.8	33.3	35.1	37.1	36.5	35.6	34.8	33.9	33.5	34.2	33.6	33.7
Individual retirement account	27.8	29.1	29.2	29.0	29.4	28.7	28.9	30.8	31.6	32.4	34.8	36.2	37.2	39.3	39.9
Panel B: Cash balance plans double															
Defined benefit	39.4	38.6	38.6	38.2	37.0	35.9	33.8	32.1	32.1	32.1	30.4	29.3	27.6	25.9	25.3
Defined contribution + cash balance	33.0	32.3	32.3	32.8	33.5	35.3	37.3	37.0	36.1	35.4	34.7	34.5	35.1	34.6	34.7
Individual retirement account	27.6	29.1	29.1	29.0	29.5	28.8	28.9	30.9	31.8	32.5	34.9	36.2	37.3	39.5	40.0
Panel C: Assuming a less aggressive long-term asset allocation															
Defined benefit	39.2	38.8	38.8	38.8	38.0	37.0	35.1	33.8	34.0	34.1	32.7	31.8	30.1	28.6	27.9
Defined contribution + cash balance	33.1	32.3	32.2	32.5	33.0	34.8	36.6	36.1	35.3	34.5	33.5	33.2	33.9	33.3	33.4
Individual retirement account	27.7	28.9	29.0	28.7	29.0	28.2	28.3	30.0	30.8	31.5	33.8	35.1	36.0	38.1	38.6
Panel D: Assuming terminated vested defined benefit participants are not cashed out															
Defined benefit	41.0	40.5	40.3	40.0	39.0	37.8	35.7	34.3	34.3	34.3	32.9	31.9	30.0	28.5	27.7
Defined contribution + cash balance	32.1	31.3	31.4	31.8	32.4	34.2	36.1	35.7	34.8	34.0	33.2	32.8	33.5	33.0	33.1
Individual retirement account	26.9	28.2	28.3	28.2	28.6	28.0	28.1	30.0	30.9	31.6	34.0	35.3	36.4	38.5	39.2
Panel E: Assuming prohibition of preretirement cashouts from defined contribution plans and IRAs															
Defined benefit	38.3	37.1	36.2	35.2	33.7	32.4	30.2	28.5	28.2	27.6	26.0	24.7	22.6	20.8	20.2
Defined contribution + cash balance	32.6	31.1	30.4	30.2	30.1	31.5	32.8	31.9	30.6	29.4	28.1	27.3	27.1	25.9	25.8
Individual retirement account	29.1	31.7	33.4	34.6	36.1	36.0	37.0	39.6	41.2	43.0	45.9	48.0	50.3	53.3	54.0

Source: Employee Benefit Research Institute retirement income projection model

Figure 6-8. *Composition of Estimated Retirement Wealth for Males at Social Security Normal Retirement Age under Baseline Assumptions, by Birth Cohort, 1936–64*

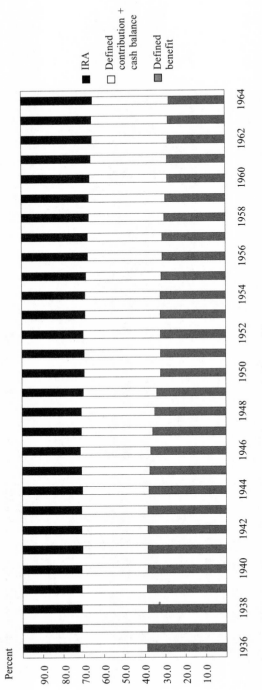

Source: Employee Benefit Research Institute retirement income projection model.

Table 6-2. Composition of Estimated Retirement Wealth for Females at Social Security Normal Retirement Age

Percent

Type of Plan	1936	1938	1940	1942	1944	1946	1948	1950	1952	1954	1956	1958	1960	1962	1964
Panel A: Baseline assumptions															
Defined benefit	49.7	48.9	47.1	45.7	44.7	44.6	43.2	42.7	42.7	41.1	40.5	39.3	39.9	37.9	37.2
Defined contribution + cash balance	32.5	32.0	32.6	34.0	34.9	34.3	34.1	33.6	33.3	33.8	32.9	32.1	32.0	32.6	31.9
Individual retirement account	17.8	19.1	20.3	20.3	20.4	21.1	22.7	23.7	24.0	25.1	26.6	28.7	28.1	29.4	30.9
Panel B: Cash balance plans double															
Defined benefit	49.7	48.9	47.0	45.7	44.6	44.4	43.2	42.2	41.8	40.0	39.2	37.9	38.6	36.9	36.3
Defined contribution + cash balance	32.5	32.0	32.6	34.0	35.0	34.4	34.2	33.9	34.0	34.6	34.0	33.3	33.2	33.6	32.8
Individual retirement account	17.8	19.1	20.3	20.3	20.5	21.1	22.6	23.8	24.2	25.3	26.8	28.8	28.1	29.5	30.9
Panel C: Assuming a less aggressive long-term asset allocation															
Defined benefit	49.8	49.2	47.5	46.3	45.5	45.4	44.2	43.9	44.0	42.7	42.2	40.9	41.6	39.7	39.1
Defined contribution + cash balance	32.4	31.8	32.4	33.6	34.4	33.9	33.8	33.1	32.6	32.9	32.0	31.4	31.3	32.0	31.2
Individual retirement account	17.7	19.0	20.1	20.1	20.2	20.7	22.0	23.0	23.3	24.5	25.8	27.7	27.0	28.3	29.8
Panel D: Assuming terminated vested defined benefit participants are not cashed out															
Defined benefit	53.2	52.2	50.1	48.5	47.6	47.3	45.9	45.2	45.1	43.4	42.8	41.5	41.8	39.7	39.0
Defined contribution + cash balance	30.3	29.9	30.8	32.2	33.1	32.6	32.6	32.1	31.9	32.5	31.7	30.9	31.0	31.8	31.0
Individual retirement account	16.5	17.8	19.1	19.3	19.4	20.1	21.6	22.7	23.0	24.1	25.5	27.6	27.1	28.6	30.0
Panel E: Assuming prohibition of preretirement cashouts from defined contribution plans and IRAs															
Defined benefit	53.0	51.8	49.4	47.4	46.3	45.7	43.9	43.1	42.7	40.6	40.0	38.4	38.5	36.4	35.7
Defined contribution + cash balance	30.2	29.7	30.4	31.5	32.2	31.5	31.2	30.7	30.2	30.4	29.7	28.6	28.6	29.2	28.4
Individual retirement account	16.8	18.5	20.1	21.1	21.6	22.8	24.9	26.2	27.1	29.0	30.3	33.0	32.9	34.4	35.8

Source: Employee Benefit Research Institute retirement income projection model.

Figure 6-9. *Composition of Estimated Retirement Wealth for Females at Social Security Normal Retirement Age under Baseline Assumptions, by Birth Cohort, 1936–64*

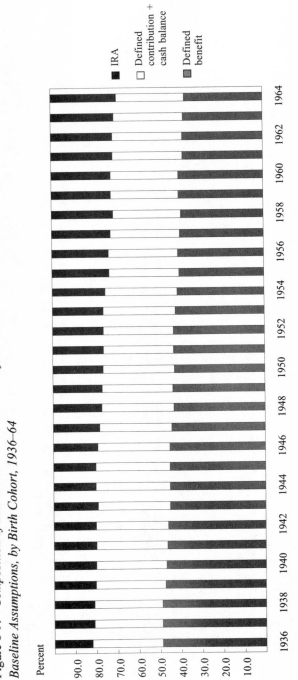

Source: Employee Benefit Research Institute retirement income projection model.

Cash-Balance Plans

The Bureau of Labor Statistics reports that 6 percent of full-time employees in medium and large private establishments had a "cash account" benefit formula.[32] Since this was the most current number available, it was used in the baseline estimates. However, a significant amount of conversion activity has taken place since that time. Elliot and Moore report that 16 percent of the pension plans among Fortune 100 companies in 1998 were cash balance plans and that, more generally, cash balance plans have increased from 5 to 12 percent of all DB plans since 1998.[33]

Given these trends, it is reasonable to assume the percentage of defined benefit participants covered by a cash balance plan may have doubled between 1997 and 2000. In an attempt to model the potential impact of this change, the distribution of DB plan types for jobs taken after the year 2000 was modified by taking a pro rata reduction across all the final average categories to rebalance to 100 percent.[34]

The results for panel B in tables 6-1 and 6-2 are generated with the same assumptions as panel A, with the exception of the new assumption for cash balance plans. There does not appear to be much impact in the short run, given the model's assumption with respect to transition provisions. However, for males in the 1964 birth cohort, the average proportion of retirement wealth estimated to be derived from (noncash balance) defined benefit plans decreases from 26.4 percent to 25.3 percent—a 4.1 percentage decrease (table 6-3). The long-run results for females suggest a 2.6 percent decrease in the importance of pension wealth for DB plans other than cash balance. As expected, most of the offsetting increase is found in the defined contribution and cash balance plan component: the 1964 birth cohort is estimated to experience a 2.9 percent increase in retirement wealth in these categories for both males and females. The impact on the IRA percentages is estimated to be de minimis for both genders.

Long-Term Asset Allocation for Defined Contribution Plans

To the extent that some defined contribution plan participants do not actively rebalance their asset allocations to reflect abnormally high recent

32. U.S. Department of Labor (1999).
33. Elliot and Moore (2000).
34. This implicitly assumes that transition provisions allow everyone in a traditional defined benefit plan that is converted to cash balance to remain in the current plan until they change jobs. This assumption will be relaxed in a future version of the model.

Table 6-3. *Percentage Change in Composition of Estimated Retirement
Wealth at Social Security Normal Retirement Age for Various Scenarios
Relative to the Baseline Assumptions: 1964 Birth Cohort, by Gender*
Percent

Type	Male	Female
Panel B: Cash balance plans double		
Defined benefit	−4.1	−2.6
Defined contribution + cash balance	2.9	2.9
Individual retirement account	0.3	0.0
Panel C: Assuming a less aggressive long- term asset allocation		
Defined benefit	5.9	4.9
Defined contribution + cash balance	−0.8	−2.1
Individual retirement account	−3.3	−3.7
Panel D: Assuming terminated vested defined benefit participants are not cashed out		
Defined benefit	5.2	4.7
Defined contribution + cash balance	−1.8	−2.7
Individual retirement account	−1.9	−2.9
Panel E: Assuming prohibition of preretirement cashouts from defined contribution plans and IRAs		
Defined benefit	−23.4	−20.5
Defined contribution + cash balance	−23.4	−20.5
Individual retirement account	35.2	45.9

Source: Employee Benefit Research Institute retirement income project model.

experience in the equity markets, it appears that using the current asset allocation of equities by age for long-run asset allocation may be artificially inflating the estimated equity percentages. Preliminary analysis of rebalancing was undertaken with the EBRI/ICI 401(k) data last year, and while additional analysis remains to be completed, it appears that there may be a larger discrepancy between active rebalancers and passive investors among older employees.[35]

For purposes of this sensitivity analysis, an ad hoc reduction in equity percentage was applied to reflect what is likely to be more of an equilibrium asset allocation by age. The equity reduction for purposes of this chapter was arbitrarily assumed to increase from a 0 percent reduction for twenty-year-olds to a 10 percent reduction for sixty-five-year-olds.

The results of this sensitivity analysis are shown in panel C of tables 6-1 and 6-2. As expected, the decreased equity concentration results in a long-term

35. See VanDerhei, Holden, and Quick (2000).

decrease for both DC plans and IRAs.[36] Overall, there was estimated to be a 0.8 percent decrease in the DC plan percentage component for males in the 1964 birth cohort and a 2.1 percent decrease for females. IRAs were estimated to decrease by 3.3 percent and 3.7 percent for males and females, respectively. Defined benefit plan benefits do not change under this new assumption; however, the relative importance of defined benefit plans for the 1964 birth cohort increases by 5.9 percent for males and 4.9 percent for females.

Defined Benefit Terminated Vested Plan Participants

In certain situations, defined benefit plan sponsors have the ability to automatically cash out former employees. When a worker separates from employment prior to normal retirement age, the present value of the accrued benefits is computed and compared with the statutory threshold for mandatory cashouts at the time. Under the baseline scenario in this model, it is assumed that employers will cash out these amounts whenever possible, and that the assets will not be retained in the retirement system. However, there does not appear to be a source of time series information on the employer's propensity to avail them of this option.[37] Therefore, this sensitivity analysis relaxes that assumption and assumes that departing employees are not cashed out and remain in terminated vested status until normal retirement age when they receive their deferred retirement benefits.

The results are shown in panel D of tables 6-1 and 6-2. As expected, this new assumption increases the importance of DB plans relative to the baseline assumptions. For males born in 1964, there is an estimated increase of 5.2 percent, while their female counterparts are estimated to have a 4.9 percent increase. Defined contribution plan and IRA benefits do not change under this new assumption; however, the relative importance of DB plans for the 1964 birth cohort decreases by 1.8 percent and 1.9 percent, respectively, for males, while the decreases for females are estimated at 2.7 and 2.9 percent.

---

36. IRAs are assumed to have the same asset allocation as defined contribution plans in the model.

37. Hurd, Lillard, and Panis (1998) find that "among DB plan holders with a lump-sum distribution option, 48 percent started collecting benefits, 31 percent expected to draw benefits in the future, 4 percent took an LSD [lump-sum distribution] and rolled it over into an IRA, and only 16 percent cashed out their pension rights." This information is limited to a relatively older population (the 1931–41 birth cohort), and the authors confine their analysis to reports of plan dispositions for respondents who left their jobs between waves 1 and 2 of the Health and Retirement Study.

Simulating the Impact of a Prohibition of Preretirement Cashouts from Defined Contribution Plans and IRAs

The relative incidence of cashouts and rollovers among participants taking distributions from their previous employer's defined contribution plans has been documented extensively elsewhere.[38] However, there has been a lack of data with respect to the long-run behavior of individuals who—at least initially—leave their account balances with the previous employer when they change jobs. Therefore, industry data are combined with SCF data to estimate the relative likelihood that the balances are rolled over to an IRA, left with the previous employer, transferred to a new employer, or used for other purposes.[39] These probabilities are used to estimate the baseline scenario in panel A of tables 6-1 and 6-2.

One way to demonstrate the first-order impact of preretirement cashouts on eventual retirement income is to simulate the impact of a proposal that would force all DC plan funds not either retained in the previous employer's plan or transferred to the new employer's plan at job termination to be rolled over to an IRA on a mandatory basis.[40] However, this provision alone would not be sufficient to ensure that the funds remained in the retirement system if individuals retained the rights to withdraw from their IRAs without restriction. Therefore, it is assumed here that all preretirement access to IRAs would be prohibited.

38. See Yakoboski (1997) for an example.

39. To calculate stay behinds from SCF, the total number of rollovers from pension plans plus the total number of previous pension plans with assets or rights left behind was determined. The percentage of stay behinds was then the number of previous pension plans with assets or rights left behind relative to the combined total described previously. Fidelity (2001) provides an analysis of their experience with respect to participant choices after termination. Based on 1999 job terminations, they found that the percentage of assets that remained in the plan until the end of the year varied from 33.7 percent for participants with account balances of less than $10,000 to 68.7 percent for those with account balances in excess of $200,000. However, as they point out, this may not be sufficient time to observe the long-term incidence, especially for those that terminate late in the year. Hurd, Lillard and Panis (1998) also investigate cashout behavior among defined contribution plan participants; however, it is subject to the same limitations mentioned in footnote 36 above.

40. An estimate of the true impact of such a proposal would need to account for, inter alia, the potential impact that such a reform would have on: (1) the relative likelihood that employers would want to continue sponsoring such a plan and, if they did, how their contribution formulas may need to be restructured, and (2) how employees (especially those designated as nonhighly compensated employees under IRC Sec. 414(q)) would decrease their participation or contributions if they were not able to withdraw the funds prior to retirement age.

The estimated results of such a modification to the current system are shown in panel E of tables 6-1 and 6-2. As expected, there is a sizable increase in the importance of IRAs at the expense of the other two types of plans. Given that (a) the likelihood of rollover to an IRA in the baseline scenario increases with account balance, and (b) males tend to have larger account balances than females, all else constant, it is not surprising that the impact of this change would be larger on females. For females born in 1964, mandatory rollovers are estimated to increase the relative importance of IRAs by 45.9 percent, while the importance of both defined benefit plans and the combination of defined contribution and cash balance plans would decrease by 20.5 percent. Their male counterparts are estimated to experience an increase of 35.2 percent in the importance of IRAs, while the other two categories each decrease by 23.4 percent.

Poterba, Venti, and Wise estimated the impact of preretirement withdrawals on 401(k) asset accumulations and concluded that it reduces average 401(k) assets at age sixty-five by about 5 percent.[41] Comparing the results from this scenario (for the combination of IRAs, defined contribution, and cash balance plans) with the baseline assumptions, a much larger impact is found for the 1964 birth cohort: 41.6 percent for males and 40.0 percent for females. The differences between the model and the set of assumptions utilized in Poterba, Venti, and Wise and those used in this report are far too numerous to mention; however, it is important to keep in mind that their analysis was limited to the 401(k) market and that they did not include the impact of the ancillary restriction on preretirement withdrawals on IRAs.

Discussion

The results show a clear increase in the income retirees will receive that will have to be managed by the retiree. This makes the risk of longevity more central to retirees' expenditure decisions. Therefore, they will have to understand that life expectancies are merely averages and that wide variation beyond the average is possible.

To illustrate, according to projections from the 2000 Social Security Trustees' Report, a sixty-five-year-old male in the year 2000 is expected to live another 16.4 years (to age eighty-one), while a female is expected to live to about age eighty-five, an additional 19.6 years of life. Yet approximately 12 percent of the males and 8 percent of the females who reach sixty-five will die before they reach seventy, while about 17.5 percent of the males and 31.4

41. Poterba, Venti, and Wise (1999).

percent of the females who reach sixty-five will live until they reach ninety. Other important considerations are medical advances from research, such as the Human Genome Project, and the increase in health care needs that are associated with old age. Consequently, retirees will need to understand how much—or little—they can spend or to explore other avenues to reduce the risk of longevity (such as the purchase of annuities).

How Much Can Individuals Spend?

Since many sixty-five-year-old males will live longer than the projected average 16.4 years, an individual must make expenditure decisions based on a longer time horizon. Cooley, Hubbard, and Waltz estimated various payout (withdrawal of assets) percentages that would be sustainable for a different number of years.[42] Across the three asset allocations examined, only a 3 percent withdrawal rate was found to have a high probability (80 percent) of not depleting one's assets before thirty years. The more aggressive investments in equities would support a 4 percent withdrawal rate for having a high probability for assets to last thirty years. Thus what most people would consider to be rather low withdrawal rates would be necessary to protect people against outliving their assets.

Annuities

Even using the small withdrawal rates suggested above, the risk of outliving one's resources is not eliminated completely. The insurance vehicle for insuring against outliving one's resources is a life annuity. This type of annuity pays regular payments for the length of one or more persons' lives. While the market for life annuities other than Social Security and private pensions is currently small, annuities could play an important role in addressing the issue of the growing amount of "nonguaranteed" assets that retirees will hold in the future and the risk of outliving one's resources.[43] Jeffrey Brown addresses the issues surrounding annuities in chapter 7 of this book.[44]

Conclusion

Most analysis and public discussion of retirement plans over the last twenty years have focused upon the growth of defined contribution plans and the

---

42. Cooley, Hubbard, and Walz (1998).
43. The American Council of Life Insurers (2000) reported that 2.75 million individuals were covered by an individual immediate annuity policy in 1999.
44. Brown (2000).

decline of defined benefit plans. Little analysis has been available of the long-term implications of this change on the composition and levels of future retirement income.

This chapter provides a clear picture of the implications for the baby boom generation. Our model estimates that for today's retirees with either defined benefit, defined contribution, or IRAs, approximately 39.0 percent of pension wealth for males would be available from defined benefit plans and 49.7 percent for females; defined contribution and cash balance plans would provide 33.2 percent for men and 32.5 percent for women; while IRAs would provide 27.8 percent for men and 17.8 percent for women. For the youngest baby boom males (born in 1964) this analysis estimates that 26.4 percent of their pension wealth will be provided through defined benefit plans (a decline of 32.4 percent), while their female counterparts will see their defined benefit pension wealth fall to 37.2 percent (a decline of 25.0 percent). Defined contribution plans will provide 33.7 percent of the retirement wealth for men in this birth cohort and 31.9 percent for women. IRAs will expand their role the most, reaching 39.9 percent for men and 30.9 percent for women.

The implications for retirees are major:

—Most of their non–Social Security retirement income will be subject to the retirees' control regarding the rate of spending, rather than arriving like a regular paycheck for life.

—Rather than the assets that back up their income being managed by the sponsor of the pension plan, which would bear the risk of investment losses, individuals will have to self-manage the assets or select someone to do so.

—Rather than having the sponsor of the pension plan bear the risk of a retiree living to one hundred years of age, retirees will either need to purchase an annuity that transfers that risk to an insurance company or to carefully manage their individual rate of spending to avoid outliving the assets.

Most Americans have not faced these challenges in the past, nor has the nation focused on financial education and financial literacy in a sustained and comprehensive way. Much remains to be done, even though increasing attention has been paid to these issues since passage in 1997 of the Savings Are Vital to Everyone's Retirement (SAVER) Act, which was aimed at advancing the public's knowledge and understanding of the importance of retirement savings.

This analysis suggests that, at a minimum, financial issues in retirement must become a higher education priority in the future. Most Americans have relied on Social Security to provide a basic monthly annuity for life and the life of a spouse. Should the nation move to individual accounts in Social Security in the future, these same issues of asset management, rate of spending, and financial literacy may apply to that program as well. Thus this report makes it clear that the individual responsibility model for retirement income will be tested in the decades ahead, and it appears that a tag line from the Choose to Save® education program will become more relevant with each passing year: Save now or work forever.

References

Allen, Everett T., Jr., Joseph J. Melone, Jerry S. Rosenbloom, and Jack L. VanDerhei. 1997. *Pension Planning: Pensions, Profit Sharing, and Other Deferred Compensation Plans*, 8th ed. Homewood, Ill.: Richard D. Irwin.

American Council of Life Insurers. 2000. *Life Insurers Fact Book.* Washington.

Bassett, William F., Michael J. Fleming, and Anthony P. Rodrigues. 1998. "How Workers Use 401(k) Plans: The Participation, Contribution, and Withdrawal Decisions." *National Tax Journal* (June): 263–89.

Brown, Jeffrey R. 2000. "How Should We Insure Longevity Risk in Pensions and Social Security?" Center for Retirement Research at Boston College, *An Issue in Brief* 4 (August). Reprinted within as chapter 7.

Clark, Robert, Gordon P. Goodfellow, Sylvester J. Schieber, and Drew A. Warwick. 2000. "Making the Most of 401(k) Plans: Who's Choosing What and Why." In *Forecasting Retirement Needs and Retirement Wealth,* edited by Olivia S. Mitchell, P. Brett Hammond, and Anna M. Rapport, 95–138. University of Pennsylvania Press, for the Pension Research Council.

Cooley, Philip L., Carl M. Hubbard, and Daniel T. Walz. 1998. "Retirement Savings: Choosing a Withdrawal Rate That Is Sustainable." *AAII Journal* (February): 16–21.

Copeland, Craig, and Jack VanDerhei. 2000. "Personal Retirement Plans: An Analysis of the Survey of Consumer Finances." Employee Benefit Research Institute, *EBRI Issue Brief* 223 (July): 1–25.

Elliot, Kenneth R., and James H Moore Jr. 2000. "Cash Balance Pension Plans: The New Wave." *Compensation and Working Conditions* (Summer): 3–11.

Fidelity Investments. 2001. *Building Futures: Opportunities and Challenges for Workplace Savings in America.* Boston.

Holden, Sarah, and Jack VanDerhei. 2001. "401(k) Plan Asset Allocation, Account Balances, and Loan Activity in 1999." Employee Benefit Research Institute, *EBRI Issue Brief* 230 (February): 1–29.

Hurd, Michael, Lee Lillard, and Constantijn Panis. 1998. "An Analysis of the Choice to Cash-Out, Maintain, or Annuitize Pension Rights at Job Change or Retirement." *RAND Working Paper.* DRU–1979–DoL (October).

Kusko Andrea L., James M. Poterba, and David W. Wilcox. 1994. "Employee Decisions with Respect to 401(k) Plans: Evidence From Individual-Level Data." Working Paper 4635. Cambridge, Mass.: National Bureau of Economic Research (February).

McCarthy, Mike, and Liz McWhirter. 2000. "Are Employees Missing the Big Picture?" *Benefits Quarterly* (First Quarter): 25–31.

Papke, Leslie. 1995. "Participation in and Contributions to 401(k) Pension Plans." *Journal of Human Resources* 30 (Spring): 311–25.

Poterba, James M., Steven F. Venti, and David A. Wise. 1999. "Pre-Retirement Cashouts and Foregone Retirement Saving: Implications for 401(k) Asset Accumulation." Working Paper W7314. Cambridge, Mass.: National Bureau of Economic Research (August).

Quick, Carol. 1999. "An Overview of Cash Balances." Employee Benefit Research Institute, *EBRI Notes* 7 (July): 1–8.

Sabelhaus, John. 2000. "Modeling IRA Accumulation and Withdrawals." *National Tax Journal* 53, no. 4 (December): 865–75.

———." 1999. Projecting IRA Balances and Withdrawals." Employee Benefit Research Institute, *EBRI Notes* 5 (May): 1–4.

U.S. Department of Labor, Bureau of Labor Statistics. 1998. *Employee Benefits in Medium and Large Private Establishments, 1995* (www.bls.gov/special.requests/ ocwc/oclt/ebs/ebb10015.pdf).

———. 1999. *Employee Benefits in Medium and Large Private Establishments, 1997* (www.bls.gov/special.requests/ocwc/oclt/ebs/ebb10017.pdf).

VanDerhei, Jack L., and Craig Copeland. 2001. "A Behavioral Model for Predicting Employee Contributions to 401(k) Plans: Preliminary Results." *North American Actuarial Journal* 5 (January): 80–94.

VanDerhei, Jack L., Sarah Holden, and Carol Quick. 2000. "401(k) Plan Asset Allocation, Account Balances, and Loan Activity in 1988." Employee Benefit Research Institute, *EBRI Issue Brief* 218 (February).

Yakoboski, Paul J., and Jack L. VanDerhei. 1996. "Contribution Rates and Plan Features: An Analysis of Large 401(k) Plan Data." Employee Benefit Research Institute, *EBRI Issue Brief* 174 (June).

Yakoboski, Paul J. 1997. "Large Plan Lump-Sums: Rollovers and Cashouts." Employee Benefit Research Institute, *EBRI Issue Brief* 184 (April).

7

How Should We Insure
Longevity Risk in Pensions
and Social Security?

Jeffrey R. Brown

A S BABY BOOMERS APPROACH retirement, individuals and policymakers are increasingly concerned about retirement income security. Thanks to dramatic advances in life expectancy, today's sixty-five-year-old man and woman can expect, on average, to live to ages eighty-one and eighty-five, respectively. Perhaps even more impressive, more than 17 percent of sixty-five-year-old men and more than 31 percent of sixty-five-year-old women are expected to live to age ninety and beyond. Most people would agree that increasing life expectancy is highly desirable. However, *uncertainty* about length of life carries the risk that individuals may outlive their resources and be forced to substantially reduce their living standards at advanced ages.

Fortunately, financial products exist that allow individuals to protect themselves from this risk. In particular, a *life annuity* is an insurance product that pays out a periodic (for example, monthly) sum of income that lasts for life, in exchange for an up-front premium. The primary appeal of the life annuity is that it offers retirees the opportunity to insure against the risk of outliving assets by exchanging these assets for a lifelong stream of guaranteed income.

In the United States the two primary sources of life annuities for most retirees are the Social Security system and employer-provided, defined benefit (DB) pension plans. The first and most important of these, the Social Security system, is facing significant future financial imbalances that have led to

Reprinted with permission, Trustees of Boston College, Center for Retirement Research. All rights reserved. The research reported herein was performed pursuant to a grant from the U.S. Social Security Administration (SSA), funded as part of the Retirement Research Consortium. The opinions and conclusions expressed are solely those of the author and should not be construed as representing the opinions or policy of SSA or any agency of the federal government or the Center for Retirement Research at Boston College.

numerous proposals for reform, including supplementing or partially replacing the existing system with a personal accounts program. The effect of such proposals on overall retirement security will depend in part on how withdrawals from these accounts are regulated. While many personal accounts proposals to reform Social Security would mandate some form of annuitization, this provision is not universal.

If personal accounts are adopted, it will in many ways mirror the dramatic shift that has already occurred with private pension plans over the past quarter century. Since the passage of the Employee Retirement Income Security Act (ERISA) in 1974, the U.S. pension landscape has been dramatically altered from one in which most retirees receive life annuities through DB pension plans to a system of defined contribution (DC) plans, such as 401(k) plans, in which individuals have more control over the disposition of these assets. The majority of workers covered by private DC plans are not offered an annuitization option. While alternative distribution mechanisms, such as lump-sum payments or periodic withdrawals, offer retirees a high degree of flexibility, they do not provide a formal mechanism by which individuals can insure against longevity risk.

The extent to which individuals insure their mortality risk has a number of important policy implications. First, by providing a guaranteed minimum level of income, annuities ensure that individuals will not outlive their retirement resources. Second, the provision of a minimum income floor directly affects the extent to which retirees, and elderly widows in particular, are at risk of falling into poverty. As such, the degree of dependence on means-tested programs such as Supplemental Security Income (SSI) and Medicaid will be affected. Third, because assets that are annuitized are no longer available for bequests, the extent of annuitization can affect the size of intergenerational transfers.

This chapter begins with a brief discussion of how annuities work and why they are important to retirees. It also discusses many of the institutional features of annuity markets in the United States, highlighting the fact that few individuals annuitize resources outside of Social Security and DB pension plans. It then explores a number of reasons for this limited annuity demand, followed by a discussion of the benefits and costs of mandating annuities. This chapter concludes with a discussion of policy implications for pensions and Social Security.

What Are Annuities and Why Are They Important to Retirees?

Annuities are generally defined as contracts that provide periodic payments for an agreed upon span of time. They include *annuities certain*, which provide periodic payouts for a fixed number of years, and *life annuities*, which provide such payouts for the duration of one or more persons' lives. This chapter is primarily concerned with life annuities, the principal insurance role of which is to protect individuals against outliving their resources.[1]

In order to understand the value of a life annuity, imagine a sixty-five-year-old woman preparing to retire with a significant stock of accumulated assets, in a world without the existing Social Security system or a DB pension. If she knew her date of death with certainty, it would be a fairly simple exercise to optimally allocate this wealth over her remaining years. In the presence of uncertainty about length of life, however, determining how much to consume is a more difficult calculation because she must consider two competing risks. The first is *longevity risk*, or the risk that she will live significantly beyond her expected life span and thus run out of money. One way to solve this problem is for her to consume very conservatively to ensure that she will not run out of money even if she lives to an extremely advanced age. For example, if she consumed only the interest on her wealth, and never consumed out of the principal, she would never run her wealth to zero.[2] This approach, however, exposes the individual to the risk that she will die with a substantial amount of wealth left unconsumed. In what sense is this a risk? Because the unconsumed wealth is a lost consumption opportunity—were it not for the uncertainty about length of life, the individual could have consumed more in every period while alive, presumably making her better off.[3]

These risks arise from the fact that there is substantial variation in length of life. Table 7-1 shows that an average sixty-five-year-old man in the year 2000 can expect to live an additional 16.4 years to age eighty-one, while a typical sixty-five-year-old woman has a life expectancy of an additional 19.6 years to nearly age eighty-five. As the table illustrates, however, 12 percent of men and 7.7 percent of women will die prior to their seventieth birthday, while 17.5 percent of men and 31.4 percent of women will live to age ninety or beyond.

---

1. *Annuities certain* contracts, because they are paid for a fixed number of periods regardless of the survival of the insured, offer no insurance against outliving one's resources.

2. In a model with finite-lived, egoistic consumers, the strategy of consuming interest only is never optimal. However, even more complex consumption rules that avoid running out of wealth provide a consumption stream that is strictly dominated by actuarially fair annuitization. Readers interested in a more formal treatment can consult Yaari (1965); Mitchell et al. (1999) or Brown (2001b).

3. For the time being, this discussion ignores any desire to leave a bequest to one's heirs. As will be discussed below, strong bequest motives will reduce the value of annuitization.

Table 7-1. *Remaining Life Expectancy and Probabilities of Survival to Selected Ages for 65-Year-Olds, 2000*

Probability of surviving to age	Men	Women
	16.4 years	19.6 years
70	.880	.923
75	.737	.821
80	.560	.685
85	.359	.513
90	.175	.314
95	.058	.135
100	.012	.036

Source: United States life table functions and actuarial functions at 3 percent interest for males and females born in 1935 based on the Alternative 2 mortality probabilities used in the 2000 *Trustees Report of the Social Security Administration.*

This highlights the significant uncertainty faced by individuals in allocating their retirement wealth across their remaining lifetime.

A life annuity solves the retiree's wealth allocation problem. A life annuity allows her to exchange a stock of wealth for a guaranteed stream of income that will be paid as long as she is alive and thus removes the risk of outliving her resources. In addition, an annuity solves the problem of the lost consumption opportunity by providing the annuitant with a higher level of income than she could receive in the absence of annuitization, in exchange for making the receipt of this income contingent upon living. In short, the provider of the annuity (that is, the government, the employer, or the insurance company) uses the assets of those who die early to pay a higher rate of return to those who are still living.

To illustrate the value of an annuity more clearly, consider two identical sixty-five-year-old men with $100,000 of accumulated retirement wealth. The first of these men purchases an actuarially fair life annuity, which, with a nominal interest rate of 7 percent, would pay the retiree $929.38 a month for as long as he lives.[4] The second of these men chooses not to annuitize but tries to maintain the same living standard by consuming $929.38 a month while alive, keeping the balance of his wealth earning 7 percent interest. The second man can do this for thirteen years and eight months, at which time he would run out

---

4. These calculations use mortality rates for the general U.S. population as used in the 2000 *Trustees Report of the Social Security Administration.* For a sixty-five-year-old in the year 2000, the 1935 birth cohort life table is used. It is assumed, for purposes of this illustration, that the maximum possible age of life is 118 years.

of money with a 60 percent chance of still being alive. Without annuitizing, the sixty-five-year-old would have to consume only $623.85 a month (33 percent less) in order to avoid running out of money by age one hundred, and even then there is a 1.2 percent chance of still being alive.[5]

For these insurance reasons, economists have long viewed annuities as an important component of any retirement portfolio. In fact, the earliest theoretical results suggested that life-cycle consumers with an uncertain date of death should annuitize *all* their retirement wealth that they wish to use for financing future consumption, leaving unannuitized only that wealth that they wish to leave behind as a bequest. Simulation results using this model suggest that such hypothetical consumers would find access to actuarially fair annuities equivalent to a 50 to 100 percent increase in wealth. Naturally, this theoretical model omits a number of important factors that would rationally lead individuals to annuitize less than their full wealth, such as other sources of uncertainty, a desire for liquidity and control, and market imperfections, all of which will be discussed below. Nonetheless, economic theory suggests that a high level of annuitization, rather than a low level, ought to be the natural benchmark.

The Size of the Annuity Market in the United States

By far the most important source of annuity income in the United States is the current Social Security system. Once an individual claims a Social Security benefit, this monthly income is paid in the form of a life annuity. This benefit is indexed to the CPI, so that the purchasing power of this annuity income remains constant. In 2000 the Social Security program paid out approximately $408 billion in benefits to more than 45 million recipients. While the majority of this amount was paid out to retired and disabled workers, a substantial fraction was paid to dependents and survivors.

Private pensions represent the second largest source of annuity income to U.S. households. Tabulations from the September 1994 Health and Pension Benefit Supplement to the Current Population Survey indicate that of the 17.4 million individuals over the age of fifty-five who were retired from private sector jobs, 7.2 million (41.3 percent) reported that they were receiving annuity income from a private pension plan. The mean annual annuity payment for this group was $9,714, and the total amount of annuity income was $70 billion.

---

5. Some might argue that this overstates the value of annuitization because the individual could simply invest his nonannuitized wealth in a higher-yielding portfolio, including corporate equities. This argument is somewhat misleading, for reasons that will be discussed later in this chapter.

The overwhelming trend among providers of private pension plans in the United States is the switch away from DB plans to DC plans, such as 401(k)s. One implication of this switch is a decline in the opportunities for annuitization within the pension plan. For example, in 1997 only 27 percent of 401(k) plan participants had an option to choose a life annuity as their method of distribution. Lump-sum withdrawal is the most common distribution option available, followed by some form of phased withdrawal. Figures for other DC plans appear to be similarly low. As a result, more than 70 percent of the nearly 50 million DC plan participants in the United States will be unable to withdraw their retirement account balances in a manner that directly protects them from longevity risk.

Outside of Social Security and private pensions, the market for individual life annuities is quite small. In 1998 the American Council of Life Insurance reported that there were 1.6 million individual annuity policies in a "payout phase," meaning that the policy owners were currently receiving benefits.[6] This figure actually overstates the extent of annuitization in the individual market, since some of these contracts are annuities certain rather than life annuities and because some individuals may hold multiple policies. Thus privately purchased individual annuities are trivial in importance when compared to Social Security and private pension plans.

The small size of the individual annuity market may come as a surprise to anyone who has heard about the dramatic growth in the market for deferred *variable annuities* over the past decade.[7] For instance, in the individual annuity market, variable annuities grew from only $2 billion in annual premiums in 1988 to $49 billion in 1998. An important distinction, however, is that nearly all these variable annuities are *deferred annuities*, meaning that the contract owners are still in the process of accumulating assets (see box 7-1 for discussion of annuity types). This chapter is concerned primarily with annuities in the payout phase, known as *immediate annuities*, which are currently providing a source of longevity-insured retirement income. The growth in the deferred variable annuity market will be relevant for future annuitization trends if these funds are routinely converted into life annuities in the payout

6. American Council of Life Insurance (1999a).

7. A variable annuity that is still in deferred status is similar to a mutual fund in that an individual's contributions are invested in a portfolio of assets. From an individual investor's perspective, an attractive feature of variable annuities is that the returns on these investments are tax-deferred until withdrawal. In general, what distinguishes deferred variable annuity products from mutual funds is that they generally offer some form of implicit or explicit insurance, such as a guaranteed return of principal in the event of the insured's death.

Box 7-1. *Types of Annuities Available*

The stylized examples in this chapter are representative of a product known as a "single premium immediate life annuity." There is, however, a much richer set of annuity products from which retirees can choose. In addition, it is useful to consider separately the accumulation phase and the payout phase of an annuity product. The accumulation phase is that period in which assets are being set aside for future conversion to an income stream. The payout phase is that period in which the individual receives income.

Design Features in the Accumulation Phase

—*Immediate versus deferred annuities:* Immediate annuities begin making payments immediately after the payment of the premium. In contrast, under deferred annuity contracts payments do not begin until some date in the future. Deferred annuities often receive favorable tax treatment during the accumulation phase, and there is no requirement that these assets ever be converted into a lifelong income stream.

—*Rates of return on deferred annuities:* With deferred annuities, payments will not commence until some date in the future. Before payouts begin, the premium dollars can be invested at a fixed rate or in a portfolio of risky assets in which case they are known as a "variable annuity."

Design Features in the Payout Phase

—*Number of lives covered:* Single-life annuities pay until the insured individual dies. Joint-and-survivor annuities continue to make (possibly reduced) payments as long as at least one of the covered individuals is alive.

—*Bequest options:* Many private market annuities offer period certain guarantees or refund options that provide some additional payments to a beneficiary in the event that the insured individual dies shortly after annuitization.

— *Type of payout:* Fixed nominal annuities offer payments that are constant in nominal terms. Graded annuities increase at a predetermined percentage rate. Inflation-indexed annuities rise with the rate of inflation, thus preserving the purchasing power of the income. Variable annuity payouts are linked to an underlying portfolio of assets and will rise and fall according to a predetermined relationship with that portfolio.

phase. However, there is no requirement that assets held in deferred annuities be converted to a life annuity at retirement, and existing evidence suggests that little of this conversion is taking place.[8]

Thus, to the extent that households are insured against longevity risk, it is done primarily through Social Security and defined benefit pension plans. Few individuals appear to be purchasing annuities with nonpension savings or with the balances of their DC accounts. It is thus quite plausible that the continued shift in private pensions toward DC plans, as well as some Social Security reform outcomes, could result in a substantial reduction in the amount of retiree wealth that is insured against longevity risk. Whether or not this is a troublesome trend depends in large part on why retirees do not choose to annuitize more of their assets, an issue that is discussed in the next section.

Why Don't More People Buy Annuities?

While annuities feature prominently in economists' theoretical discussions of asset decumulation, most households are not choosing to buy annuities. Why is the individual annuity market so small?

Annuitization through Pensions and Social Security

Social Security and pensions are the primary source of annuities in the United States and represent nearly two-thirds of the wealth of households nearing retirement.[9] Clearly, having a substantial fraction of wealth in this form reduces the marginal value of additional annuitization. The reason is that the benefits from Social Security and pension annuities already provide a minimum level of guaranteed income that cannot be outlived. With these benefits in place, individuals do not run the risk of running their resources to zero. Were the annuity benefits paid by Social Security to be substantially reduced or eliminated, one would expect to see an increase in the demand for annuities in the individual market. The increase in private demand, however, would likely offset the loss of Social Security by less than dollar for dollar, due to imperfections in the annuity market and decisions by some individuals not to annuitize.

The Pricing of Individual Annuities

The standard economic model that predicts high levels of annuitization assumes that individuals can purchase annuities that are actuarially fair.

8. For more discussion, see Brown and Warshawsky (2001).
9. Mitchell and Moore (1998).

However, prices in the individual annuity market, like prices in many insurance markets, diverge from their actuarially fair level for two primary reasons. First, insurance companies incur administrative and sales expenses to underwrite and market annuity products, and these costs, plus some level of profit, must be captured in the premiums that are charged. Second, individuals who voluntarily purchase annuities tend to live longer than nonpurchasers. As a result of this "adverse selection," insurance premiums must be set high enough to compensate insurers for the fact that they will have to make annuity payments for a longer period of time. As the annuity prices are raised, some individuals with shorter life expectancies may find that these actuarially unfair annuities are no longer attractive.

The extent to which adverse selection reduces the attractiveness of life annuities has been examined in a number of empirical studies of U.S. and international annuity markets. A common metric in these studies is the "Money's Worth" calculation, which measures the expected discounted value of annuity payments per dollar of premium paid. A Money's Worth of 1.00 corresponds to the case of an actuarially fair annuity. Values less than 1.00 indicate that the present value of the annuity payments will, on average, be less than the premium paid. For example, if the Money's Worth of an annuity is 0.90, this indicates that the individual can expect, on average, to receive 90 cents in annuity income for every $1 paid in premium.[10]

To calculate the Money's Worth, one needs information on annuity payouts, interest rates, and mortality rates. According to an industry trade publication,[11] the average payout available to a sixty-five-year-old male purchasing a life annuity in May 1999 with an initial investment of $100,000 would have been $734.77 a month for life. A sixty-five-year-old woman would have received $667.36 a month, with the difference attributable to lower mortality rates among women.

To transform these payment streams into a present value requires selecting an interest rate. One option is to use the interest rates that are implied by the term structure of yields for U.S. Treasury bonds.[12] These are riskless interest rates, and using them to discount future annuity payouts implicitly assumes that no default risk is associated with these payouts. The argument for using such discount rates is that insurance regulation makes the default risk for

10. Details of the Money's Worth calculation are available in Mitchell et al. (1999) and Brown, Mitchell, and Poterba (2000).

11. Annuity payout rates are taken from *Annuity Shopper* magazine (Summer 1999).

12. The data on the U.S. Treasury yield curve were collected from *Bloomberg Financial Markets* for the same dates on which the *Annuity Shopper* data were collected.

Table 7-2. *Money's Worth of Single Premium Immediate Annuities Offered to 65-Year-Olds, 1999*

Percent

	Men		Women	
	Population	*Annuitant*	*Population*	*Annuitant*
Treasury rates	0.85	0.97	0.87	0.95
Corporate rates	0.78	0.88	0.79	0.86

Source: Author's calculations.

annuity providers very low. In addition, annuity buyers in most states are protected against insurance company defaults through state insolvency funds. While these funds do not make all annuity purchases riskless, they do further reduce the chance that an annuity buyer will not receive the promised payouts. One can argue, however, that riskless interest rates generate discount rates that are too low, since life insurance firms generally invest their portfolios in risky corporate bonds. Thus table 7-2 also reports results using the term structure for Baa-rated corporate bonds.[13]

Due to the fact that mortality rates of annuitants differ from those of the general population, it is useful to calculate the Money's Worth using two sets of mortality tables. The first set uses survival probabilities for the population at large, taken from the birth cohort mortality rates used in the Social Security Administration's Trustees' Report.[14] The second set of results acknowledges that annuity purchasers tend to have longer life expectancies than the general population. As a result, insurance companies have developed a second set of mortality rates that describe the mortality experience of those who actually purchase annuities.[15]

13. As defined by Moody's Investors Service, bonds that are rated Baa "are considered as medium-grade obligations (that is, they are neither highly protected nor poorly secured)." The bond rates in table 7-2 were also taken from *Bloomberg* on the same dates as the annuity price quotes and correspond to a *Bloomberg* bond rating of BBB-2.

14. This report is formally called the *2000 Annual Report of the Board of Trustees of the Federal Old-Age and Survivors Insurance and Disability Insurance Trust Funds.*

15. Mitchell et al. (1999) develop an algorithm that combines information from the Annuity 2000 mortality table described in Johansen (1996), the 1983 Individual Annuitant Mortality table, and the projected rate of mortality improvement implicit in the difference between the Social Security Administration's cohort and period mortality tables for the population. This algorithm generates projected mortality rates for the set of annuitants purchasing annuity contracts in a given year. These calculations use an updated version of that algorithm that incorporates the most recent Social Security data.

Figure 7-1.   *Population and Annuitant Mortality Rates*

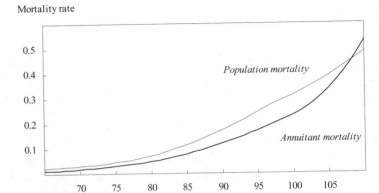

Mortality rate

Age

Source: Population mortality rates from unpublished data used in the 2000 *Trustees Report of the Social Security Administration* and annuitant mortality rates from the Society of Actuaries (with some adjustments made by author).

The population and annuitant mortality tables differ substantially. Figure 7-1 shows the projected mortality rates in 1999 for sixty-five-year-old male annuity buyers and sixty-five-year-old men in the population at large. Between the ages of sixty-five and seventy-five, the mortality rate for annuitants is roughly half of that for the general population. The mortality differential is somewhat smaller at older ages. Because cash flows in the first few years after annuity purchase contribute importantly to determining the expected present discounted value of the annuity payout, the large mortality differential between ages sixty-five and seventy-five generates significant differences in Money's Worth calculations when switching from one mortality table to another.

Table 7-2 reports results of the Money's Worth calculation. Using the population mortality table and discounting using the Treasury rate, the Money's Worth is 85 cents on the dollar for men and 87 cents on the dollar for women. This suggests that sixty-five-year-olds can expect to receive 13 to 15 cents less in annuity payments than they paid as an initial premium. If one instead discounts using the higher corporate bond rate, the Money's Worth is reduced considerably to 78 cents on the dollar for men and 79 cents on the dollar for women, suggesting a differential of more than 20 cents on the dollar.

If the Money's Worth is calculated using mortality rates of typical annuitants, however, the ratios are higher. Using a Treasury rate, the Money's Worth is 97 cents on the dollar for men and 95 cents on the dollar for women. Therefore, individuals with mortality expectations like those of typical annuitants appear to receive an actuarially attractive price, with only 3 to 5 cents on the dollar being attributed to administrative costs of the insurance company. The 10 cents on the dollar difference between the Money's Worth using the population and the annuitant tables, however, is a measure of the cost of adverse selection. This number is important because if all individuals were forced into the private annuity market with an annuity mandate, the adverse selection component would likely disappear. This suggests that an annuity mandate might raise payouts by as much as 10 percent.[16]

Bequest Motives and Self-Insurance within Families

If retirees wish to leave an inheritance to their children or other relatives, then this desire would reduce the incentive to annuitize at retirement. With an ordinary life annuity, the value of the annuity contract is zero upon the death of the insured. While a number of "bequest" options are available, such as guarantee periods or refund options, generally the easiest method of providing for a bequest is to annuitize only partially and leave some wealth in assets that can be inherited.

The strength of bequest motives and their implication for financial behavior of elderly households are issues of continued debate in the economics literature. It is clear that many households leave wealth behind to their children, but it is less clear whether these bequests are intentional—the result of poor financial planning on the part of the decedent or due to limited market options for annuitization. Some researchers have argued that the large magnitude of bequests, the presence of life insurance in many household portfolios, and the choice of survivor options in pensions are suggestive of intentional bequest behavior.[17] Still others have demonstrated that couples with children do not behave in a manner consistent with a bequest motive.[18] Further research is needed to resolve this debate.

Risk pooling within families may be another reason that people do not fully annuitize in the formal insurance market. Researchers have looked at this effect in two ways. First, one can think of a family as a miniature annuity market. Annuity markets operate by transferring the resources of an early decedent to those who live for a longer period of time. Family members who share a

16. One would also need to consider whether administrative and selling expenses would be different in a large, mandated annuity market than in the currently small market dominated by high-income individuals.

17. Examples include Laitner and Juster (1996) and Bernheim (1991).

18. Examples include Hurd (1987, 1989) and Brown (2001a, 2001b).

common budget essentially do the same thing. For example, if the husband dies with unannuitized assets, his resources are not wasted but rather are available to his wife or children for consumption. Obviously, the ability to pool risks in a couple or a small family cannot completely substitute for an efficient annuity market with many participants, but it can come surprisingly close. In fact, simulations suggest that a two-person household can achieve just under 50 percent of the utility gains that would accrue from an actuarially fair annuity market.[19] A second view is that the risk of both members of a couple dying in any given year is obviously lower than the risk of any one of them dying in that year. Since annuity payments are inversely related to mortality risk (that is, an insurance company can pay more each month when the risk of dying is higher), the extra return that a joint life annuity provides is lower, making annuities somewhat less attractive relative to alternative investments.

The Desire for Flexibility

With few exceptions, the decision to annuitize one's wealth is largely irreversible. The reason for this is quite simple—if individuals had the ability to cash out their annuity at any time, they would always try to do so right before death. This would be a severe form of adverse selection and would make it financially impossible for an insurance company to offer attractive annuity rates.

As a result of this irreversibility, individuals who annuitize give up flexibility and essentially impose a liquidity constraint on themselves. In a recent survey, financial planning professionals were asked why so few individuals choose to annuitize. Of 321 financial planners surveyed, 31 percent cited the loss of control of principal or lost flexibility as the primary reason for low annuitization rates, as shown in table 7-3. This response is far higher than any other response.

Presumably one of the main reasons that individuals desire flexibility is that they are uncertain about future expenditure needs. This uncertainty is particularly true with regard to uninsured medical expenses, such as for prescription drugs or long-term care. For example, studies have estimated that 35 to 40 percent of sixty-five-year-olds will spend some time in a nursing home before they die. While Medicare will often pay for stays up to one hundred days, many nursing home stays are of longer duration. Given the extremely limited coverage by private long-term care insurance in the United States, most expenses must be paid out of pocket by the individuals or by Medicaid after the

19. Kotlikoff and Spivak (1981); Brown and Poterba (2000).

Table 7-3. *Financial Planner Responses as to Why Few Retirees Take a Lifetime Income Option*
Percent

Loss of control of principal/locked in	31
Want money to go to heirs/loss of assets	18
Low payout	15
No adjustment for inflation	12
Better ways to make money	11
Poor advice/not well informed	9
Bad idea/don't need it	5

Source: American Council of Life Insurance, "Positioning and Promoting Annuities in a New Retirement Environment," 1999.

individuals have spent down their resources. It is clear that older Americans recognize health care costs as an important source of financial risk. Venti and Wise report results from a health and retirement survey question that asks "In thinking about your financial future, how concerned are you with health care costs?"[20] Fifty-two percent of respondents indicated a high level of concern, significantly more than are concerned with other sources of uncertainty, such as job loss or financial market collapse.

Inflation

Outside of Social Security and a limited number of DB plans, most annuities in the United States are fixed in nominal terms, meaning they do not include any provision to protect the individual against the risk of inflation. Inflation has two undesirable effects on fixed nominal annuity streams. First, even modest rates of inflation will erode the real value of the income stream over time. For instance, at a 3.2 percent annual rate (which is the average U.S. inflation rate over the 1926–97 period), the real value of a constant nominal annuity will be cut in half in twenty-two years. If inflation were constant and expected, however, this would easily be remedied by the use of a *graded* or *escalating* annuity product that increases the nominal payout by a fixed percentage each year. The second effect, however, arises from inflation *uncertainty*. If inflation varies from year to year, it will induce variation in the real purchasing power available to retirees. This is true even if the product is escalating at a fixed percentage rate each year.

In the United States inflation-indexed annuities are largely not available to consumers. Historically, this scarcity was due to the lack of inflation-indexed investments with which life insurance companies could underwrite policies. In

20. Venti and Wise (2000).

1997, however, the U.S. government introduced TIPS inflation-indexed government bonds. Since the introduction of these securities, two companies have made inflation-indexed annuities available to consumers. TIAA-CREF, the principal and longstanding retirement system for the nation's education and research sectors, offers a variable annuity linked to an "inflation linked bond account." While this product does not guarantee a fixed real income stream due to several design features, it does offer a very high degree of inflation protection.[21] However, this product is not available to individuals outside of the education and research sector. A second U.S. company, Irish Life of North America, offers a true CPI-indexed annuity, but as of this writing they had no sales of this product. It is unclear whether this lack of demand is due to unattractive prices, poor marketing, or a genuine lack of demand for inflation-adjusted products. If demand for inflation-indexed annuities were to increase in the future, such as through a Social Security or pension reform that mandated inflation-indexed annuities through the private sector, the availability of TIPS should enable life insurance companies to meet this demand.

Outside the United States, other nations have more experience with inflation-indexed annuities. For example, index-linked bonds have been available in the United Kingdom for two decades, allowing insurance companies to offer inflation-indexed annuities. Even so, approximately 90 percent of individuals purchase level annuities and do not opt for any sort of inflation protection. Part of the lack of demand may be due to the high costs; the Money's Worth of real annuities in the United Kingdom appears to be 8 to 10 percent lower than that of nominal annuities.[22] The experience of other nations, such as Israel and Australia, confirms that the private sector is able to offer real annuities but at a significant additional cost relative to fixed nominal annuities.

Higher-Return Portfolio Choices

It is sometimes argued that individuals can do better than an annuity by investing the funds on their own in higher-return assets, such as a portfolio of equities. The logic of this argument is that bond portfolios generally back fixed

21. These features include: (1) TIAA annuities are "participating" and thus change value based on the mortality experience of the contract owners; (2) the value of the underlying portfolio is marked to market daily, and thus the value will vary; and (3) the nominal portfolio return must exceed 4 percent plus the rate of inflation in order not to decline in real terms.

22. See Murthi, Orszag, and Orszag (1999) and Finkelstein and Poterba (1999).

annuities, and over the long term stocks have historically earned a higher rate of return than bonds.[23]

This argument is misleading for two reasons. First, even a well-diversified portfolio does not insure a retiree against longevity risk. Stock returns are higher than bond returns on average, but these returns come at the cost of increased risk. A recent study found that even with an optimally chosen, diversified portfolio, if a person tries to replicate the stream of annuity payments, the probability of running out of wealth is still significant.[24]

Second, an individual who wishes to invest in a more diversified portfolio can do so without sacrificing longevity insurance by purchasing variable or equity-linked annuities. Variable annuities invest the premium in an underlying portfolio of assets, and the monthly payment from the annuity rises or falls depending on whether the asset returns are higher or lower than the *assumed interest rate* that was used to determine the initial annuity payment. Equity-indexed annuities invest a fraction of the premium (for example, 90 percent) in a fixed annuity and use the remaining premium to purchase call options on a stock index, such as the Standard & Poor 500. With this product, individuals are guaranteed never to receive less than the value of the fixed annuity portion, but they can capture some of the "upside" potential of equities if returns are high enough. Both of these products preserve the longevity insurance feature that individuals will continue to receive payments for as long as they live.

Lack of Understanding of the Benefits of Annuitization

A final reason that individuals may not choose to annuitize is that they fail to fully understand the benefits of annuitization. This could arise either because they underestimate the probability of living to advanced ages or because they fail to understand how annuities operate to insure against longevity risk.

The limited evidence available to assess subjective survival probabilities suggests that, on average, these subjective probabilities behave a lot like actual probabilities derived from life tables and mortality data.[25] Thus, while individuals may have an inaccurate assessment of their mortality risk, the data suggest that people are just as likely to overstate as to understate their survival

23. For a detailed discussion of the equity premium, see Diamond (1999).

24. Milevsky (2000).

25. See Hamermesh (1985) and Hurd and McGarry (1995).

probabilities. Based on these data, it is unlikely that the lack of annuity demand is due to people systematically underestimating their length of life.[26]

A more likely scenario is that individuals simply do not understand how an annuity operates or why it is beneficial. A task force of the American Council on Life Insurance has concluded, based on qualitative consumer research, that consumer knowledge of annuities is low.[27] Their report suggests that the least understood aspect of annuities is how risk sharing can allow insurers to offer lifelong income. Consumers tended to focus on the risk of dying early and therefore receiving less in return from the annuity than they paid in, while overlooking the fact that they may live longer than expected and receive much more than they paid. In fact, some consumers equated lifetime annuity payments with gambling on their lives and believed that the odds in the gamble favored the insurance company.

Unlike many of the other reasons that consumers may not annuitize, a lack of understanding of annuity products and their benefits is particularly troubling. While more research is needed to understand the extent to which this explanation is true, one possible implication is that the lack of annuitization outside of Social Security and defined benefit pensions should not be viewed as an optimal decision by all consumers. If true, it would lend further support to mandating a minimum level of annuitization.

Spousal Considerations

While most of the discussion so far has focused on individual retirees, it is also important to consider the impact of retirement income policy on the spouses of retired workers. According to 1997 Census Bureau data, 79 percent of men and 53 percent of women between the ages of sixty-five and seventy-four were married. Of those who were not married, most were widowed. These figures underscore the importance of considering both spouses when examining retirement income security.

The Social Security Act requires survivor insurance for spouses of workers covered by Social Security. Surviving spouses generally receive between half and two-thirds of the income that was being paid by Social Security when both spouses were alive. In contrast, there is no requirement that private pensions

---

26. Even if individuals correctly estimate their life expectancy, however, the degree of uncertainty about survival rates will still affect annuity demand. For example, people who believe that they will die with certainty at age eighty-five may not desire an annuity because, according to their subjective probabilities, there is no longevity risk.

27. American Council of Life Insurance (1999b).

pay survivor benefits. ERISA, the federal law governing private pensions, only requires that pension plans that offer an annuity provide a joint and survivor option that pays the surviving spouse at least 50 percent, but not more than 100 percent, of the pension received during the joint lives of the husband and wife. Couples can waive the survivor option only if both spouses sign a notarized consent form.

Sponsors of defined contribution plans are not required to offer an annuity at all. However, if they choose to do so, they are also required to offer a joint and survivor annuity as the default option. Some practitioners have argued that this additional administrative burden is one reason that more DC plans do not offer annuities. These costs, however, must be netted against the significant social benefits of providing a guaranteed source of survivor income.

Becoming widowed has long been recognized as a key determinant of poverty rates among the elderly, especially women. The major benefit of providing survivor income is a reduction in poverty among these elderly widows. Between 1982 and 1991, for example, the median value of inflation-adjusted income from private pensions had fallen 23 percent for intact couples, primarily due to incomplete inflation indexing. For households in which the wife became widowed, the value of real pension income over this period fell 75 percent.[28] Higher levels of survivor benefits could help address this problem. A retirement system that wishes to provide meaningful income security, therefore, must be especially careful to provide for a surviving spouse.

Should We Mandate Annuitization?

One way to view the existing Social Security system is as a government-mandated annuitization system. Individuals are required to contribute to the system while working via Social Security payroll taxes and are then required to take the benefit as a life annuity. In the past, when defined benefit pension plans were far less likely to offer a lump-sum option than they are today, employees of firms with these plans had little choice but to take their pension benefit as an annuity. In short, mandatory annuitization has been the norm in the United States for many decades.

Advocates of DC plans and individual accounts applaud the broader degree of freedom that participants have to choose how to use their accumulated accounts in retirement. The absence of an annuity mandate is thus viewed positively as a loosening of constraints on individual choice.

---

28. Coile and Diamond (1998).

As is often the case, however, the question of whether or not some annuitization of retirement resources should be mandated involves a complicated set of trade-offs. The two primary benefits of mandatory annuitization are: (1) the potential to improve annuity market efficiency through the elimination of adverse selection, and (2) the decreased risk that some retirees will fail to adequately provide for their own consumption at advanced ages. Mandatory annuitization also has two important costs: (1) some individuals will be forced to overannuitize relative to what is optimal, due, for example, to poor health or strong bequest motives; and (2) mandatory annuitization can have undesirable distributional consequences. In the end, decisionmakers will no doubt differ on the answer to the mandatory annuitization question based on their different values about the importance of each of these costs and benefits.

Benefit 1: Enhanced Annuity Market Efficiency

As discussed earlier in the context of private market pricing of annuities, insurance markets often suffer from adverse selection. Because an annuity pays income for life, it will be more attractive to individuals who expect to live a long time and less attractive to those who suspect that they will not live a long time. As a result, in a voluntary annuity market, individuals who purchase annuities are likely to have longer life expectancies than those who do not. If an insurance company prices annuities based on the average mortality in the population as a whole, but only sells them to individuals who are longer-lived than average, then the company will lose money. To avoid this, insurance companies must charge more for an annuity; stated differently, they must lower the monthly payout they can provide for a given annuity premium. As they raise their price, they make annuities attractive to fewer individuals, thus "unraveling" the market.[29] As a result, annuity transactions that would be mutually beneficial to the insurance company and the individual in the presence of full and symmetric information and more detailed pricing do not take place.

Mandatory annuitization forces all risk classes into the market. As a result, insurance companies can price their annuities using average mortality charac-

---

29. Clearly, if the insurance company could accurately determine the expected mortality of each individual applicant, it could price each policy in a manner that was appropriate and profitable. In practice, life insurance companies estimate mortality for life insurance contracts, using medical exams and health histories to separate individuals into risk classes. This estimation is almost never done for annuity products, however.

teristics. This outcome serves to lower prices and increase payouts for all individuals by overcoming the adverse selection problem. As noted above, evidence suggests that mandatory annuitization could increase payouts to individuals in the United States by up to 10 percent.[30]

Benefit 2: Decreased Risk of Individuals Having Inadequate Old Age Resources

If all individuals had near-perfect information and behaved rationally, they would all adequately provide for the contingency of living to advanced ages. Unfortunately, due to factors such as imperfect information about mortality risk, imperfect annuity markets, and even myopic behavior on the part of retirees, it is quite likely that some individuals will fail to adequately insure themselves against outliving their resources. In addition to the personal costs that running out of money imposes upon these individuals, there is also a potentially large public cost in the form of government assistance programs. Individuals or couples whose income falls very low become eligible for SSI, thus increasing the financial burden on the public sector. Mandating a minimum level of annuitization that provides an income stream greater than the eligibility level for SSI ensures that this will not occur.

Cost 1: Mandate May Overannuitize Some Individuals

Individuals may wish not to annuitize for a number of rational reasons. For example, they may have exceptionally strong bequest motives. Requiring these individuals to annuitize a substantial portion of their retirement wealth could make them worse off.

Some of these situations are more troubling than others. For example, two individuals with strong bequest motives but different health conditions could face different options. Very healthy individuals can always "undo" excessive annuitization and leave a bequest by using the annuity income to pay the premiums on a life insurance policy. However, this option may not be available to individuals in poor health, since they may be unable to qualify for life insurance. Thus it is important that any annuity mandate not be excessive, or it will be of the most disadvantage to those individuals who are already "worse off" due to health considerations.

30. Mitchell et al. (1999).

Cost 2: Redistribution from Poor to Rich

Distributional considerations of an annuity mandate arise due to heterogeneity in mortality risk across the population. Annuities that ignore individual or group characteristics will result in expected transfers from high-mortality risk groups to low-mortality risk groups. While the extent of redistribution is quite sensitive to the precise structure of the annuity, in some cases it can be substantial. Mandating the use of a single life, inflation-indexed annuity leads to substantial transfers from men to women, from blacks to whites and Hispanics, and from lower education groups to higher ones. Research suggests that black males with less than a high school education would receive less than 80 cents in lifetime annuity income per dollar invested in the annuity, while white women with a college degree would receive $1.10 per dollar invested.[31] In general, within each gender these transfers tend to be from economically disadvantaged groups to groups that are better off financially.

The size of these expected transfers can be significantly reduced through the use of joint and survivor annuities, period-certain or refund options, or by "front-loading" annuity payments. However, the mechanisms that lessen the extent of redistribution often do so at the cost of reducing the income that is available to retirees. One could also attempt to offset these distributional outcomes through the use of an income-based tax or subsidy system. For example, low earners, who have higher mortality rates, could receive a government match on contributions as a way of increasing their annuity payment, while higher earners could pay an implicit or explicit tax. In order to offset the redistribution, these tax and subsidy rates would have to be set based on the correlation between income, or retirement wealth, and mortality. More research is needed to accurately quantify this relationship.

Implications for Pension Policy

Current policy toward pension plans in the United States discourages annuitization because defined contribution plans such as 401(k)s are not required to offer an annuity option. This fact, combined with the other disincentives for doing so, has resulted in a mere 27 percent of 401(k) plan participants having access to annuitization within their pension plan. While retirees have the option of withdrawing their funds from the plan and purchasing an annuity directly from an insurance company, available evidence suggests this option is rarely chosen.

Given the importance of annuitization as a way of insuring longevity risk, this lack of opportunity to annuitize within the plan is troubling. Public policy

31. Brown (2000).

could be changed in several ways to encourage annuitization, ranging from an annuity mandate to increased education of participants. The Department of Labor Advisory Council Working Group proposed to make annuities the default distribution option in defined contribution plans. Plan distributions other than in annuity form would require the active choice of the plan participant. Such a plan would probably be quite effective at increasing annuitization rates while still providing participants with the freedom to choose an alternative distribution method.

Some practitioners have argued that ERISA's "joint and survivor" requirements are partially responsible for the scarcity of an annuity option within DC plans, due to the additional administrative complexity they bring. However, policymakers should be concerned about the income security for spouses of pensioners as much as for the pensioners themselves. Joint and survivor options, by insuring that surviving spouses also have a guaranteed lifelong income stream, are an important component of retirement portfolios. The ERISA requirement allows for couples to forgo the survivor option if both spouses agree, so choice is preserved. It does, however, provide a safeguard to spouses that may protect them in the case of widowhood.

In summary, policy toward annuitization has not kept up with the realities of the changing pension landscape in the United States. Looking to the future, defined contribution pension plans will be the dominant source of retirement wealth for many households. As such, if policymakers wish to encourage annuitization, it is critical that these households have opportunities to annuitize their assets within the DC plan.

Implications for Social Security Reform

The existing Social Security system provides an important source of inflation-indexed longevity insurance that is currently unavailable in the private sector. This insurance is of substantial value to retired households, but it is often ignored in discussions of the financial returns available in the current system. This omission is unfortunate, since the benefits of annuitization are an important element of any retirement system that seeks to provide income security.

However, a desire to ensure adequate annuitization is not inconsistent with support for personal accounts proposals, since any individual accounts system can include an annuitization component.[32] Particularly if individual accounts

32. For example, the members of the 1994–96 Advisory Council on Social Security (the "Gramlich Commission") who supported the individual accounts proposal recommended that account balances be paid out through inflation-indexed annuities.

are a partial replacement for the existing Social Security program, it is important that individuals have the opportunity to annuitize these accounts. Policymakers may wish to require that individuals annuitize enough of their resources so that they are above the poverty line. Retirees could then be free to take any remaining account balance as a lump sum.

Furthermore, at least some portion of the overall retirement benefit should be protected from inflation. This protection could be provided directly by the government, as is done with the current system, or through the private market. The availability of Treasury Inflation Protected Securities should make it possible for the private market to underwrite an inflation guarantee, assuming that the U.S. Treasury will continue to provide an adequate supply of these bonds in the future.

It is also quite important that any personal accounts plan provide adequate retirement income for surviving spouses. One simple way to achieve this goal is to require that the mandated annuities be joint and survivor annuities. The government or private sector can easily provide such annuities. It would be important, however, to ensure that the level of the survivor benefit chosen be sufficient for the surviving spouse to stay above the poverty line.

It should also be recognized, however, that mandatory annuitization has potentially severe distributional consequences. This is true in the existing Social Security system and would also be true in an individual accounts system. An important difference, however, is that the current Social Security system offsets this redistribution through the use of a progressive-benefit structure. Taken together, the distributional impact of the existing system appears to be largely neutral.[33] Many individual accounts proposals, on the other hand, do not have an offsetting progressive-benefit structure. As a result, the distributional effects can be quite substantial.

Conclusion

Annuities have an important role to play in retirement portfolios as a way of insuring that individuals do not outlive their resources. From a public policy perspective, ensuring access and utilization of annuity options by retirees is one way to limit dependence on social assistance programs. In the United States the current Social Security system is the primary, and in many cases the only, source of annuitization for most households. If the private pension system continues to evolve in a manner that limits opportunities for annuitization, the inflation-indexed annuity offered by Social Security will become that much

33. See Liebman (2000) and Coronado, Fullerton, and Glass (2000).

more important as a source of longevity insurance. Given this importance, proposals that seek to supplement the existing Social Security program with an individual accounts system need to ensure that individuals will have adequate opportunities to annuitize their wealth. Proposals that seek to partially replace the Social Security system should consider requiring a minimum level of mandatory annuitization in order to overcome adverse selection and to guarantee a minimum level of retirement income for life. Mandatory annuitization, however, comes at a cost of redistributing resources away from economically disadvantaged groups toward groups that are better off financially. Fortunately, there are many policy options that would help offset this redistribution, such as contribution matches based on income.

References

American Council on Life Insurance. 1999a. *Life Insurance Factbook 1999*. Washington.

American Council on Life Insurance. 1999b. "Positioning and Promoting Annuities in a New Retirement Environment." Washington.

Bernheim, Douglas D. 1991. "How Strong Are Bequest Motives? Evidence Based on Estimates of the Demand for Life Insurance and Annuities." *Journal of Political Economy* 99: 899–927.

Brown, Jeffrey R. 2001a. "Are the Elderly Really Over-Annuitized? New Evidence on Life Insurance and Bequests." In *Themes in the Economics of Aging*, edited by D. Wise, 91–124. University of Chicago Press.

———. 2001b. "Private Pensions, Mortality Risk, and the Decision to Annuitize." *Journal of Public Economics* 82 (1): 29–62.

———. 2000. "Differential Mortality and the Value of Individual Account Retirement Annuities." Working Paper 7560. Cambridge, Mass.: National Bureau of Economic Research.

Brown, Jeffrey, Olivia Mitchell, and James Poterba. 2000. "Mortality Risk, Inflation Risk, and Annuity Products." Working Paper 7812. Cambridge, Mass.: National Bureau of Economic Research.

Brown, Jeffrey R., and James M. Poterba. 2000. "Joint Life Annuities and Annuity Demand by Married Couples." *Journal of Risk and Insurance* 67 (4): 527–53.

Brown, Jeffrey R., and Mark J. Warshawsky. 2001. "Longevity-Insured Retirement Distributions from Pension Plans: Market and Regulatory Issues." Working Paper 8064. Cambrdige, Mass.: National Bureau of Economic Research.

Coile, Courtney, and Peter Diamond. 1998. "Changes in Income and Assets in the NBDS by Marital Status." Massachusetts Institute of Technology, mimeo.

Coronado, Julia Lynn, Don Fullerton, and Thomas Glass. 2000. "The Progressivity of Social Security." Working Paper 7520. Cambridge, Mass.: National Bureau of Economic Research.

Diamond, Peter A. 1999. "What Stock Market Returns to Expect for the Future?" An Issue in Brief, no. 2. Center for Retirement Research at Boston College.

Finkelstein, Amy, and James Poterba. 1999. "The Market for Annuity Products in the United Kingdom." Working Paper 7168. Cambridge, Mass.: National Bureau of Economic Research.

Hamermesh, Daniel S. 1985. "Expectations, Life Expectancy, and Economic Behavior." *Quarterly Journal of Economics* 100 (2): 389–408.

Hurd, Michael D. 1987. "Savings of the Elderly and Desired Bequests." *American Economic Review* 77 (3): 298–312.

———. 1989. "Mortality Risk and Bequests." *Econometrica* 57 (4): 779–813.

Hurd, Michael D., and Kathleen McGarry. 1995. "Evaluation of the Subjective Probabilities of Survival." *Journal of Human Resources* 30 (supplement): S268–S292.

Johansen, R. 1996. "Review of Adequacy of 1983 Individual Annuity Mortality Table." *Transactions of the Society of Actuaries* 47: 101–23.

Kotlikoff, Laurence J., and Avia Spivak. 1981. "The Family as an Incomplete Annuities Market." *Journal of Political Economy* 89 (April): 372–91.

Laitner, John, and F. Thomas Juster. 1996. "New Evidence on Altruism: A Study of TIAA-CREF Retirees." *American Economic Review* 86: 893–908.

Liebman, Jeffrey. 2000. "Redistribution in the Current U.S. Social Security System." Harvard University, mimeo.

Milevsky, Moshe A. 2000. "Self-Annuitization and the Probability of Ruin in Retirement." *North American Actuarial Journal* 4 (4): 112–29.

Mitchell, Olivia S., and James F. Moore. 1998. "Can Americans Afford to Retire? New Evidence on Retirement Saving Adequacy." *Journal of Risk and Insurance* 65 (3): 371–400.

Mitchell, Olivia S., James M. Poterba, Mark Warshawsky, and Jeffrey R. Brown. 1999. "New Evidence on the Money's Worth of Individual Annuities." *American Economic Review* 89 (December): 1299–318.

Murthi, Mamta, J. Michael Orszag, and Peter R. Orszag. 1999. "The Value for Money of Annuities in the U.K.: Theory, Experience, and Policy." London: Birkbeck College, mimeo.

Venti, Steven, and David A. Wise. 2000. "Choice, Chance, and Wealth Dispersion at Retirement." Working Paper 7521. Cambridge, Mass.: National Bureau of Economic Research.

Yaari, Menahem E. 1965. "Uncertain Lifetime, Life Insurance, and the Theory of the Consumer." *Review of Economic Studies* 32: 137–50.

Comment by Ann Combs

Chapters 6 and 7 add important data and insight into what is an emerging and a very vital debate. Jack VanDerhei and Craig Copeland's data are extremely important, demonstrating a major effect of the significant erosion of defined benefit (DB) plan coverage, and that is a substantial diminution in the level of retirement income that is guaranteed for life.

One simple fact in the data is striking. As Copeland noted, earlier cohorts received their non–Social Security pension wealth from defined benefit plans, defined contribution (DC) plans, and rollover individual retirement accounts (IRAs), in that order. Those sources have completely flipped for those who are born after 1950—the baby boom generation, the Gen-Xers, and the new millennials coming along. Those individuals are now going to be receiving their non–Social Security pension wealth primarily from rollover IRAs; the second source will be DC plans; and the third source will be DB plans.

The figures in chapter 6 show that if you combine the IRA and DC wealth for the 1964 birth cohort, 75 percent of females' and 83 percent of males' pension wealth is in a form where annuity payouts are rare. And there is no sign that this trend is abating.

One response to this is to bemoan the demise of the traditional—that is, noncash balance or hybrid—defined benefit pension plan. While I believe in the value of such plans, and have always been a strong supporter, at this point I think it is futile and, in fact, may be a mistake to try to stem the tide and continue to argue that we need to go back and insist on traditional defined benefit plans as the only appropriate source of retirement income. That argument will not be successful. Moreover, defined contribution plans, and the new hybrid defined benefit plans like cash balance plans, are, in fact, responsive to the needs of many workers.

Government regulation, both real and as perceived by the employer community, is stifling employers' willingness to offer defined benefit plans. Defined contribution plans may be the only practical option for smaller employers who employ an increasing share of the work force. Defined contribution plans can provide meaningful retirement benefits to all covered workers—not just to those who spend an entire career with one employer, which is the group that benefits greatly from traditional defined benefit plans. Defined contribution plans also have the potential for significant wealth accumulation. The challenge before us, as Richard Berner has noted, is to sit back and try to develop policies that will recreate some of the positive features of the traditional DB plan in this new environment. One of the most important of these is the ability to receive benefits in the form of a lifetime annuity—income guaranteed for life that you cannot outlive.

The major difference between defined benefit and defined contribution plans is who bears the risk. Everyone in the policy and political communities at this point understands that investment risk is shifted to the employee in a DC plan. A number of policies have been proposed in recent years to address some of the concerns raised by that shift. Major initiatives are under way within the employer community, particularly to educate participants about investment strategies and characteristics. It is a long road, but the data show that when education is undertaken, it makes a difference. There are also legislative proposals to allow financial institutions to provide specific investment advice to plan participants, which is a positive development.

With the exception of Jeffrey Brown, Mark Warshawsky, and a few others, no one to date has focused on the other risk shifting that is going on as we move toward defined contribution type arrangements. No one is talking about the risk of outliving your assets. That risk is also being shifted to the employee when benefits are paid out as a lump sum instead of an annuity. If employees are ill-prepared to deal with investment risk, they are absolutely not prepared to deal with managing these assets to last a lifetime.

Brown's chapter points out that wealth accumulation is great, but it is not enough to guarantee retirement income security. Other factors need to be examined, and the focus of the pension debate must be broadened. Asset accumulation is essential. Incentives must be improved for people to save for their retirement, and there are several worthy of legislative proposals now pending in Congress to do that.

Policymakers begin to think about how to help people manage their assets and how to protect those assets from risk. Brown mentioned the risk of long-term care needs. One episode of long-term care can wipe out an individual's retirement savings. Another fear is outliving your assets. In essence, the challenge is to help people create private safety nets to supplement the social safety nets that are offered by Social Security and Medicare.

As Brown's chapter makes clear, this is a multifaceted challenge with both policy and public education components. The education challenge is highlighted by Brown's finding that, at the present time, even if workers are offered an annuity option in a defined contribution arrangement, most do not take it. They do not understand the value of an annuity. All the stakeholders need to work together to improve public understanding and awareness. The American Council of Life Insurers (ACLI) has conducted a number of focus groups, performed market research, and developed consumer booklets trying to promote awareness of annuities and the risk of outliving one's income. The ACLI is also proposing that participants at the National Summit on Retirement Savings, a bipartisan forum that is being convened by the Bush administration and the Congress to look at retirement security, put this and the issue of asset accumulation on the agenda. This would be a good way to get started on trying to raise awareness with the public.

The crux of the policy challenge is twofold. First, incentives need to be developed for employers to offer annuity options in defined contribution arrangements. Mandating that employees take their entire DC account balance in the form of annuity is probably not a good idea; politically it is a nonstarter. However, proposing individual accounts as part of Social Security is a different equation, particularly if these individual accounts are carved out and funded with existing payroll taxes. There is a very strong argument that those should be required to be annuitized. With individual accounts that are in addition to Social Security, like the retirement savings accounts proposed by the Clinton administration, there should be more debate about whether they should be fully annuitized or whether some minimum level of annuitization could be developed. Perhaps a rule of thumb could be created for people and financial planners to say individuals should have "X" amount of their retirement income annuitized from whatever sources. For example, if workers are fortunate enough to have a defined benefit plan, they may need less of their defined contribution plan annuitized.

In order to encourage employers to offer annuity options, the regulatory burdens that create disincentives need to be examined. One approach would be to make it clear under the law that an employer who selects a qualified annuity provider would shed any residual legal liability for those assets once they are transferred to the insurer. The insurer would assume the legal and the fiduciary responsibility for making those payments. If that is something that would make employers more comfortable about offering annuities, it is something that should be discussed.

Employers have other issues that must be dealt with, such as the administrative burdens in managing annuities. The fact that they have to be unisex is another issue for employers.

The more difficult challenge is to create incentives for employees to elect annuities. If a demand can be created for annuities, employers will respond by trying to meet employees' needs for a cost-effective annuity product. Even if the employer does not step up to the challenge and offer the annuity, the employee would still have the ability to roll funds into an IRA and purchase an annuity.

ACLI has developed a proposal that will be taken to Capitol Hill this year to create an incentive for employees to elect annuities. At this time, the proposal is limited to the individual, nonqualified market. It would not apply, as currently constructed, to distributions from 401(k)s and 403(b)s or IRAs. The proposal itself is straightforward. It would change the law to tax the income portion of a lifetime annuity payment at a lower rate, for instance, the capital gains rate. So that if employees elected to take their distribution in the form of a life-contingent payment, joint and survivor or single life, the income payout would be taxed at the capital gains rate. ACLI is not suggesting at this time that similar favorable tax treatment apply to qualified plan distributions simply because, in looking at what the revenue implications might be, it would be better to start small and lay the groundwork for this as a policy idea. Because the payouts from qualified plans are already so large, the revenue loss associated with this kind of favorable tax treatment would be substantial. So the ACLI decided to start with the individual annuity market, which is much smaller, as Brown pointed out in chapter 7. Individual annuities also are a vehicle for the 50 percent of the work force that does not have a qualified plan. They are a viable source of retirement savings for those workers, but they are being used as accumulation vehicles right now. Since no one has a lot of experience with people annuitizing individual, nonqualified annuities, it has yet to be seen if more favorable tax treatment for annuity payments can change behavior. This proposal is a good test case and the ACLI is excited about encouraging individuals to elect annuities.

Brown just touched on the issue of why indexed annuities are not more widely available, but he talks quite a bit about the inflation risk and questions why private sector inflation-indexed annuities are not available. Several reasons have been put forth. First, the issuance of indexed Treasury bonds, while a good step, is not in itself sufficient to allow insurers to underwrite inflation effectively. Indexed corporate bonds, with their larger margins, would be needed to provide a viable private market for fully inflation-indexed annuities.

Second, and perhaps the more basic issue, is that there is no demand for indexed annuities at this point. This may be because inflation has been low in recent years or because people do not appreciate the value of indexation. Some speculate that people just do not understand annuities and are resistant when they are shown the options and they see the lower initial payouts for an indexed annuity as opposed to a straight life annuity. People are not demanding inflation-indexed annuities and, without demand, it is not likely that a market is going to develop at this time. This leads the discussion back to the education point. The more the value of annuitization is explained, the more likely some progress will be made.

Both of these chapters have raised important issues. There is a need for more research in this area. Brown points out several areas where he thinks that more work needs to be done. The members of the National Academy of Social Insurance should step up to that challenge and recognize that the private pension market of the future is much more likely to be based on a defined contribution model, as Copeland and VanDerhei demonstrated. NASI members need to make sure that some of the best features of defined benefit plans can be taken and made available to workers in a defined contribution environment.

Comment by Albert Crenshaw

In listening to the discussion about choosing annuities and why they are not more popular and in demand, I am reminded of a friend who has been going down to the Outer Banks in North Carolina for vacation every summer since the 1950s. The Outer Banks in the 1950s was a wild and semi-uninhabited place in which you could do pretty much what you want and not see another person for yards or miles. This friend has not been happy with what has happened down there, and every time he comes back and I ask him how he liked the Outer Banks he always says, "There's nothing wrong with that place that a good class 5 hurricane wouldn't cure."

Listening to the discussions of the shift away from defined benefit (DB) plans to defined contribution (DC) plans and of people turning away from annuities, I am reminded of the Outer Banks story because it is the same sort of way of looking at things. We are coming off about twenty years of perhaps the best investment climate any of us will ever know. It has been the closest thing to risk-free investing we have ever seen and maybe ever will see, and it has turned the attitude of a growing block of people about retirement planning away from social insurance and toward wealth accumulation.

This can be seen both on the employer and the employee side. For example, several years ago, as the labor shortages were first starting to show up, the owner of a small metal fabrication factory in the Northeast was discussing what he was doing to attract new workers. He said that the first thing he did was get rid of his defined benefit pension plan. Why? He said that his new workers love the 401(k) plan. They get a statement every month and they see their balance going up and they think that is great. They never saw anything with the DB plan, so it was not much of an attractor when it came to bringing in workers.

This climate of expectations is making it difficult to sell many of the possible solutions that have been mentioned here. People are looking at their friends and neighbors who had 401(k) plans and who may have now a seven-digit balance to rollover from their 401(k) into their individual retirement account (IRA). Those people who have a friend or relative or who themselves annuitized fifteen, twenty, or twenty-five years ago may be feeling foolish. What is lost in a lot of this is the risk—that class 5 hurricane that has not happened. The meteorologists tell the people in North Carolina that the Outer Banks is a hurricane-prone place, it has happened before, it will happen again, and every hurricane season comes and goes and the buildings are still standing and the following year there are more of them.

That is exactly what can be seen in the defined benefit and defined contribution pension area and in the calls for a shift in Social Security to self-directed accounts—investment accounts that can perhaps be used as a path to wealth. This is showing up in political and administrative decisions. The Treasury Department's recent decisions to radically ease the requirements for IRA and qualified plan distributions has this as its background. Neither the Democratic nor Republican administration treasuries want to face a growing number of people who are confronted with what was the 1987 rules and who may be finding that they cannot figure them out. Or they do not want to hear from children who come in and say that mom saved all her life, but then she died and because she did not make some stupid election, her savings all got taxed away. Mom never noticed, but the heirs certainly cared.

The wealth accumulation factor is becoming an estate creation device. You don't see much of this in survey results, but there is a lot of interest. People do not put it first in lists of what is important to them, but when you discuss this with them at some length, you find that a lot of people say their first priority is not to run out of money. The second priority is to leave something for the kids or for a charity, and that becomes a factor in their thinking about the way these plans operate.

Finally, the people who have had annuities or who have been paying into Social Security at or near the full wage base are becoming increasingly grumpy about their investment returns, especially when they look at (a) all the taxes they have paid, and then (b) at the returns they might have gotten if they could just have put that money into the right fund. While these calculations may not be precisely accurate, if they start figuring out what they would have gotten if they had received 30 percent a year, which investors were getting the last few years, they think this is a terrible system.

What we need to think about here is that a lot of our citizens, like some economists, see a continuation of the present when they look into the future. And that leads them into planning that ignores the risks discussed in chapters 6 and 7. The risk that people will outlive their money, and the risk that they will screw up their investments. It becomes a pressure both in the public policy arena and in private pension planning by employers. Employers are happy with what they have seen out there with the performance of defined contribution plans. The better they do, the less pressure the employer feels to provide anything—to assume any of the risk or to provide any of the kinds of plans that would provide more of a social safety net. They are perfectly happy to let the employees take the risk, and when there does not seem to be much in the way of risk, the employees are happy to take it.

When you start thinking about solutions, this is not the time to be praying for disasters, such as the one my friend wished for North Carolina. It is hard to sell an extensive annuity system or any situation that compels or strongly pressures people to put their retirement savings into an annuity, unless and until we get a reminder that the stock market does not always go up and certainly does not always go up at 20 and 30 percent per annum clips.

Finally, I have been in Washington long enough to be fairly cynical about the voters' attitudes toward these kinds of situations. When the market is going up, they would like to ride. Many of them would like it in Social Security. They would like it in their private retirement plans. But when the class 5 hurricane passes through, a large number of them will then turn to the government and say, "Oops, I'd like to be bailed out, please." And they are politically active and numerous, and those are two characteristics that tend to be very effective in our political environment.

As we look at these things, the point about education is probably the most important one. We need to educate people not only about the choices that they may have, but also about the long-term consequences of these choices and the way they could be affected by ups and downs in the market. The mutual fund company T. Rowe Price and others are bringing out software that projects how well an individual would do with a given amount of money over a given period of time at a certain level of withdrawals. What you find is that the success rate is drastically different depending on the sequence of ups and downs in the market. Planners tend to say that if you get a 7 percent annual return and you withdraw 3 percent, you will end up with X. And that is true if you get the same thing every year. But if you get minus 7 percent return for eight or ten years and then you get 15 or 20 percent in the subsequent years, you will not make it. If you reverse that sequence and get bonanza returns in the first few years and then crummy returns in the out years, you still end up quite well off.

These kinds of fairly sophisticated explanations need to be driven home to the electorate and the participants in various plans. These sentiments are led by a middle-level group of people, well educated and well off, who are getting good contributions to their DC plans and who tend to vote and be politically active. They are in the best position to deal with the consequences when things go wrong, but they may have disproportionate influence and drive policies that are not in the best interest of people at the low-income end of the scale. We need to emphasize that the investment is unpredictable, and when you assume these risks, you cannot assume that we will get the 1980s and 1990s all over again.

Comment by Heidi Hartmann

Chapters 6 and 7 reinforce the idea that Social Security should be kept as a social insurance system because the private marketplace really is not taking care of our retirement needs. Jack VanDerhei and Craig Copeland document the shifts away from defined benefit and toward defined contribution based retirement benefits. They have a sophisticated data set and use some complex modeling to reach their conclusion that we are moving toward defined contribution. Their main contribution is trying to get a precise estimate of what the distribution of income will be in retirement as a result of this shift. However, their chapter understates the gender differences in retirement, a point that will be discussed below.

Jeffrey Brown's chapter is a useful discussion of annuities and the role they might play in protecting people against risks, such as the risk of living too long. For the most part, privately available annuities do not play that role now. What is playing that role is Social Security, which is under challenge, and defined benefit plans, which are disappearing. In contrast to welfare, where "we don't like it as we know it," we like Social Security as we know it, and we should really work hard to keep it.

Women are still at much higher risk of poverty than men after age sixty-five. The results of an analysis of the New Beneficiary Survey done by Lois Shaw at the Institute for Women's Policy Research (IWPR) show high rates of poverty for women who are long-term divorced and separated.[1] In 1982 these women had a 23 percent rate of poverty; in 1991 that figure was 27 percent. Adding in the near-poor raises the rate of those women in poverty to 52 percent, even with the benefits they are already getting from Social Security and other programs.

Those rates of poverty are much higher for women than men who are older. Even single women have higher rates of poverty than single men. Part of the reason men are less poor is that more of them are married in old age than are women. More women are alone.

The differences between women and men in their pension participation and their behavior tend to be underestimated. An analysis of the 1993 Survey of Income and Program Participation (SIPP), by Catherine Hill and Lois Shaw, shows a 10 percentage point difference between older men and older women participating in any kind of employee plan.[2] The good news is that the younger

1. Lois Shaw, Diane Zuckerman, and Heidi Hartmann, *The Impact of Social Security Reform on Women.* Washington, D.C.: Institute for Women's Policy Research, 1998.

2. Lois Shaw and Catherine Hill. *The Gender Gap in Pension Coverage: What Does the Future Hold?* Washington, D.C.: Institute for Women's Policy Research, forthcoming.

age group shows only about 5 percentage points difference for full-time workers.

This might suggest that the pension gap in the future will not be as big. However, analysts need to look beyond the data on plan participation to women's and men's patterns of work. Part of women's problem is that a lot of the time they are not working, and a lot of the time they are working, they are working part-time. That has enormous impacts for their pension. I want to ask Copeland and VanDerhei how they dealt with that in their model.

A cross-section of prime age workers in the 1996 Current Population Survey shows that 75 percent of the men are working full-time for the full year and only 7 percent have no work. Of women in the prime ages, 20 percent had no work that year and less than 50 percent worked full-time year round. The implications for pensions are clear.

Moreover, many women and men do not participate in the pension plans that are offered. The reason given most often for both women and men is that they are not with the current employer long enough to participate. The next biggest reason for women is that they did not work enough hours; 24 percent of women give that reason as compared to only 13 percent of men. Slightly more than 30 percent of women indicate that they "chose not to enroll." The reason is often affordability, when the plan requires a contribution of their own.

Data from the 1993 SIPP for those workers who were near retirement, ages forty-five to sixty-four, show that about 25 percent of men are not expecting a pension from any work-related program, not counting Social Security, but more than 30 percent of women are not expecting a pension from any source. We know from the data on the size of pensions that women receive much smaller pensions because of their low earnings and their lesser work history over their lifetimes.

Near-retirement workers are better off in terms of their expectation of employment-related pensions than are the retired workers. Some of these may not be lifetime pensions. They may have access to a spouse's pension just after retirement; that access may disappear when the spouse dies or outlives the benefit. Only 30 percent of retired women are now getting any pension income, which includes those benefits they receive as spouses, from their husband's pensions, not from their own work. Given women's special role as the family caretaker and as the one more likely to take off from work for those needs, there really have to be protections for women like those provided by the Social Security system.

In the VanDerhei and Copeland chapter, the gender differences are somewhat disguised because they calculate the expected pension accumulation relative to their lifetime earnings. Women's earnings are much lower than men's. If that base is just a one-year earning rather than a whole lifetime earning, this will understate the fact that over their lifetimes they earned very little. I would like to see VanDerhei and Copeland add in the dollar value of what the expected pension accumulation means for men and women. Until now (and probably for sometime into the future), women's main access to retirement income may be through a husband.

Since its peak in 1997, the female/male wage ratio has fallen to 72 percent for year-round, full-time work. Women are working more, compressing childbirth, and having fewer children. An article by Tim Smeeding, Carol Estes, and Lou Glass published in 1999 by the Gerontological Society of America shows that the future of women in retirement is going to be just as bleak as it is now, but for different reasons. More women are going to be working and their lifetime earnings will probably increase. However, increasingly women are going to enter retirement never married, divorced, or widowed. The New Beneficiary Survey shows that more than 50 percent of all women in retirement are living without men. So whatever women are gaining in earnings in terms of their own economic security, they are going to lose in marriage as a source of their economic security.

This background leads to the most important policy implications of the chapters: the main conclusion is that Social Security and defined benefits are the major source of lifetime annuity incomes, and Social Security is virtually the only source of inflation-adjusted lifetime annuity income. This means that to increase the use of annuities, employers must be required to offer annuities and incentives to workers to participate. In view of Title VII of the 1964 Civil Rights Act, unisex annuity schedules would be required.

Brown claims that 70 percent of people with private pensions have no option at all to easily convert to an annuity, so this clearly is a serious problem to be solved by policy. For the most part, annuities do not have inflation protection, so we would want that to be required to be built in.

All the things that you would have to do to annuities to make them better are already done by Social Security. Brown points out that if people live longer, they are transferring money from the poor to the rich when everyone is required to have an annuity. Social Security requires everyone to have an annuity, but it balances for that with its progressive benefit formula. It also takes care of spouses because it requires a joint and survivor option.

My conclusion is that these analysts tell us what could be done in the private market to improve the availability of private annuities. However, the author's work points overwhelmingly to the conclusion that U.S. citizens absolutely cannot afford to lose their public annuity, the Social Security system.

PART IV

The Future of Unemployment Insurance

T HE UNCERTAIN ECONOMY and increases in unemployment insurance claims have policymakers paying attention to unemployment insurance. Due, in part, to efforts of the individuals who contributed to this section, Congress and the administration will be paying close attention to unemployment insurance and unemployment insurance reform.

In chapter 8, Janet Norwood, the presidentially appointed chairman of the Advisory Commission on Unemployment Compensation, summarizes the unemployment insurance issues that policymakers have been debating in this field for the last ten years and highlights what might be upcoming in the next year or two. The commentaries that follow her chapter provide a clear picture of the issues that policymakers need to understand. Rich Hobbie of the National Association of State Workforce Agencies moderated the conference session. He noted that the advisory commission wrote several excellent reports in the mid-1990s that updated and summarized the issues and commission debates. Recommendations to Congress and the president from the commission were never acted on, however.

In 1998 the Department of Labor set up a work group, which included representatives of business, labor (both organized labor and other types of workers), and federal and state government. That work group reached an agreement in June 2000 on a comprehensive bipartisan package on unemployment insurance reform that was presented to the House Ways and Means Committee. That package still is before Congress, and advocates are discussing its provisions with the business community and the new secretary at the Department of Labor. The hope is that Congress will seriously consider it in the coming session.

8

Issues in Unemployment Insurance

Janet L. Norwood

T HE UNEMPLOYMENT INSURANCE (UI) program, a fundamental part of the nation's safety net for those who lose
their jobs through no fault of their own, was a radical departure from the past
when it was established as a part of the Social Security system sixty-five years
ago. The system was one of the first—and today is one of the most successful—
federal-state cooperative programs in the social area. Employers, workers and
their unions, state governments, and the federal government each played
important roles in the system—and each continues to do so today. For the most
part, the federal government required that a program for unemployment
insurance be established in each state, prescribed the broad outlines of the role
of the various players, and established overall funding procedures; the states
established rules for the operation of the program—eligibility, benefits, procedures, and finance levels. For many years, the program, established to provide
basic income to workers to tide them over relatively brief periods of joblessness during an economic downturn until business conditions picked up, served
its purpose reasonably well.

But much has happened to the labor market since the late 1930s, when the
program was designed. The UI program has not kept up with the significant
changes that have occurred in labor market conditions, especially since World
War II. These trends have occurred with remarkable speed in recent decades.
A comprehensive review of the program was ordered when Congress in the late
1970s provided for a National Commission on Unemployment Compensation.
That commission, which was chaired by Wilbur Cohen, made an extensive list
of recommendations, but no federal legislative action was taken to put them
into effect.[1]

---

1. National Commission on Unemployment Compensation (1980).

Advisory Council Established

It took more than a decade for Congress to act again. Concluding that it was time to conduct a careful and complete review of the entire UI program, Congress enacted in November 1991 the Emergency Unemployment Compensation Act of 1991 (P.L. 102-164), which provided for an Advisory Council on Unemployment Compensation (ACUC). The ACUC had a broad mandate to "evaluate the unemployment compensation program, including the purpose, goals, countercyclical effectiveness, coverage, benefit adequacy, trust fund solvency, funding of state administrative costs, administrative efficiency, and any other aspects of the program and to make recommendations for improvement."[2]

The law provided for a council of eleven members appointed by the president, Senate, and House of Representatives. The Senate president pro tempore, in consultation with the chair and ranking member of the Finance Committee, was to appoint three council members—representing business, labor, and state governments. The Speaker of the House, in consultation with the chairman and the ranking member of the Committee on Ways and Means, was to name three members chosen to represent the same three groups. The president was to name five persons, who would represent business, labor, state government, and the general public. The president was also to appoint the chairman of the council from among its members. The ACUC was given $1,200,000 and six staff persons for its work, was to meet about five times each year, and was to report its findings to the president and Congress within four years, starting with an interim report that was to focus especially on the extended benefits (EB) program.

Once Congress and the White House appointed the members, the ACUC began its work in May 1993. The council's first report in February 1994 responded especially to congressional questions posed to it on the extended benefits program. The second report, issued a year later in January 1995, considered issues relating to benefits, financing, and coverage. The final report, issued in January 1996, reviewed many of these issues and considered the administrative aspects of the program, in particular the federal and state roles in UI insurance. The three reports contain a useful summary of the operation of the UI program—both the parts that are working well and those that could be improved.

The Labor Market Conundrum

The new advisory council recognized immediately that the unemployment insurance program confronted a labor market that bore little resemblance to

2. Advisory Council on Unemployment Compensation (1994, pp. 167–69).

that of the 1930s. Significant change had occurred in the demographic makeup of the work force, in the composition of the nation's industrial establishments, and in the importance of our competitive position with foreign countries. Issues relating to work force diversity had become increasingly important as African Americans and Hispanics became a much larger portion of the work force. The labor force participation of women—married as well as single—had risen considerably, and with their larger numbers came an increased need for attention to the interaction of work and the family. Significant numbers of workers frequently found it difficult to qualify for benefits, especially if they were low-wage workers, those employed part-time, or those who served as temporary contract workers.

Thus the unemployment insurance program, which had begun primarily as a program to support male factory workers who worked to support themselves and their nonworking wives and families during recessionary periods, had to operate in an entirely different economy. UI benefits also had to be available to large numbers of workers employed in service-producing activities with different hiring practices and business cycle effects.

Looking at the situation today (using data from November 2000), 64.3 percent of the population is working—a significant number. Nearly 7.5 million are multiple job holders who have found it necessary to have more than one job to make ends meet. About 80 percent of those working have jobs in the service-producing sector, with only about 14 percent of nonfarm workers employed in the nation's factories. This industrial shift is important because the swings in employment during recession tend to be somewhat different in service indus-tries than in manufacturing. Recessions take a somewhat longer time to affect employment in services, and the job reductions frequently are not as sharp and steep as in the goods-producing industries. An additional problem is that, as competition has expanded in recent years, forcing manufacturing establish-ments to become more efficient, a number of the nation's factories have permanently downsized, and some have closed down entirely. As a result, some factory workers have no real assurance that they will be hired back once the economy picks up.

Added to all this is the changing profile of the labor force itself. The number of working women in the labor force has continued to rise and, at nearly 66 million, has been fast catching up with the number of men. Even more marked has been the change in the race and ethnic profile of the nation's workers. Today more than 20 percent of the persons in the labor force are either black or Hispanic, and the numbers are growing. In fact, the government projects that the Hispanic labor force will increase four times faster than the rest of the labor force over the next eight years or so. These demographic trends are important because minority men and women tend to be less experienced in the work force than white workers are, and the educational attainment of both the black and Hispanic work force is somewhat lower than that for their white counterparts. As a result, they frequently find it harder to meet the increasing demands of employers for educational and cognitive skills.

Each of these changes will have a profound effect on the UI program of the future. Despite the fact that the economy has been growing steadily for many years, unemployment—at nearly 5.7 million in November 2000—continues to be a matter of concern. Many workers who lose their jobs are often not hired back because their jobs have been abolished, because the duties of the position have changed completely, or because inefficient plants have been shut down and eventually gone out of business entirely. In addition, long-term unemployment causes special problems for workers. In November 2000 nearly 25 percent of the unemployed were unemployed for fifteen weeks or more, and more than 10 percent of all unemployed workers were without jobs for more than six months.

A recent complicating factor is that of welfare reform. Those formerly on welfare tend to have less work experience and less education than their more affluent counterparts. They frequently lack the work experience or education that many of today's jobs require. As a result, they frequently have more spells of unemployment than other workers, and, in many cases, they may not qualify for UI benefits under current eligibility rules.

The ACUC considered all these developments; held nine sets of public hearings around the country, where more than 160 witnesses presented testimony on the UI program; conducted focus group discussions with unemployed workers; talked with employers; and visited a number of state UI offices. The panel held meetings in nine cities, selected to represent different types of labor markets, and held research conferences in Portland, Maine; Ann Arbor, Michigan; and Burlington, Vermont.

Council members represented many different perspectives. Owen Bieber, Thomas Donahue, Leon Lynch, and Guy Rodrigues were from labor; Ann Duncan, William Grossenbacher, and Tommy Thompson represented state views; John Stephens and Robert Mitchell were from business; and Lucy Williams and the author represented the public.

Major Advisory Council Findings

The ACUC did a great deal of research and analysis and made a large number of findings of fact—all of which formed the foundation for its recommendations. These covered such issues as the increase in the length of unemployment, the steady decline in the UI recipiency rate, the variations in rules for UI eligibility and benefit levels among the states, the problems faced by low-wage and part-time workers, and the solvency of the state UI trust funds. The council also considered the contribution of UI benefits to pump-priming the economy during economic downturns and carefully reviewed the roles of the federal government and state governments in the unemployment insurance system.

Major Recommendations of the ACUC

The ACUC made fifty-two recommendations for reform of the unemploy-ment compensation program in its three reports in 1994, 1995, and 1996.[3] Although many different perspectives were represented on the council, most of the recommendations were unanimous. They focused on such important matters as the program's coverage, benefit levels, financing, utility to workers, pump-priming effects for the economy, triggers for the extended benefits program, federally mandated requirements, the different roles of the federal and state governments, and administrative arrangements.

The recommendations, some of which were very detailed, can be found in a summary pamphlet of ACUC findings and recommendations published in 1996.[4] This chapter will focus only on seven major areas that this author believes demonstrate the most critical need for reform.

Trust Fund Solvency

Having agreed that the unemployment insurance system played an impor-tant role in pump-priming the economy in recession as well as in providing income to workers during periods of joblessness, the council concluded that the solvency of state UI trust funds is critical to the effective operation of the unemployment insurance system. Funds must be accumulated during periods of prosperity so that benefits can be paid out in periods of economic decline; some states had done so, but others had not. The countercyclical effect of raising money during recession means that states that do not have sufficient trust funds to handle payments during a period of recession might be forced to curtail benefits or reduce eligibility, neither of which would carry out the purposes of the program. The ACUC, therefore, recommended that:

---

3. Advisory Council on Unemployment Compensation (1994, 1995, 1996b).
4. Advisory Council on Unemployment Compensation (1996a).

Congress should establish an explicit goal to promote . . . forward funding of the . . . system. In particular, during periods of economic health, each state should be encouraged to accumulate reserves sufficient to pay at least one year of Unemployment Insurance benefits at levels comparable to its previous high cost" where high cost is defined as the average of the 3 highest annual levels of benefits paid in any of the previous 20 years.[5]

Moreover, to accomplish this end, the council recommended that incentives be provided to encourage states to achieve the high-cost multiple. First, the current practice of interest-free loans to state trust funds should be terminated for all states that have not made progress on the forward-funding goal.[6] States should be paid an interest premium on that portion of the trust fund in excess of one high-cost year of reserves. The cost of the premium, the council suggested, should come from a reduction on the portion of a state's reserve that is less than one high-cost year.[7]

Eligibility of Low-Wage and Part-Time Workers

A number of witnesses at the ACUC hearings described problems they had with both monetary and nonmonetary eligibility for unemployment insurance. Since the basic eligibility rules are determined by the states, the ACUC found considerable variation in treatment among the states. Of particular concern were the differences in eligibility between full-time and part-time workers and between low-wage and higher-wage workers. In some states, for example, those working part time the full year were ineligible for UI benefits even though those who worked full time, part year (that is, with the same total number of hours) were qualified. Earnings for the most recent quarter—which might have qualified some of these workers for benefits—were frequently not available at the time of the claim.

The council, therefore, recommended that all states "use a moveable base period" when its use would affect a claimant's ability to meet the state monetary eligibility requirements. This change could, the ACUC believed, easily be achieved with the use of modern technology, which should make it possible to get data more quickly than had been the case in the past.

Because of its concern that low-wage workers might still not meet the monetary requirement in some states, the ACUC recommended that the "base

---

5. Advisory Council on Unemployment Compensation (1995, p. 2).
6. Advisory Council on Unemployment Compensation (1995, pp. 2–6).
7. Advisory Council on Unemployment Compensation (1995, pp. 2–6).

period earnings requirement should" be set so that the "requirements do not exceed 800 times the state's minimum hourly wage, and so that its high quarter earnings requirements do not exceed one-quarter of that amount." Furthermore, the council proposed that workers who met the state monetary eligibility requirement should not be denied benefits "merely because they are seeking part-time, rather than full-time, employment."[8]

Benefit Adequacy

Federal law has never specified what amounts to adequate payments under the UI system; indeed, the question of benefit adequacy has been debated since the inception of the UI program. The council felt that "each state should replace at least 50 percent of lost earnings over a six-month period, with a maximum weekly benefit amount equal to two-thirds of the state's average weekly wages.[9]

Taxable Wage Base

Recognizing that the taxable wage base, as well as the UI tax rate, directly affects trust fund solvency, the ACUC gave a great deal of consideration to the issues of financing UI benefits. It found that a number of states had indexed the taxable wage base to average wages in the state and that a number of other states had specifically raised the wage base upon which the UI tax is paid. In fact, only eleven states still used a taxable wage base as low as the federally established $7,000 minimum figure. Accordingly, a majority of the council recommended that "the federal taxable wage base should be raised to $9,000, with an accompanying elimination of the two-tenths percentage point Federal Unemployment Tax Act (FUTA) surcharge. The federal taxable wage base should be adjusted annually by the Employment Cost Index."[10]

Database Development for Research and Evaluation

The ACUC, surprised to find that the data needed for research and evaluation of the UI program were frequently not available or needed improvement, made several recommendations:

---

8. Advisory Council on Unemployment Compensation (1995, pp. 17, 18, 20).
9. Advisory Council on Unemployment Compensation (1995, p. 22).
10. Advisory Council on Unemployment Compensation (1996b, p. 20).

—A change should be made in the calculation of both the number and the rate of the insured unemployed. Both numbers overstate the number of individuals who actually receive unemployment insurance benefits in a given week because they include all who filed claims even if they did not receive benefits for the period covered.[11]

—The UI replacement rate should be based on the "actual replacement rate for individuals who receive unemployment insurance. . . . by dividing the weekly benefits paid to individuals by the average weekly earnings paid to those individuals prior to unemployment" and not by the wages of all covered workers.[12]

—There is need for a . . . comprehensive information system of UI data that are comparable in definition and format for all states," including coverage and eligibility by earnings level and type of worker; labor market attachment; levels and duration of benefits paid; extent and causes of nonmonetary disqualifications; labor market information at federal, state, and local levels; extent of trust fund forward funding; and continued development of the wage record database.[13]

Extended Benefits Program

Because changes in the economy and labor force mean that workers laid off from their jobs are less likely than before to be hired back to their previous jobs, the ACUC recommended expansion of the EB program "to enhance the Unemployment Insurance system to provide assistance for long-term unemployed workers" but suggested that separate funding should be used to finance job search and training for the long-term unemployed.[14]

The ACUC found that threshold requirements for extended benefits triggered on too late and triggered off too early in states with the highest unemployment. As a result, it recommended reform of the EB program. The council majority recommended that the overall state unemployment rate rather than the insured rate be used as the trigger for the extended benefit program.

Federal-State Roles in the UI Program

ACUC staff research raised considerable concern among some ACUC members that states might have lowered UI tax levels to attract—or to keep—

11. Advisory Council on Unemployment Compensation (1995, p. 16).
12. Advisory Council on Unemployment Compensation (1995, p. 24).
13. Advisory Council on Unemployment Compensation (1996b, p. 12, 15).
14. Advisory Council on Unemployment Compensation (1994, pp. 1, 2).

business in the state. It seemed that this "race to the bottom" sometimes resulted in either a tightening of eligibility or a lowering of benefit levels. While recognizing the federal-state character of the program, the council agreed that the federal government must provide leadership in protecting several important elements of the UI program:
   —promote forward funding of state trust funds
   —ensure minimum levels of eligibility and of benefits
   —maintain an extended benefits program with effective automatic triggers
   —monitor and coordinate development of labor market information
On the other hand, it seemed clear to the members of the council that the federal government needed to eliminate or sharply reduce a number of detailed oversight and reporting requirements in areas that should be left entirely to the states.[15]

Recent Developments

The ACUC spent three years in its review of the nation's unemployment insurance program. Our hope, which may have been too optimistic, was that Congress would consider the report quickly and legislate at least some of the most important recommendations. Since the country was going through a period when the demands on the UI system were relatively low, this seemed a time when planning for the future should be undertaken.

To date, however, that hope has not been realized, although the Subcommittee on Human Resources of the House Ways and Means Committee has held several hearings on UI issues. One, in April 1997, chaired by Representative E. Clay Shaw Jr. (R-Fla.), considered several proposals, although the representative emphasized that no bill had yet been introduced. But the proposals discussed at the hearing were aimed primarily at increasing state authority over UI funding and decreasing federal authority, with little consideration of problems with the solvency of state trust funds. Only a few of those who testified at that hearing pointed out the importance of reform and modernization of the UI program.[16]

Early in 1998 Representatives Sander Levin (D-Mich.), Phil English (R-Pa.), and Charles Rangel (D-N.Y.) introduced administration-supported proposals based on the ACUC recommendations; the same bills were introduced again in 1999. The House subcommittee once again held hearings, this time on two bills that had been introduced—H.R. 3684, about increasing state flexibil-

15. Advisory Council on Unemployment Compensation (1996b, pp. 15–19).
16. Norwood (1997).

ity and control over UI finance, and H.R. 3697, the bill that had been introduced by Representatives Levin and English.[17]

Meanwhile, early in 1998, the Department of Labor began a dialogue with the states and a broad group of other UI stakeholders, including business and labor. The department convened sixty-five dialogues all over the country to discuss reforms, and the president's budget for FY 2000 and 2001 provided for the department to continue to work with stakeholders to develop a bipartisan, comprehensive proposal.

The Interstate Conference of Employment Security Agencies (ICESA) organized a work group of representatives of employers and labor, state agencies, and the Department of Labor to develop a consensus for legislative change. In June 2000 the House subcommittee held another hearing at which some of the proposals considered by that work group—as well as several other bills targeted on specific aspects of the program—were discussed.[18]

Finally, on September 7, 2000, the House subcommittee heard testimony on the proposals developed by the ICESA work group that were at that time in the process of conversion to legislative language. The proposals covered several—but not all—of the ACUC recommendations and, in addition, went further in proposing administrative state funding changes than the council had done. Among the major proposals discussed at the September 2000 hearing were:

—reducing the EB trigger from a 5 percent state insured unemployment rate to 4 percent and eliminating several federal eligibility requirements

—expanding UI coverage for part-time workers

—using wage data for the most recently completed quarter in determining UI monetary eligibility

—repealing the 0.2 percent federal unemployment tax (FUTA surcharge)

—improving arrangements for distributing funding for the UI system and for employment services

Conclusion

The nation's unemployment insurance system continues to function as a part of our social safety net; for more than sixty years it has served the nation well, as it has provided some measure of economic security to workers who have become unemployed through no fault of their own. The system is, in fact, a prime example of cooperation between the federal government and the states and is generally accepted by both business and labor. However, we must ensure

17. Norwood (1998).
18. Interstate Conference of Employment Security Agencies (2000).

that the program continues to meet the needs of workers who work today in a labor market that is considerably different from that of the past.

In the last twenty years, Congress and the president have received recommendations for change from two commissions, which considered the views of all of the stakeholders involved in the program and of the general public. The research and fact-finding has been done. It is time now for reform of the program. Indeed, it should be easier to reform and modernize the UI program now when the unemployment rate is lower than it has been in many years and when the demands on the UI system are relatively low.

The efforts of the Department of Labor and the Interstate Conference of Employment Security Agencies to bring together all the stakeholders to develop issues that they can all support are extremely encouraging. Those proposals—especially the ones to lower the trigger for extended benefits and to repeal several federal requirements for EB recipients, to extend eligibility for part-time workers, and to help low-wage workers through use of more recent wage data—should be enacted quickly.

But these proposals are not enough. Stronger, more courageous action is needed. Much more attention needs to be given to the establishment of minimum requirements for forward funding state trust funds and for techniques to encourage states to meet those minimum goals with some reward for good behavior. The federal government should establish minimum standards for eligibility for unemployed workers to receive UI benefits, and agreement should be reached on minimum levels of wage replacement to be received by those eligible for UI benefits. These are major issues that require reform. The ACUC recommendations in these areas are important, and hopefully they will be revisited soon.

This is an era of increasing devolution of authority from the federal government to the states, and reform of the UI program must take account of these trends. Once having established minimum requirements of the kind outlined from the ACUC deliberations, the federal government should eliminate many process-oriented reporting and audit requirements that can best be left to the states.

An improved data system is also needed so that the results of the program and how it affects different workers can be better assessed. The U.S. labor market has changed considerably in the last sixty-five years, and it can be expected to develop further in the future. Under the Workforce Investment Act of 1998, the development of a more extensive federal-state cooperative employment statistics program has begun, but more data on results achieved in the unemployment insurance program are needed.

We have an opportunity now to strengthen the entire unemployment insurance program as a federal-state cooperative program that produces results for workers who lose their jobs through no fault of their own. Unemployed workers have a right to a modernized UI program, one that recognizes changes that have occurred in the makeup of the work force and in employment conditions. They have a right to expect that the unemployment insurance system will continue to assist them in periods of economic distress. They have a right to an unemployment insurance program that will be better able than it now is to function to help those workers who need it in the future.

References

Advisory Council on Unemployment Compensation. 1994. "Report and Recommendations." Washington (February).
————. 1995. "Unemployment Insurance in the United States: Benefits, Financing, Coverage." Washington (February).
————. 1996a. *Collected Findings and Recommendations, 1994–1996.* Washington.
————. 1996b. "Defining Federal and State Roles in Unemployment Insurance." Washington (January).
Interstate Conference of Employment Security Agencies. 2000. "Joint Comprehensive Unemployment Insurance-Employment Service Reform Proposal." Washington (June 27).
National Commission on Unemployment Compensation. 1980. *Unemployment Compensation: Final Report.* Washington (July).
Norwood, Janet L. 1997. Testimony before the Subcommittee on Human Resources of the House Committee on Ways and Means, Hearing on Unemployment Compensation Reform. Washington (April 24).
————. 1998. Testimony before the Subcommittee on Human Resources of the House Committee on Ways and Means, Hearing on Unemployment Compensation Reform. Washington (June 23).

Comment by Eric Oxfeld

My organization, UWC-Strategic Services on Unemployment and Workers' Compensation (UWC), is the only national association of employers that is exclusively dedicated to public policy advocacy relating to unemployment and workers' compensation. UWC has led a coalition of employers who have been working hard to address several of the problems associated with the failings of the unemployment insurance (UI) program. The National Academy of Social Insurance (NASI) wisely has included employers in this discussion of social insurance, as employers are the taxpayers who finance the UI program, or at least are the ones who are required to write the checks to pay the two taxes that finance it.

UWC was the business representative at the four-party working group—comprised of members from the Department of Labor, the states, organized labor, and business—that resulted in the 2001 compromise reform proposal. Business supports the state UI program. Although there is great commonality to how business and labor view UI, there are some differences in views on the purposes of the program. Business supports unemployment insurance as a program that provides limited wage replacement to workers who are seeking suitable new employment, who have a strong attachment to work, and who lost their jobs because their employer no longer had work for them. That has been the precept of the unemployment insurance program since its inception. In the view of employers, there is no reason why that should change.

State and not federal laws should determine basic benefits, eligibility, and tax levels, and the federal role in the system should be limited. While there is an appropriate limited federal role in the system, in many ways the federal presence in the UI system has not been a positive force in recent years. This adverse federal role is likely to continue into the foreseeable future, unless something is done to change it.

Because of the way the federal government has fulfilled its role within the system, employers are overtaxed. State UI administrative agencies are not getting the resources they need to provide the services employers are paying for through their federal unemployment taxes, and workers are not being well served either. This is a major reason why the average duration of unemployment claims, at a time when unemployment rates are at a thirty-year low, is running almost three weeks longer than would be expected for comparable periods of low unemployment.

To address the concerns of employers, UWC has mounted a political effort to try to get legislation in Congress that deals with two concerns. The first is the level of the federal unemployment tax. The second is the way that money is distributed back to the states to finance the agencies that administer the system. Employers are paying almost $7 billion now in taxes under the Federal Unemployment Tax Act (FUTA), and only about half of that revenue actually comes back to the states, which is the principal if not exclusive purpose for levying that tax. The percentage coming back to the states is actually shrinking each year.

Although our proposal had the support of thirty-four states and major business organizations throughout the country, unfortunately it did not have the political muscle in the 105th or 106th Congresses to get enacted. One stumbling block was a lack of support from some key states that did not like the way the money would be allocated among the states.

Another reason was that the Clinton administration and representatives of organized labor had concerns that the proposal, which we call the coalition proposal, would have vested increased authority in the hands of states. There is strong support on the part of labor representatives for an increased federal presence in the system. They also felt that the proposal lacked anything to address their concerns about what the Department of Labor in recent years has called "equity in access" for low-wage workers.

Equally important, the impact of doing something about the way the federal unemployment tax is levied and distributed would have had an effect on the federal budget process. The Office of Management and Budget is the hidden presence behind the negotiation table, as they are clearly a major factor in what happens on any UI-related proposal.

When it became clear that the UWC/states coalition proposal was not going to get enacted, and thus employers were going to be stuck for another year with a federal unemployment tax that was clearly higher than necessary to run the program properly, discussions were initiated with the Department of Labor and labor unions and states. UWC played a large role in initiating these discussions. These discussions followed a year of public discussions in the working group organized by the National Association of State Workforce Agencies, and those discussions frankly had reached deadlock. There was an impasse. They had broken down. UWC took the initiative to say, since we are very bottom-line oriented as a business organization, that we wanted to see something happen. We wanted to see that federal unemployment tax reduced. We wanted to fix the major problems with the way administrative financing is handled and dealt with, and that simply was not going to occur. We just could not tolerate another year of inaction. Accordingly, we attempted to strike a compromise that addresses our concerns, as well as the concerns of organized labor. Although we did not fully agree with them, we were cognizant of the concerns that labor had and were able to strike a deal that in our judgment would have been a win-win-win for everyone.

The compromise had significant benefit for business. It dealt with administrative finance reform and the federal unemployment tax, which were our two major goals. From our point of view as employers, there was a political price for that—benefit expansions, changing the triggers for the extended benefits program and the eligibility criteria for it, addressing part-time workers, and using more recent wages to determine eligibility for UI benefits.

We are clearly opposed to any of those benefit expansion proposals on their merits. We do not agree that those are appropriate things to do, but they are at least within the legitimate scope of a UI system, and there are states that do all those things. States are free to do that if they choose.

From the other point of view, we have an equally great philosophical concern about expanding the federal role in the state UI system. We respect, although we respectfully disagree with, those who feel that the states have too much control over it currently.

Despite the fact that we were able to reach this compromise, it is a political reality that there were others who did believe that this agreement would result in the positive changes that we expected. Although there was substantial support for the compromise proposal in the business community, there also was substantial dissent, particularly in the retail, restaurant, and hospitality industries, which have a lot of part-time workers. Frankly, the whole issue of part-time workers hit a nerve with many employers, most of whom are not knowledgeable about unemployment insurance and how UI eligibility is handled. They were concerned that the proposal might be a precedent that would have led to other kinds of mandated employee benefits for part-time workers, a topic that NASI is attentive to as well.

There was a legitimate concern from those in the UI system that some workers would be able to abuse the system. Many regular part-time workers also have some full-time employment, for example at Christmas, and then return to their regular part-time jobs in January. There was concern that the proposal would allow them to collect unemployment benefits for the partial unemployment by merely going back to their normal working hours.

Because of all those factors, and because of time constraints in putting this package together and getting it drafted and introduced in Congress, it did not pass. While we were disappointed that it did not pass, we now find ourselves in a completely different environment: the economy, the new administration, and Congress, where many of the people who were involved on these issues are no longer there. And so we are now taking a look at where are we going to go on

202 THE FUTURE OF UNEMPLOYMENT INSURANCE

this. Where is the Bush administration going to go? Where is Congress going to go? Can the business community unite around one set of proposals that has a chance of passage and is acceptable to the other people who are players in this system?

While we have the greatest respect and admiration for Commissioner Norwood, we respectfully have a different point of view on several of the issues she discussed. Raising the FUTA wage base is one proposal that employers do not believe has merit, and there is even greater concern about indexing it further. We do not need the money for the FUTA-funded programs, since twice as much money is already being collected than is being spent. We do not need that money, so raising the wage base is an unacceptable way to address the solvency problem, which is a legitimate topic for people to be talking about, although again we respectfully disagree on the solution.

When the federal government raises the wage base, the states are thereby forced to raise the wage base under the state system. That is not a particularly effective way to get more money into the state trust funds because the government can, of course, lower their tax *rates*, which would offset the wage base increase and create a whole lot of chaos in between. We do not believe that the federal government is particularly well positioned to tell states how much money they should have in their state trust funds. The federal government does have an important role to play in calling attention to states whose trust fund balances look dangerously low. Everyone would agree that that is important and necessary to do. But a federal one-size-fits-all solvency standard for state unemployment insurance is not something that either makes good sense on the merits or will have the political muscle to ever be adopted.

The unemployment trust fund is a triple misnomer. We have practically no unemployment. There are no funds because trust fund balances are really nothing more than IOUs since the current budget rules take this money and spend it on other programs. There is no "lock box" for the UI system, to use a term from the 2000 presidential campaign. And there is no trust in the federal government. Having the federal government increase its presence and tell states what to do with their money is a particularly injudicious way to go.

Unemployment insurance is not and was not meant to be a substitute for the welfare program. It is legitimate for states to consider how much attachment to work a worker must have in order to qualify for benefits. Different states have drawn the line in different places. That is a subject that deserves to be reexamined from time to time. States need to look at how many people are eligible and how much attachment they must have in order to qualify. On the other hand, this decision creates a lot of problems. Wherever those lines are drawn, abuses are created as well. For example, people who have little attachment to work are sometimes able to get into the system and collect benefits even though they have not been working what most people would consider to be a long amount of time. To ask employers to provide unemployment benefits to people who have actually had little work attachment is not something that will find acceptance among taxpayers.

There are a lot of reasons why the recipiency rate for UI benefits can vary, some of them related to the UI program and some of them completely unrelated to it. For one thing, there may be an apples-and-oranges comparison, because the recipiency rate is a comparison to the total unemployment rate, not the rate of unemployment among people eligible for unemployment insurance. There are timing issues because the UI system uses the insured unemployment rate, which is based on a different set of criteria and timing from the total unemployment rate. Interstate problems arise when people live in one jurisdiction and work in another, such as areas like the Washington, D.C., metropolitan area. This can affect the recipiency rate as measured by the Department of Labor. In addition, people who are new entrants to the work force, people who have exhausted their UI benefits, and people who have been disqualified for various types of misconduct are never properly considered within the recipiency rate.

With signs of a softening economy, with a new administration in place, with legitimate concerns on the part of worker representatives as to how well the system is serving workers, and with the real concerns on the part of employers about how well it is serving employers and their employees, it is commendable for NASI to undertake an examination of what is the right future course of the UI program.

There is a lot that needs to be done. The demanding and serious issues that affect people's lives do not get as much attention as they deserve from public policymakers, whether it is in the business community or otherwise.

Comment by Wayne Vroman

The discussion here focuses on the individual aspects of the consensus proposal, which Janet Norwood has fully described in chapter 8, and on some of the other undertakings of the Advisory Council on Unemployment Compensation (ACUC) during its period of existence, in particular its recommendations regarding the tax base and the funding of the program. Finally, other aspects of benefits worthy of consideration for change in the unemployment programs currently in use in the states are discussed.

Because Eric Oxfeld and Charity Wilson represent institutions with definite perspectives on many questions regarding unemployment insurance (UI) programs, some of their comments may be anticipated. This discussion is aimed at material that may not be covered by the others.

The funding situation of the programs in the states is the first topic for review. As of September 30, 2000, the UI programs in the aggregate had nearly $55 billion available for the sole purpose of paying benefits to unemployed workers. In the last few years, the program in the aggregate has been taking in about $20 billion in taxes annually and paying out $20 to $22 billion in benefits. Thus the total reserves currently in the state trust funds are approximately 2.5 times the annual payout of the last several years.

The funds have been building during the decade of the 1990s, but they have not been growing much more rapidly than the overall growth in the economy. The economy of the 1990s was extraordinarily robust. In fact, if the cost rate of unemployment insurance in the aggregate is compared to the payrolls of covered workers, the lowest cost year in the entire post–World War II period extending through 1999 was 1999. The data from 2000 show that costs were even lower than in 1999.

That cost rate is just a bit more than 0.5 percent of covered payroll. For the decade of the 1990s, the average cost rate for unemployment insurance was about 0.8 percent of payroll. And during the worst year of the recession of the first part of the decade, the payout rate was 1.2 percent of payroll.

How big is $55 billion compared to potential payouts? In the past, the serious recessions have had payout rates exceeding 2 percent of payroll. Aggregate covered wages at the economy's current level of operation is roughly $3.6 trillion. Paying out 2 percent would total $72 billion. If the economy experiences a repetition of 1975 or 1982, more in the aggregate would be paid out than the total in the trust funds right now. The ACUC's concerns with fund adequacy are certainly well placed.

Even with a payout rate during the next recession of 1.5 percent of payroll, that would roughly match the total funds that have been accumulated by the states during the current decade. And, of course, the situation in individual states differs widely. New York and Texas would go broke very quickly. Many other states, like Mississippi and certain large states, would have funds that would last quite a while. So the suggestion that Norwood mentions of having the ability to lend from one state to another would help to spread the existing reserves in a useful way should there be a serious recession.

The UI tax base for many state programs should be higher. Roughly ten states still operate with the lowest permitted base of $7,000. It would be a straightforward technical matter to raise the base for the federal UI tax to, say, $10,000, and through the operation of a conformity requirement all states would have to move to at least this level. That would help increase funds in the short run, but the longer-run effect would be small due to the operation of experience rating.

One of the characteristics of the funding experiences of the 1990s is the lack of large-scale trust fund building. Since 1960 the economy has had three long periods of economic expansion: 1961–69, 1983–89, and 1992–2000. Trust fund building has taken place in each of those expansions. But the rate of accumulation for the decade of the 1990s was low. The reserve ratio—reserves as a percent of covered payroll—at the end of the decade was about 1.5 percent of covered payroll. That was not too much different than it was about five years earlier, and considerably lower than it was before the last recession in 1989 (roughly 1.9 percent). So again, there is good reason for concern about the adequacy of trust fund balances.

How many reserves are needed? We have all heard the new economy arguments, but a more responsible variant of the new economy arguments needs to be discussed. Macroresearch over the last three to four years has started to document the increased stability of the macroeconomy as compared to earlier periods of time. At the January 2001 economics meetings in New Orleans, there were three sessions dealing with economic stability and prolonged economic expansions. To quickly summarize, one of the papers from that research found that for the period 1984–99, the output variability of the economy was about half of what it had been in the previous thirty years. There is objective evidence suggesting that the economy is now more stable, which may mean that UI programs can now operate with lower reserves relative to payroll than in the past.

When the major sectors of the economy were examined, the sector with the biggest change in behavior and performance was durable manufacturing. Durable manufacturing has declined as a share of employment, but it still accounts for a lot of output in the economy. Compared to nondurable manufacturing, services, and construction and structures, durable manufacturing now operates with a different inventory principle (just-in-time) than it used to, and that seems to have changed the performance of output in terms of its variability since about 1984. An argument can be constructed to say that UI trust funds might be smaller relative to payroll than they have been in the past because the economy is not going to have as much variability.

Here is one way to think about this: suppose the economy were to completely cease having cyclical variability. Unemployment insurance would still need trust funds because of seasonality in benefit payouts and periodic regional perturbations. When the economy is doing well in one region, it is not necessarily doing well in all other regions. However, the economy could probably operate with lower reserves than in the past. Trying to document how much more the economy can tolerate in the way of low reserves is worthy of further research. The U.S. Labor Department's Office of Workforce Security should devote some resources to this question.

In the same economy that has had more output stability, there have been changes in the labor market. In the time path of overall unemployment rates going back to 1960 the three long economic expansions can be seen in unemployment rate decreases. This is obvious in data from the 1990s and the year 2000.

Examining five-year moving averages of unemployment duration, measured in weeks, shows that both in the monthly labor force survey (the survey of about 50,000 households) and in unemployment insurance data, average unemployment duration has increased in the last two decades. The effects of the business cycle—duration increases in recessions—are obvious. In addition, average duration has higher plateaus during the last two decades. There have been changes in the labor market of the 1980s and 1990s that are reflected in unemployment duration, for example, an increased pace of worker dislocation from jobs of long tenure. It can be concluded from the duration data that a concern about unemployment duration as related to the UI program is fully justified.

For the last three decades, potential duration of benefit collection has consistently been about twenty-four weeks. Thus variation in the ratio of actual to potential duration arises from increases in actual duration in benefit status. Actual duration was higher for the 1980s and the 1990s than it was for the previous three decades. The exhaustion rates—the share of people who fully use up their entitlements relative to the number of people flowing into the system—have been high in the 1990s. The highest exhaustion rates for any of the cyclical episodes occurred during the early 1990s. Exhaustion rates have exceeded 30 percent in all recent years. There is a problem of increasing unemployment duration that is reflected in both actual duration and in exhaustion rates.

Finally, a project studying interstate variation in the receipt of unemployment insurance benefits is at the concluding stages. For the overall economy, the ratio of the average number of beneficiaries to the average number unemployed has averaged about 0.30. The research showed very strong stability in these ratios for individual states from year to year. In addition, the states with low recipiency rates during the 1970s and 1980s also had low recipiency rates during the last decade. Some states stand out. New Hampshire is particularly dramatic, standing out in New England for its low recipiency. Similarly, Indiana stands out in the Midwest. In the Southwest the message about unemployment insurance does not seem to fully have penetrated. All states in this region (except Nevada) have low recipiency.

The project tried to develop an explanation for this interstate variation. Very briefly, UI administration as executed in the states was strongly linked to differences in recipiency rates. The research approach involved both working with data that the states submit to the national Office of Workforce Security and conducting site visits in nine states, with a focus on the states with low UI recipiency. Denials because claimants engaged in what was deemed misconduct were very important in explaining interstate differences in the share of the unemployed that collect benefits. In short, there are identifiable reasons why recipiency varies so much and why recipiency is systematically different in some regions of the country compared to other regions.

Comment by Charity Wilson

There are two natural adversaries in unemployment insurance (UI) policy negotiations: worker groups and business. People think that worker advocates emphasize eligibility and benefit levels. However, they also recognize that there has to be a system to serve those people to help get them back to work, into training, or into education programs. Advocates representing workers came away from last year's policy negotiation convinced that a proposal was coming forth that had accomplished two major goals: to address the issues of low-wage workers for eligibility and to address the issue of administrative financing. The proposal did not have everything that worker advocates wanted, but then neither did it have everything that any of the other parties wanted.

Great strides were made in reaching these dual goals. Janet Norwood's statements about the appropriate federal role underscores why it was so necessary for worker advocates to be part of this process. State federations, along with worker groups, women's groups, civil rights groups, low-wage worker groups, and some states had, in a piecemeal fashion, addressed things such as coverage for part-time workers. Eleven states have the alternative base period, after long and hard-fought legislative battles that worker advocates lost in a lot of states where they tried to get them.

As Wayne Vroman noted, there are great differences in recipiency rates among states. In some states this rate has a great deal to do with a state's readiness to negotiate for coverage of part-time workers. It was very important that states reached a point where they said there is an important overriding public policy interest that part-time workers seeking part-time work receive unemployment benefits if they meet the other criteria. Requiring that the most recent quarter of work completed be used to calculate eligibility was a huge win. And workers' advocates would have broader gains, such as including coverage for part-time workers who were full-time going to part-time and some issues around trailing spouses. However, it was a give-and-take negotiation, and these were some of the things that were not addressed.

Norwood's chapter says that the U.S. work force deserves a modernized UI system. In order to do so, there has to be more money fairly distributed to states. Therefore, it was felt that the proposal accomplished an important reform to administrative financing.

There is a laundry list of things that workers' advocates did not accomplish in the UI policy negotiation in 1999. Advocates are still not finished fighting for low-wage worker issues, and when the Temporary Assistance for Needy Families (TANF) reauthorization comes to the floor, these issues are going to become even more important. Research by Heidi Hartmann shows that 80 percent of unemployed women nationally do not qualify for UI benefits. It is a fact that women have lower recipiency rates for UI than men, and people of color have lower recipiency rates than white males.

These are real circumstances in the current economy. These are the people most likely to be affected when there is a recession. TANF recipients would face being out of a job, not having the money, and perhaps not qualifying for UI. They would also face going back on TANF and using up their lifetime eligibility. A significant effect is projected for the state's work percentages under TANF.

Workers' advocates would like to see these issues addressed now, during the current economic slowdown in certain industries, instead of waiting for a recession. Advocates will continue to work to get a better extended benefits trigger, one that uses total unemployment rate instead of insured unemployment rate. However, the current policy "patch" is a substantial first step down a long road that will culminate in an equitable system for all working people as they transition from unemployment to work.

PART V

Reflections on Welfare Reform

B EFORE 1996, cash assistance for low-income people was known as AFDC (Aid to Families with Dependent Children) or more commonly as "welfare." The Personal Responsibility and Work Opportunities Reconciliation Act of 1996 created a new program of cash benefits under the name Temporary Assistance for Needy Families, or TANF, whose chief goal was to assist adult beneficiaries to enter the work force.

Peter Edelman moderated a lively conference luncheon discussion that reviewed preliminary results of TANF. He posed questions to two former staff members of the House Ways and Means Committee, Ron Haskins and Wendell Primus. Both are probably the best-informed former staffers on cash assistance issues. Primus is also a former colleague of Edelman in the Clinton administration. Primus and Edelman resigned from the Department of Health and Human Services in protest when TANF was enacted.

Chapter 9 presents their discussion in dialogue format with reference to key chart presentations of the data used by both presenters to make their different points.

9

Welfare Reform
after Five Years

*Peter Edelman, Wendell Primus,
and Ron Haskins*

Peter Edelman: This panel features two of the most well-informed and influential policymakers on the question of cash assistance for low-income people. Like the artist formerly known as Prince, this is the program that was formerly known as welfare.

Ron Haskins, who was one of the major architects of the Personal Responsibility Act in 1996, is now a senior fellow in the Economic Studies program at the Brookings Institution. He was the staff director for the Subcommittee on Human Resources of the Ways and Means Committee for the past six years, counsel for the Republicans on that committee before that, and on the faculty at the University of North Carolina in Chapel Hill previous to that.

Our second speaker is Wendell Primus, who has been at the Center on Budget and Policy Priorities for four years. Wendell has been working on expanding the center's research efforts in areas that include Social Security and unemployment insurance, income and poverty trends, and the implementation of the 1996 law. He was deputy assistant secretary for human services policy at the Department of Health and Human Services. We worked together there and I treasure the experience that we had together. Wendell has worked on these issues for many years. He was chief economist for the Ways and Means Committee and then staff director for the Subcommittee on Human Resources.

The first question is for both Wendell and Ron. We've had Temporary Assistance for Needy Families (TANF), the 1996 law, on the books and in operation around the country for four and a half years. Tell us, in your judgment and based on your experience with it, where are we now?

Wendell Primus: I think Ron and I agree on many things. There are a few facts here that are basically indisputable. Clearly, case loads have gone down dramatically. In fact, they have fallen by about half since March 1994, when they were at their peak. Food stamp case loads are down by one-third.

It is also clear that employment and earnings have gone up tremendously among never-married mothers. Their labor force participation has gone up somewhere between 17 and 20 percentage points. The pretransfer poverty gap—in other words, how much increased earnings there are—has gone down by $17 billion.

I think the only dispute between Ron and me would be how much of that is due to a very strong economy where we have seen unemployment go down a lot during the 1990s, to the point where real persistent wage-rate increases are now occurring at the bottom of the wage-rate distribution. We have also had make-work-pay policies, substantial expansions of the earned income tax credit (EITC), and substantially more resources being put into child care, for example. Which of those factors should get the most credit for these fairly significant employment increases?

The other thing we know is that food stamp utilization and participation is down. As a result, many families at the bottom of the income distribution— single-mother families—have lost ground.

I'm going to focus on the earnings of mothers in the bottom quintile—that is, the about two million mothers with children whose incomes are below 75 percent of poverty, as you can see in table 9-1.

Poverty today is $17,000 for a family of four. It is about $13,000 or $14,000 for a family of three. So these are the mothers below 75 percent of poverty. Their earnings have gone up, but on average they are still behind by $300 or $400 in terms of where their income was in 1995.

The second quintile—mothers between 75 percent of poverty and about 115 percent of poverty—are doing well. Each of these two million mothers is earning about $4,000 more in earnings. Yet their bottom-line disposable income after the EITC, after payroll taxes, after food stamps, and so on, is up $1,000.

The question is how happy should we be with a success story where everyone of these has increased earnings by $4,000, but their bottom-line disposable income has only increased $1,000? How many of you would like it if your employer gave you a $4,000 raise, but only $1,000 of it showed up in the paycheck? The focus over the next round of welfare reform has to be on increasing the income while maintaining these employment increases.

Ron Haskins: First, we ought to make it clear that Wendell would not mind too much if you earned a $4,000 raise and you only got $1,000 in your paycheck, because the other $3,000 went to the government and he could have more social programs and more spending. We ought to establish that right at the beginning.

The bill that Congress passed in 1996 had five characteristics that were almost completely unlike anything passed before (box 9-1). First, the new law

Table 9-1. *Average Income of Female-Headed Families by Quintile (in 1999 dollars)*

	1993	1994	1995	1996	1997	1998	1999	Percent change	
								1993–95	1995–99
Total disposable income									
Quintile 1	7,877	8,490	8,721	8,384	7,976	8,207	8,405	10.7	-3.6
Quintile 2	13,954	14,548	16,069	15,202	15,815	16,420	17,109	15.2	6.5
Quintile 3	18,633	19,792	21,126	20,542	21,038	22,375	22,507	13.4	6.5
Quintile 4	26,735	27,700	28,965	28,109	28,517	30,103	31,491	8.3	8.7
Quintile 5	45,903	45,461	48,095	51,101	51,150	52,709	55,867	4.8	16.2
								Dollar change	
Quintile									
Earnings	1,322	1,373	1,744	1,688	1,578	1,899	2,360	422	616
Mean-tested income	5,547	5,941	5,614	5,187	4,967	4,695	4,279	68	-1,335
Disposable income	7,877	8,490	8,721	8,384	7,976	8,207	8,405	843	-316
Quintile 2									
Earnings	3,445	4,101	5,171	4,918	5,946	7,643	9,092	1,725	3,921
Mean-tested income	8,482	8,129	8,179	7,282	6,250	5,342	4,535	-303	-3,644
Disposable income	13,954	14,548	16,069	15,202	15,815	16,420	17,109	2,116	1,040

Source: CBPP as stated by ASPE, Department of Human Health and Human Services.
Note: Families sorted by ratio of comprehensive income definition to poverty threshold with an equal number of people in each quintile. Includes unrelated subfamilies.

Box 9-1   *Overview of the Temporary Assistance for*
Needy Families Programs

—Elimination of cash welfare entitlement
—Block grant funding
—Work participation standards
—Sanctions
—Five-year time limit

ended the entitlement to cash welfare. That was the first time that had ever happened. The nation's previous philosophy was that if people lived in America, even if they weren't U.S. citizens, they were entitled to welfare benefits. Roughly speaking, all they had to do was to have children they could not support and refuse to work and they were entitled to a package of benefits worth about $12,000 in cash, food stamps, and Medicaid. Note that Congress left the food stamps and Medicaid entitlements intact and ended the entitlement only to cash welfare.

Second, Congress turned the federal funding mechanism for cash welfare into a block grant. Previously, if states added more people to the welfare rolls, the federal government gave them more federal dollars; if the states helped people leave the rolls, the state received fewer federal dollars. This might be called "financial incentives to do the wrong thing." Under the block grant, states now get a fixed amount of money, so if states can help get people off the rolls, they have more money left over to work with the hardest cases or provide whatever support to low-income families they prefer. Thus, states have an incentive to help get people off the rolls.

Third, the new law included very strong work requirements. Previous law had weak work requirements, but the new law spelled out the work requirements in great detail, stipulating exactly what the states and individuals had to do and what counted as work.

Fourth, there were sanctions on both individuals and on the states if they did not meet these new work requirements. By 2002 states had to have half their caseload in work programs or suffer cuts in their federal funding. Similarly, states were required to reduce and had the option to terminate cash payments to families that did not meet work requirements. The vision of Congress in writing this law was that people on welfare would be giving something back to society because they would be participating in work programs and trying to get off welfare. There was some allowance for education, but the bill had a bias against education and in favor of work.

Finally, there was a five-year time limit, a very infamous part of the bill. In accord with the message conveyed by the time limit that welfare is not permanent, Congress renamed the program *Temporary* Assistance for Needy Families. There are some exceptions to the time limit, but there is for the first time a limit in the nation's cash welfare law.

The final vote on these unprecedented provisions, by the way, was bigger than the vote for Medicaid and Medicare in 1965. A lot of people take that to show that Democrats are smarter at catching on when they are going to lose than Republicans are; nonetheless, it was a huge bipartisan vote, and the bill was signed by a Democratic president.

What has happened since 1996? I would like to turn the tables a little bit on Peter. I would love to hear what Peter has to say about some of these results because he has written widely about how this legislation is the worst thing Bill Clinton, and presumably the Republican Congress, has done.

Here is the basic logic of the position that Republicans took. Back in 1995 and 1996, many senior Republican members would haul big charts to the floor and argue with Democrats and say, "Look at this chart, if you are on welfare, you cannot get out of poverty." They argued that Congress had created a system in which people were confined to poverty as long as they stayed on welfare. By contrast, if recipients get a job, even a low-wage job, and then government subsidizes their income, using what I will call the *work support system,* the mothers are approximately twice as well off financially as they were on welfare.

I do not want to pull the wool over your eyes here. There are work expenses, social security taxes, child care expenses, and so forth. This is not the whole picture, but this will give you an idea of what the basic argument was: there was tremendous financial incentive for people to work because of the work support system Congress created.

As you look at figure 9-1, you can see that the welfare rolls actually increased during the economic expansion of the 1980s. Many economists claim that a hot economy in which employment increased by a net of 19 million jobs would reduce the welfare rolls. But that did not happen during the 1980s. In fact, the opposite happened. During one of the biggest economic expansions the nation has ever had, the welfare rolls increased 12 percent. So a hot economy does not necessarily suck people off of welfare.

In the 1990s, at the beginning of the economic recovery, the welfare rolls were still growing. But then, after states started to implement welfare reform, and especially after 1996 when the federal law passed, the rolls plummeted. Where did those mothers go? To me, this is the most important figure (see

Figure 9-1. *AFDC/TANF Caseload, 1959–2000*

Millions of families

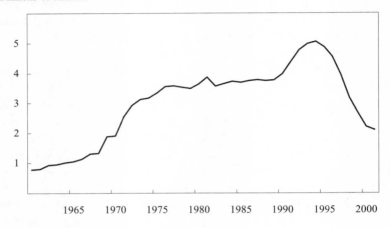

Source: Congressional Research Service.

figure 9-2) and the one that I would really like to hear our moderator and Wendell talk about.

The percentage of married women with jobs has increased since the end of World War II, although the increase drops marginally in the late 1990s. By contrast, the number of single mothers working was virtually flat during the 1980s and 1990s, up to about 1995, and then increased very substantially. Never-married mothers, who are the ones most likely to go on welfare, least likely to graduate from high school, and most likely to have long welfare spells, showed a huge 40 percent increase in work after 1996. Nothing like this had ever happened before.

This increase in work by single mothers led to increases in earnings and, because of the work support system and especially the earned income tax credit (EITC), increases in total income for poor and low-income female-headed families. Between 1993 and 1999, these mothers increased their earnings almost every year. Here is a single and accurate way to think about this pattern: welfare income down, earnings and total income up. That's a nice outcome of welfare reform and exactly what the American people want.

Which brings us to the child poverty. During the 1995–96 congressional debate, Wendell invented a statistical method to show that the Republican bill was going to put a million children in poverty. The *Washington Post* picked up on the study and referred to it often. So did Senator Moynihan and many others

Figure 9-2. *Married, Single, and Never-Married Mothers Working,*
1985–2000

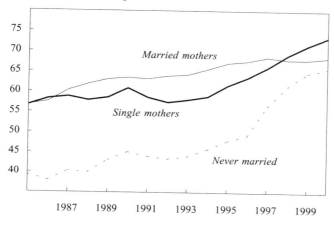

Percent of mothers working

Source: Burtless (2001).

opposed to the bill. So let's look at the actual data to see what happened to child
poverty from 1993 to 1999.

The declines in the welfare rolls during this time period are greater than in
any previous period in the history of welfare (figure 9-3). Yet every year as the
welfare rolls were plummeting, so was poverty; welfare is down and poverty is
down because earnings are up and the earned income tax credit is up. In fact,
black child poverty fell more than ever before; by 1999 it had reached its lowest
level ever.

As encouraging as these poverty numbers are, they actually do not tell the
whole story. They tell a minimum story about the changes in child poverty. A
broader measure of poverty is shown in figure 9-4. This is also a Census Bureau
measure. In computing family income, this measure includes income from the
EITC and food stamps, which are not included in the official poverty measure.
The point to take from this figure is that during the 1980s children's poverty
declined from about 21 to 18 percent or about 15 percent.

By contrast, during the 1990s poverty declined 35 percent, more than twice
as much. The reason is that Congress has created a new national strategy to
fight welfare dependency and poverty—one that Peter and Wendell opposed.
It is a strategy of doing everything possible, including using somewhat harsh
measures, to get low-income mothers into the labor force and then subsidizing
their income. As you can see, the effects on child poverty are considerable.

Figure 9-3. *Welfare Caseload and Children's Poverty Decline Simultaneously, 1995–2000*

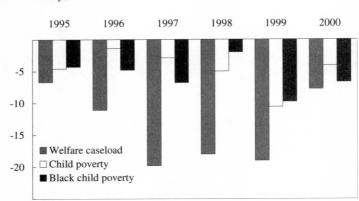

Decline

Source: Caseload data from Congressional Research Services; poverty data from Census Bureau.

Finally, figure 9-5 shows how the expansion of several programs between 1984 and 1999, including child care, the state child health insurance program (SCHIP), the child care tax credit, Medicaid, and the EITC, led to increased federal spending on families that work but have low incomes. If Congress had not expanded any of those programs or, in some cases, like the tax credit and SCHIP, literally created them, then in 1999 the federal government would have spent less than $6 billion subsidizing low-income working families. But because Congress expanded or created these programs, the Congressional Budget Office (CBO) estimates federal spending of $52 billion supporting low-income families that work.

In the end this is a very nice story, and this is why Wendell and I get along so well. On the one hand, we have very tough work requirements. The states actually use sanctions. They make people go to work rather than sit around and collect welfare benefits. On the other hand, taxpayers are willing to subsidize the earnings of low-income workers by helping them pay for their child care and giving them additional cash and other benefits. As a result of work and the government's expanding work support system, earnings are up and poverty is down.

The new strategy of encouraging and, where necessary, forcing work, and then subsidizing income from work is much more effective at reducing poverty and increasing income among single-parent families than simply providing

Figure 9-4. *Decline in Children's Poverty by Broad Definition, 1983–89 and 1993–2000*

Percent in poverty   Percent deline

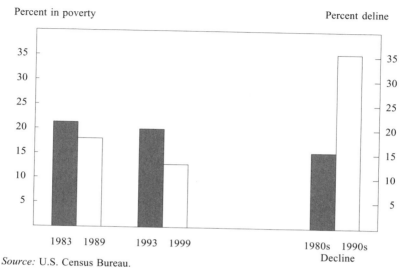

Source: U.S. Census Bureau.

welfare. If we had not tried this, we would be back where we were in the 1980s, and welfare dependency and child poverty would still be at much higher levels than they are now.

Edelman: Because you invited it, Ron, I will say a word in response, even though I was not going to take that role. And Wendell will say a couple words in response.

Basically, Ron has concentrated on what happened in one story when there are really two stories.

There is no question that the people who got jobs are somewhat better off than they were. That is the better part of the story, particularly because what needs to be done to improve the policy in that area is very clear. But even as to the people who are working, approximately half of those who have jobs after being on welfare do not have full-time jobs. Depending on the study you look at, the average number of hours being worked is thirty to thirty-five. The average wage nationally is around $7.00 an hour.

There are a few people who have great jobs, and there are many people who really are not any better off. That is what is shown in Wendell's numbers, although those people are helped by the EITC and other spending that Ron was talking about. No question that there is a lot more money rolling around the system to help you if you are working.

Figure 9-5. *Support for Working Families Increases Dramatically, 1984–99*

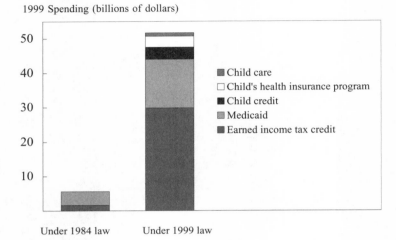

1999 Spending (billions of dollars)

■ Child care
□ Child's health insurance program
■ Child credit
▨ Medicaid
■ Earned income tax credit

Under 1984 law   Under 1999 law

Source: Congressional Budget Office

If that was the only story, I would say it is a pretty good story, although I would emphasize what Wendell noted earlier: you cannot tell how much of this story is the hot economy and how much is the welfare policy. But when the hot economy helps people get jobs, there is this additional supplementation that Ron showed you. I do not argue with that. Even as to that, though, on the top of figure 9-5 there is a very thin line that reads "child care." We could spend a lot of time on that piece of the story—the number of people who have tremendous trouble finding good child care and those that lose jobs because their child gets sick and cannot go to child care.

The bad part of the story deals with the people who are completely out. That is a big number. Nationally—again, this is looking at all the studies and making a synthesis—approximately 60 percent of the people who went off welfare have a job on any given day when they are snapshoted in the "leaver" studies, as they are called. Whether it is a good job is a different issue. These are big numbers because the decline in the welfare rolls was from more than fourteen million people in the early 1990s to approximately six million people now. That is a big decline.

If on any given day 40 percent of the leavers have neither a job nor cash assistance, that amounts to a million plus moms and two million plus children. Why is this such a big number? Because welfare is no longer an entitlement and states can do as they like. People are regularly pushed off the rolls or cannot get on now because the state has a "diversion" policy.

Many of these three million plus people have lost their food stamps improperly and sometimes their Medicaid. Ron's argument does not take into account whether people actually get the food stamps and the Medicaid that they are supposed to have. That is where Wendell's numbers in the bottom quintile come from, because they are the translation of all these people who neither have work nor cash assistance.

My biggest beef is not about the people who have gone to work, although much more needs to be done there. My biggest beef is that we destroyed the safety net and that we have mothers and children out there who are in really bad shape. The homeless shelters for moms and kids are bursting at the seams in this hot economy all over the country.

It is true that the number of children in poverty has gone down to one in six from where it was before. That is still unconscionable. Plus, there are even worse problems among the poorest of those who are still in poverty. The number of African Americans in poverty is down to an "all-time low." Well, the number of African Americans in poverty is still 23.4 percent in the 1999 figures. I think that is unacceptable. Even though it is true that this is the lowest figure since we started counting, it is not anywhere near where it should be.

Primus: I think what you have to remember about this debate between Ron and me is that TANF had the good fortune of being implemented in a strong economy. Yes, we would expect poverty to go down when our unemployment rate is going down from 7 to 4 percent. What we cannot do is roll the clock back and say what would have happened if we had kept the old law going and we had the states doing their bit in terms of reforming welfare.

When the welfare act was signed, the CBO said there was going to be $55 billion in savings. Those were not in TANF or the Aid to Families with Dependent Children program that Ron and I have spent most of the time talking about. They were in the food stamp program, $27 billion, and in immigrant cuts, primarily in Supplemental Security Income (SSI).

In 1997 Congress rolled back a good portion of those SSI cuts for the disabled. A lot of those elderly women getting SSI, $4,000 or $5,000 a year, were living with families with children. That is what drove our predictions of the fact that this bill was going to hurt low-income children.

The support sources shown in figure 9-5 would be great if it worked. A lot of the families are not showing up at the food stamp office for that $2,000, and they are incurring work expenses that are not on there, such as child care costs of $2,000 or $3,000. Only 20 percent of the mothers leaving welfare, according to the Urban Institute, actually get child care assistance.

Table 9-2.   *Impact of the Safety Net on the Poverty Gap for Families with Children*

					Percent change	
Measure	1993	1995	1997	1999	1993–95	1995–99
Poverty gap (billions of 1999 dollars)						
Before taxes and transfers	85.0	73.0	69.6	55.9	–12.0	–17.1
After taxes and transfers	32.0	24.8	26.3	22.5	–7.2	–2.3
Percent reduction in poverty gap						
Social insurance	16.9	16.6	18.8	18.3	–0.3	1.7
Means-tested benefits	44.3	45.0	37.7	34.3	0.7	–10.7
Federal taxes	1.1	4.4	5.7	7.1	3.3	2.7
Total	62.3	66.0	62.2	59.7	3.7	–6.3

If it theoretically works like that, yes, these families are ahead. But the truth is that less than half of working poor families get food stamps, and I think what we have to be about in our next round of welfare reform is reengineering the delivery, not so much the structure of these benefits, so that more of the working poor actually get the food stamp assistance, the child care assistance, and the Medicaid assistance that this figure would have you believe.

Ron in his writings does recognize that some families have lost ground. We think about 13 or 14 percent of single-mother families are actually worse off compared to their counterparts three or four years ago. They have lost ground despite this very strong economy.

If you look at table 9-2 and concentrate on the changes in the last two columns, this is the poverty gap before taxes and transfers. This is what happens when families earn income. During this time trend the poverty gap is declining significantly. Between 1993 and 1995 it declined by $12 billion. The bottom line poverty gap after taxes and transfers—this is all families with children—declined 7.2 percent.

Between 1995 and 1999 the families again were making huge progress, with the poverty gap declining $17 billion. Their bottom-line income only increased 2.3 percent. That, in essence, is what I am saying is good about welfare, the economy, and make-work-pay. We have gotten more work effort.

But that poverty gap after you count all taxes and transfers—and Ron really has not disputed this with any of his statistics—really has not improved nearly as much as that work effort deserves.

Edelman: The next question is for Ron Haskins. Where do we go from here? I am looking especially at the five-year clock when I ask that question,

Table 9-3. *Changes in Returns to Work and Welfare, 1986 and 1998*
Dollars

Welfare or work	Earnings	Federal taxes	AFDC/ TANF and food stamps	Earned income credit	Total income	Medicaid coverage?
1986[a]						
Welfare	0	0	8,747	0	8,747	yes
Work	10,000	−956	2,584	728	12,356	no
Difference	10,000	−956	−6,163	728	3,609	
1998						
Welfare	0	0	7,870	0	7,870	yes
Work	10,000	−765	4,240	3,756	17,231	yes
Difference	10,000	−765	−3,630	3,756	9,361	

a. Estimated 1986 numbers are based on those shown in the House Ways and Means Committee's *1986 Green Book* (Government Printing Office) for a worker with $7,000 in earnings in Pennsylvania. Taxes and benefits were then adjusted for inflation from January 1986 to July 1998. Calculations for 1986 assume no 33 percent deduction but do assume the standard deduction of $75, the $30 deduction, and $160 child care deduction. Federal taxes are income taxes and FICA taxes. Calculations made by the Congressional Research Service.

but please add whatever else you would like, because Wendell and I have said a number of things.

Haskins: We have the battle of the figures here. A big part of the argument Congress had in 1996 was whether work pays more than welfare. In the 1992 presidential campaign Governor Clinton said, "Make work pay." That is what Congress and President Clinton did.

Look at table 9-3. This analysis was conducted by the Congressional Research Service and is untainted by Republican hands. This table shows changes in the incentive to work between 1986 and 1998 by comparing the net income from welfare and earnings for a mother leaving welfare for work in a minimum wage job in each of the two years. Because of changes in welfare and in the work support system, the mother gets $9,361 more if she works in 1998 as compared with only about $3,000 in 1986. Clearly, the combination of changes in welfare and the work support system have vastly improved the incentive to work.

Wendell complains because we have an entitlement to food stamps, but many families leaving welfare do not get their food stamps. We have food stamp offices all over the nation and yet parents do not go in there and get those food stamps. What an outrage. The government, I guess, needs to pick them up at their houses and take them down to get the food stamps. You have to factor personal responsibility into your thinking about the kind of system that we have created, and the commitment policymakers and the public have to helping low-income families. Yes, we should make it easier to get food stamps, but parents and advocates have a responsibility to be more aggressive in making sure that working families get food stamps.

Having said that, I agree with Wendell. I have no problem in working with the states in doing everything we can to make it easier to apply for and get food stamps. Wendell is concerned that food stamp benefits have gone down for the poorest female-headed families. Me too. If this problem can be solved, income in these families would increase by an average of $2,000 per year.

But I want Wendell to make an equal commitment to the five-year time limit, to the mandatory work requirements, and to the sanctions, and say, "Welfare recipients must behave in accord with the new system. You have to help yourself."

What Peter and Wendell don't like is risk. They are offended because we created a welfare system in which there are some losers. Now, anybody here who knows of a policy that creates all winners and no losers, raise your hand. What policy can we have that does not create any losers?

So there are some losers. But you have seen the effects of the new system in increasing employment and earnings and reducing poverty. Peter says nothing to dispute these data, nor does Wendell. On average, low-income, female-headed families that used to live on welfare are better off, and they have lower levels of poverty, period.

Now, let us talk about details. We have a group at the bottom. Absolutely. I've written about this. House Republicans published a paper, with the Speaker's signature on it, before the administration would even acknowledge this problem, saying that the food stamp program was a problem, that Medicaid was a problem, and that there is a group at the bottom that has lower income.

But who is that group? They are a group that not only does not work but also does not meet the welfare requirements. In the old days, under Peter's system, they could go on welfare and stay forever, and they did. There is no dispute about this. Sixty-five percent of the families on welfare in 1986 would eventually be on welfare eight years or more, and the average length was twelve years. That was the old system, and they were not in deep poverty, but they stayed on welfare for a long time. We ended that system.

If recipients are stubborn about their lifestyle and will not even meet the requirements so they can stay on welfare and get their welfare benefits, the only system that will help them is one in which we simply give benefits away and ask for nothing in return.

So I vote for risk. I want to help poor families. I would be willing to spend money and Republicans have supported more spending, but only if recipients also help themselves—or at least they try. We need risk in the system because it disciplines human behavior. Without that risk we will have families living on welfare year after year, and their children will live on welfare. We have broken that system and the future is positive, not negative.

Primus: I think we made a little progress. Ron is for making sure that these families get food stamps. In the state of California, where I was recently, they make the food stamp families come in every month. They fill out a long form. It is like filling out your 1040 twelve times a year. How many of you would like to do that? Again, I think we have to support working families. I did not resign because I was against work. I think in addition to placing all this emphasis on getting mothers to work, we have to look at the other side of the equation, the males.

If we have done such a good job, Ron, with the female side of this, why don't we also work on making sure that the fathers of these children also get to work and that when they pay child support, all of that child support goes to the family. I know you and I both worked on a bill, so I know you are partially for that, but that is one place where I think we can go.

Time limits is a different issue. In fact, there are two issues here. First, if we have a mother who is working twenty or thirty hours a week, why should she not be able to keep some cash assistance? She is doing the right thing. We would all agree that we want her to be working.

There is a real conflict in the law between a mother who has been working. Several states—Maryland, Illinois, and a couple others—have said that when a mother is doing the right thing and working, we are going to stop the clock. I think that is a policy that we ought to discourage.

Second, the mothers at the bottom are floundering. Sheldon Danziger and others have done a lot of work on this. Who are these mothers? These are mothers who for the most part have multiple barriers. They have not completed high school. They may be mentally depressed. They may be the victim of domestic violence. They may be a long way from work. They may have two or three preschool children. The point is that the mothers who are not making it now are mothers with multiple barriers. Do we want to spend the money to get those mothers fully into the labor force, and how many additional requirements are we going to put on this fairly small population? We could approach some of this on a cost benefit analysis and say where it makes the most sense to put our employment services, with the dads, with the mothers, with the youth, or elsewhere.

Again, I'm not against work. I think that we cannot issue time limits and put requirements on people who cannot comply. The time limit is wrong, but recognizing political reality, if we kept the 20 percent, which would be about a million mothers—20 percent of what the caseloads were in 1996—plus stop the clock for the working mothers, we would have gone a long way.

Let me just say one or two other things about where we should go. We need to increase family income. That needs to be our emphasis in the next round, while maintaining our emphasis on keeping these families employed, so we do make food stamps easier to access.

We must make sure that more of the working parents today who get cut off from the rolls in some states at 30 percent of poverty, or 40 percent of poverty, get Medicaid or get access to CHIP. We have to make sure that more of these families get child care so that we improve our work support system.

I have already said some things about noncustodial parents and the need to help them into the labor force, as well as to encourage them to support their children. And when they pay—if we really believe in these dads paying child support—why do we have a 100 percent tax on it? It is a mandatory payment of which the government receives the entire benefit.

If we believe in it, I would like to change that 100 percent tax rate to a subsidy rate so that if a low-income dad was making a payment of $150 or $200 a month, we match that payment maybe dollar for dollar or a dollar for every 50 cents. Then it would flow to the mother. I think we have to do a lot more on that side of the equation.

Finally, two-parent families. I'm for two-parent families, but our welfare system does not serve them today. Half of the children who are born out of wedlock in this country come home to a two-parent family. The poverty rate for those families is high. But for the most part, because of the culture of our system, those families do not get support in terms of employment, food stamps, Medicaid, or TANF. I think we have to help those two-parent families strengthen their relationships, and we need to serve them.

Edelman: Ron, you did not get a chance to state your views on what should happen next. The law is coming up for reauthorization in 2002, and Wendell has given some suggestions. TANF provides $16.5 billion a year, and when one adds in the state maintenance of effort, there is $27 billion out there annually. One thing I would like you to address is whether we need to continue spending, in your judgment, that level of funding and whether that federal/state combination is the right one.

Haskins: There is a lot to conserve in this bill, including the money. I would not take any of the money out of the TANF program. It is a $16.5 billion block grant, and Congress should be absolutely certain that the money is untouched. I would do everything possible right from the beginning to make it clear that the money will not be reduced. Nor would I reduce the child care money, which is now more than $6 billion per year, if you include all the TANF money spent on child care and all the money that goes into the child care block grant.

I agree with almost everything Wendell said. I do not have any problem with making food stamps easier to get. I do want to point out that Democrats controlled the House and Wendell was on the staff of the Ways and Means Committee when we made up the rules about child support enforcement. The government keeps part of the money for a very good reason. The original justification for child support enforcement was in part to pay back the government because taxpayers paid for mothers to be on welfare. That was an essential part of the child support program.

But we should remember that Republicans, as part of the welfare reform law of 1996, changed the child support rules. Before 1996, when a mother left welfare, the money that was collected to pay for past-due child support could be, and usually was, kept by federal and state governments. House Republicans tried to change the law so that all this past-due support would go to families, but the Senate would not go along, so Congress wound up splitting it 50/50 between government and former welfare families. That gave about $3 billion over six years to families.

The bill authored by Nancy Johnson and Ben Cardin that Wendell mentioned, which passed the House 405-18, would have followed the original Republican bill and given all the past-due support to the mother and children. The Johnson-Cardin bill should be enacted this year. Congress should make sure that mothers and children get all the money that is paid by the fathers.

I agree with Wendell that the other major thing Congress should do is stress policies that favor marriage. However, it warps the meaning of the term *family* to include parents who cohabit.

Cohabitation is not the same as marriage. Research shows that the marital dissolution rate is 50 percent and that the cohabiting dissolution rate is way above that. We have to do something to help those cohabiting families stay together. Children need the stability of a married-couple family; a series of parental relationships based on cohabitation will hurt children.

Wendell and I agree on a number of the policies to promote marriage, like reducing the marriage penalty in the earned income tax credit. But we also need to change our rhetoric. This is what really bothers me about the debate we had this year on the floor in the House—that there is an unwillingness among our elected officials to admit that both adults and children are better off in married, two-parent families and that we should set increasing rates of marriage, especially among the poor, as a national goal.

Our ministers, politicians, other public officials, and adults who have regular contact with children should say that single-parent families are not the way to raise children to maximize their development or to maximize the health or happiness of adults. The research on these issues is now very clear, and we ought to set a clear priority that every child should be reared in a married, two-parent family, and we should adjust our policies to achieve that goal.

Edelman: We will take a few questions.

Nancy Coleman: I am at the American Bar Association. I am very concerned about the issues of people's ability to get services and cash payments that they might be entitled to. We have seen through the SSI outreach program, and through the food stamp and CHIP programs, that people do not come forward for entitlements that they are entitled to, especially those who have been cut off from something.

How in this new era of no welfare and benefits can we get people to go in and sign up if, in fact, we do not have one-stop shopping? If, as Wendell suggested, you have to go in once a month and fill out a 1040-type form to get food stamps in California, you still have to do that to get your Medicare supplements paid and to be eligible for SSI when you were on social security, and so on.

Haskins: I have one thing to add very quickly. Governor Tommy Thompson, now Secretary Thompson, changed the SCHIP program in Wisconsin by getting a federal waiver. The essence of the waiver was to make parents, mostly single mothers, eligible for SCHIP benefits. Guess what? Enrollment went way up. There is self-interest involved here. Parents are more willing to sign up their children if they, too, get the benefit. This is something Congress and the states can do to help people get their benefits even after they leave welfare.

Here's another example: The Ways and Means Committee had a hearing last year about the kids who did not get their Medicaid. We invited three states—Florida, Oklahoma, and Ohio—all of which described in great detail the administrative actions they took to increase the percentage of eligible families that actually received Medicaid coverage. The general thrust of the administrative actions they took was to make it as easy as possible for families to sign up for Medicaid. As a result, their Medicaid enrollments went way up above where they had been even before welfare reform.

Clearly, there are administrative actions the states can take that will make a big difference. There are policy changes, such as making the adults eligible, that will also have a big impact.

Primus: I agree with the premise of the question. Just before the Clinton administration left town they issued some interesting food stamp regulations that said, for example, asset tests are made much simpler. Also, once you establish income for one month, that holds for six months. There are a lot of things we can do just to make the delivery of these benefits much simpler and easier.

Edelman: I would just connect the two comments by saying that one of the challenges for everybody who is concerned about this as an advocate, commentator, or worker on the Hill is to try to work with this new administration to get, at the very least, stronger encouragement and help to the states so that more states would do what Ron was talking about, at a minimum.

Participant: I am interested in the child care aspect of welfare reform. One of the considerations back in 1996 was that many of these children already do not have fathers. If the mothers are out sweeping up the streets or picking up cigarette butts, then who is going to take care of the kids?

Maybe this was answered in part by a report that appeared in the *Washington Times*, January 23, 2001, citing a study from the Manpower Demonstration Research Corporation (MDRC) of New York saying, "Welfare reform is okay for children. Whoever is taking care of them, it is working out."

This seems to me a bit counterintuitive, but maybe that is my problem. It seems a little too good to be true. Am I wrong, or is there a lurking variable around here somewhere?

Primus: That is a very good study, but you should not have confused the term *welfare reform* with the programs that are being analyzed there. They took a look at New Hope, the Minnesota Family Investment Program (MFIP), and programs that supplemented work substantially. They found that programs that increased employment and supplemented work with government subsidies, for lack of a better term, increased the performance of their children. It was not that this welfare reform, this federal act, was generating these positive school performances.

In fact, it contrasted MFIP and New Hope with what was going on in Grand Rapids and Atlanta and some of the other programs that MDRC has analyzed. The programs just increased employment and had no effect on school performance, basically. I would urge you to get hold of a copy of that study and read it carefully.

Haskins: These findings are exceptionally interesting, especially because the MDRC studies are big, random-assignment, high-quality studies. I am going to make up a number. MDRC has not given a number on total income in these families. So I do not want to associate what I am going to say now with them, but here is what I think the finding is. Mandatory work, just like the kind that we talked about here, plus state and federal income supplements of the type Wendell and I have discussed brought the families to about $18,000 in total income. The system that we have now without any further supplements gets families to around $16,000 or $17,000. If $18,000 or $19,000 is the goal, we are very close to that goal under the current system, if they get everything they deserve. Trying to get these working families as much income as possible so they have the chance to achieve these wonderful effects on marriage and children is another reason I am so concerned about food stamps.

Edelman: Is that a full-time minimum wage job, Ron, in that statement?

Haskins: Very few of the families in Minnesota (or elsewhere) have minimum wage jobs. As you pointed out, the average is about $7.00 an hour. Families tend to work about thirty or thirty-five hours rather than forty hours a week. But they usually don't work year round. I would say that most of these families earn around $10,000 per year.

MDRC thinks there is a level of income that will produce these effects on children. Now, really and truly, think about this. We spend billions a year on educational interventions directly with children, and these interventions produce very little. So you ignore the kids, concentrate on the parents, and do everything possible to ensure that the parents have enough money to rear their children decently.

MDRC research shows that if they are working, if their income is being supplemented, and if their income is at least $18,000 or so, marriage increases and the kids do better. In three out of three studies of this type, their school performance increased. In one of these studies, divorce decreased and marriage increased. Getting the families to $18,000 in income is a very big thing, and that is why this work support system is so important.

Second point, child care. In 1996 Congress did two very good things that even Wendell agrees with. One is we got rid of a bunch of programs and gave the states one big program to run, so we got rid of a ton of red tape. Second, we increased the amount of money by $4.5 billion over six years. And we gave the states flexibility to transfer money out of the TANF program into child care. They are doing that now to the tune of about $3.5 billion or $4 billion per year. We have a lot more money for child care. Child care has not been a problem so far.

Advocates will argue, and you will see articles in the paper now and again, that the quality of child care is low, that it harms the children, and so forth, and I'm sure that happens in some places. On average, however, you cannot make a case, based on data, that child care harms the children's development.

The families make their own child care arrangements. Most of them are informal arrangements with relatives or other people in their neighborhood. Far less than half the families use any government child care money. There is virtually no evidence that this system harms the children in any way. The Republican attitude toward child care was: "Give the states more money and more flexibility and rely on them to figure out child care."

There is not a national problem here that requires a national solution. More money is okay, but Congress should not pass regulations and should not try to say that states have to improve child care because child care is harming children. The evidence is not there.

Edelman: I just might add, before we close, that Ron's argument is based on the assumption that all the ducks line up in a row. If we look at all the people who have gone to work and ask if all their child care needs are being met, the answer is absolutely not.

We have a long way to go on child care, whether it is shortages of infant care, because in most states mothers have to go to work when their child is three months old, or whether it is swing shift care, because so many jobs are in the evening and overnight. Whether it is sick child care, as I mentioned earlier. Whether it is a decent wage for child care workers. Whether it is the fact that in state after state the subsidized child care cuts off soon after a person goes to work.

Very few states—Illinois, parts of California, Minnesota, and a couple of others—actually provide child care assistance for every family where there is a need, whether or not they have been on welfare. This is really the way we ought to look at it, helping *all* people who need subsidization to get child care.

So we have a long way to go on child care, although there is no question that there is a lot more money in the child care system now than there was, and it is somewhat better organized because of the pulling together of the federal money.

PART VI

The Future of Medicare

FIVE YEARS AGO the National Academy of Social Insurance launched a project called Restructuring Medicare for the Long Term, divided into seven study panels. At that time it was becoming increasingly apparent that with rising health care costs and demographic pressures, some fundamental change would be required in the future if Medicare was to provide the same type of security and support to the elderly and disabled as it had in the past. Robert D. Reischauer, president of the Urban Institute, who chairs that project's steering committee also moderated the conference session on which this section is based.

Three of the seven panels have completed their reports, and the steering committee also released an interim and subsequent report. The second group of panels has been working more recently on issues described in the next chapters.

Chapter 10 reports on the panel dealing with long-term financing issues, chaired by chapter author Marilyn Moon. Chapter 11 reports on a second panel dealing with issues of governance and management in the Medicare program, chaired by author Sheila Burke. Medicare and markets were the focus of the third panel, chapter 12, as related by panel chair Mark Schlesinger. Finally, chapter 13 by Gerard Anderson describes new work on chronic care and Medicare.

It is particularly timely that the conference focused on these issues because President George Bush has made a commitment to bring forward a plan to restructure Medicare for the long term. So many of the issues studied over the last five years, and that these panels will look at in the future, will be part of the public debate.

10

Medicare's Long-Term Financing

Marilyn Moon

T HE VALUE OF the panels convened at the National Academy of Social Insurance (NASI) conference is in finding a way for people with different backgrounds, opinions, and views to come together and reach some consensus—not on the full set of solutions but rather on how to characterize the problem, put some bounds on the problem, and at least narrow the range of debate to a more realistic set of options. In that sense the Study Panel on Medicare's Long-Term Financing succeeded well.

The Study Panel's Charge

The charge of the panel was to look at financing options, but very quickly and early on members decided that this could not be done without first looking at two possible avenues for changing the program over time, that is, finding new savings and potential expansions of the program. Those possibilities were included in this analysis and helped substantially in terms of the final product, although it took some time to get to some of the tough financing questions.

Agreement was finally reached on the most important conclusion: that new revenues will be necessary to avoid eroding the financial protection that Medicare now provides.[1] If the program is cut back substantially, additional financing is, of course, not necessary, but it is required for Medicare to retain its same general level of support.

It was also concluded that the magnitude of the additional revenues needed is not unmanageable. That is also an important piece of the issue, as no magic solution will arise from taxes, either. There are advantages and disadvantages associated with the tax options considered. The panel did not try to settle on one

---

1. Gluck and Moon (2000).

desirable approach, recognizing that this is going to be a tough discussion that needs to go on.

Timing is important and was the subject of discussions and our conclusions. Uncertainty is still there and, in fact, the focus did not go beyond 2030. The panel believed that it would be unrealistic to try to talk about solutions that might be put in place in the next few years without causing new problems or changes for Medicare over the next twenty-five or thirty years. Even within that 2030 window, other changes were discussed as things went along because of the great uncertainty about some of these projections. The changes in health care, added onto the other uncertainties of long-term projections, make this a difficult task indeed.

The Substantive Findings

As indicated, the panel decided to look beyond the baseline projections and instead to think about both adding benefits and achieving bigger savings. Some of the things that were determined and found are suggested here, but more findings are available in the full report.

Projections for 1998, which are now a little dated, were used. Most of the changes that occurred in Medicare in the last few years really occurred between 1997 and 1998 with the Balanced Budget Act that altered the program. The economy has improved and other things have changed the outlook since then, but the trends are pretty much the same.

Using 1998 projections, which are now more pessimistic than people would use these days, it was found that by 2030, under current law, if nothing else was changed, revenues would need to be increased by 111 percent from the base of current revenues (see table 10-1).

The panel did not just examine Part A, hospital insurance, which a lot of analysts do, but also looked at Part B. It was assumed that general revenues under Part B would be the share of gross domestic product (GDP) that existed in 1999 and that people would continue to pay Part B premiums. So, in that sense, this is an artificial revenue stream used for illustration. Revenue increases in table 10-1 are increases above and beyond our artificial baseline.

Using the preliminary Breaux-Thomas proposal—which is code for proactive efforts to reduce the level of spending on Medicare by restructuring the program, raising the age of eligibility, and making a number of other changes—revenues would still have to be raised by 86 percent.

Breaux-Thomas was used as one of the indicators even though that estimate was preliminary and not their final recommendation. It was, however, one of the more ambitious savings proposals that have been offered and uses optimis-

Table 10-1. *Estimated Increases in Taxpayer Contributions to Medicare in 2030 Compared to 1998*[a]

Percent

Provisions	Approximate increase needed
Current law, projected spending in 2030[b]	111
Changes in Medicare designed to produce savings	
Interim Breaux-Thomas proposal to the Medicare Commission[c]	86
Defined contribution: hold per beneficiary increases in Medicare spending to growth in the consumer price index (CPI)	52
Raise age of eligibility to 67[d]	105
Raise age of eligibility to 70	93
Expansions in Medicare[e]	
Outpatient prescription drug coverage ($200 deductible, 20% coinsurance, $2,000 maximum benefit)	136
Outpatient prescription drug coverage ($200 deductible, 20% coinsurance, $2,000 stop loss)	171
Stop loss of $3,000 per year	123
Stop loss of $5,000 per year	119
Allow buy-in at ages 62–64	116
Allow buy-in at ages 60–64	115
Changes in cost sharing	
$300 Part B deductible tied to CPI, one annual hospital deductible, no hospital coinsurance, 10% home health coinsurance	103
$300 Part B deductible tied to CPI, one annual hospital deductible, no hospital coinsurance, 10% home health coinsurance, $3,000 stop loss	117
$300 Part B deductible tied to CPI, one annual hospital deductible, no hospital coinsurance, 10% home health coinsurance, $5,000 stop loss	111

Source: Gluck and Moon (2000).

a. Taxpayer contributions are defined as all Medicare expenditures except for the 25 percent of Part B costs paid by beneficiaries themselves in premiums. Payroll taxes and general tax revenues make up the bulk of the taxpayer contributions. This table represents the percent increase over 1998 in taxpayer contributions to Medicare as a percentage of gross domestic product (GDP). Because tax revenues tend to rise at the same rate as GDP, estimates in the table are a reasonable approximation of how much revenues would need to rise over their 1998 level to meet Medicare spending needs under each of the illustrative scenarios presented in the table.

b. Baseline projection of 1998 by the Social Security and Medicare Trustees of Medicare costs in 2030.

c. The "interim" Breaux-Thomas proposal contained a provision for an income-related premium for Medicare subsequently dropped from the final version voted on (but not adopted) by the bipartisan commission. Hence the revenue needs of the final version would have been larger than those shown here for the interim proposal. The subsequent Breaux-Frist legislation (S. 106-1895 and S. 106-2807) also differs from the version of Breaux-Thomas analyzed here. Box 2-3 in Gluck and Moon (2000) discusses those differences.

d. All analysis from this row down to the end of the table based on cost estimates developed for the National Academy of Social Insurance by Actuarial Research Corporation, Springfield, Virginia.

e. The estimates assume all features of the Medicare program other than the specific expansions noted remain as under current law.

tic savings assumptions, which led the panel to look at that as a possible lower bound on needed spending increases.

If prescription drugs were added, either of two prescription drug proposals could be looked at—one less generous than what was described by both parties in the 2000 presidential campaign and one more generous. The range of increases would have to be from 136 percent, not enormously higher than increases needed for current law, to 171 percent. That provides a sense of the task before the study panel.

The panel looked at what it would take to achieve various spending targets. As indicated, it was assumed that Part B premiums and Part A revenue would be as projected. Then the 1999 share of Part B general revenues was used. If general revenues needed to rise further, that increase was included in the projections for higher revenues.

In looking at the baseline, requiring a 111 percent increase, estimates were that the payroll tax would have to go from 2.9 percent to 4.84 percent if that was the only thing that changed. An income tax surtax of 8.43 percent would be needed on top of what people now pay. It should be noted that since income taxes are being reduced, this latter projection is now out of date.

If Medicare benefits were taxed, about half of the shortfall would be taken care of. That would be a fairly progressive way of asking beneficiaries to pay more.

Those are some of the key findings. When the report came out, there was some criticism that it was using 1998 data. It was hard enough to pull these numbers together when using one consistent year and then to try to update things. It would have been very difficult to try to update all our numbers.

Building on the Panel's Work

After the report came out, some colleagues and I did some work published in *Inquiry*.[2] We did things a little differently. All three years—1998, 1999, and 2000—were used to look at what a difference changing projections make through time. The panel focused on 2025, a little bit earlier, and assumed a slightly higher share of GDP from general revenues because all changes were assumed to start in 2002, including locking in the level of general revenue at that point.

We found that for 2025, using 1998 projections—which is a little different way of looking at this on a pay-as-you-go basis—the revenue gap would have been 1.9 percent of GDP. In 2000 the gap had gone down to 0.8 percent. That is,

2. Moon, Segal, and Weiss (2000–01).

the revenue gap of what would have to be made up after Part B premiums and other revenues are accounted for would be approximately 0.8 percent of GDP, substantially lower than the 1998 numbers. The long-term outlook has improved.

The pay-as-you-go approach is probably the most pessimistic way to look at financing because it assumes you are just paying every year what is needed in that exact year.

We also looked at a combined trust fund in an artificial way. In that case, we had a goal of a balance of a year and a half of combined Part A and Part B spending left in 2025, so the program does not just come to a screeching halt in 2025. We found that in this case the payroll tax would have to go from a combined tax of 2.9 to 3.5 percent using the 2000 estimates.

If you increased the premium that individuals pay, which will be about 12 percent on a combined basis of A and B, over time, to 15 percent, the payroll tax would have to go only to 3.2 percent from 2.9. These are very modest changes. Finally, taxing the actuarial value of Medicare would be enough to get to the baseline.

Conclusion

What does this all mean? First of all, it means any kind of numbers can be shown if you work long enough at it and use different assumptions. It means that even with a better outlook in 2000, there will likely need to be additional revenues. However, the revenues are not that intimidating. Also, between now and 2025 there will be approximately a 70 percent increase in the number of beneficiaries on this program. It should not be surprising to think that revenues might have to be raised, if we are going to take care of not only a rising number but also a rising share of the population.

Continued efforts will be needed to improve efficiency and to think about modest increases in beneficiary effort elsewhere. Colleagues of mine and I have done some analysis of the burdens that will take place for seniors, and even with no policy changes, the costs to beneficiaries will be high.[3]

A better economy over time, which is largely what drove the improvements from 1998 to 2000, is very important in making all of this more affordable. A better economy even allows potentially for some increases for items such as prescription drugs.

This is not a doomsday scenario. There are going to be some challenges. It is going to be hard to do in some ways, but it is certainly not an unsustainable program in the way that some people discuss it.

3. Maxwell, Moon, and Storeygard (2001).

References

Gluck, Michael, and Marilyn Moon. 2000. *Financing Medicare's Future. Final Report of the Study Panel on Medicare's Long-Term Financing.* Washington, D.C.: NASI (September).

Moon, Marilyn, Misha Segal, and Randall Weiss. 2000–01. "A Moving Target: Financing Medicare for the Future." *Inquiry* 37 (winter): 338–74.

Maxwell, Stephanie, Marilyn Moon, and Matthew Storeygard. 2001. *Reforming Medicare's Benefit Package: Impact on Beneficiary Expenditures.* New York: Commonwealth Fund (May).

11

Medicare Management and Governance

Sheila Burke

T HIS CHAPTER AIMS to do essentially four things. First, it describes the origins of the study, and what we are doing on this panel. Second, it will detail the timetable and composition of the panel to give you a sense of the people engaged in this work and what is intended to be produced. Third, it will air some of the issues that are being examined. It is a work in progress and we are anxious to be sure that we are, in fact, asking the right questions. Fourth, it will provide a sense of what we anticipate, given the fact that the country is in a transition from the Clinton to the Bush administrations. There are a number of new chairmen on both the House and Senate sides, and we are not yet certain as to where they are likely to go and how we should incorporate that into this process.

Origins of the Study

All four of the previous panels raised the issue of the management of the Medicare program as one of the greatest challenges facing the program in going forward both in its management and in its governance. That is true for both traditional fee-for-service Medicare, as well as for any kind of system of capitated or managed-care plans, either Medicare + Choice or some other competitive program that might be suggested by either party.

In looking at those issues and in looking at the reports, it becomes clear that issues of management and governance underlie many of the questions that have to be asked about the solvency of the program. A good summary of those challenges is contained in a report that William Scanlon prepared last spring for the General Accounting Office in which he examines Medicare management.[1]

---

1. Scanlon's report is based on testimony he presented before the Committee on Finance, U.S. Senate, "Medicare: 21st Century Challenges Prompt Fresh Thinking about Program's Administrative Structure" (General Accounting Office, 2000).

In brief, Medicare is an inherently difficult program to manage, regardless of its governance structure. Any entity administering a public program of Medicare's size and with its vast universe of stakeholders is going to be the target of affected parties that feel disadvantaged and harmed by the decisions that are made.

However, there are key problems that impair the ability of the Health Care Financing Administration (HCFA), now called the Centers for Medicare and Medicaid Services, to manage Medicare effectively, and they are, we believe, amenable to solutions. Currently, first, there is no one senior official in HCFA that is responsible for managing only Medicare. Instead, HCFA's administrator oversees Medicaid and a variety of other state-centered programs, worthy competitors for an agency's interest and concerns and management attention.

Second, there have been frequent changes in the agency leadership. The frequency with which the administrators of HCFA have changed and the relatively brief periods of time any one of them, in fact, have been in charge of the agency make it difficult to develop and implement a consistent long-term set of strategies and a long-term vision.

Third, the constraints on HCFA's ability to acquire appropriate resources and expertise have limited the agency's capability and capacity to modernize Medicare's existing operations and carry out the program's growing sense of responsibilities.

One of the issues we are contending with is that there have been additional responsibilities added to Medicare over time in terms of the breadth of the activities that they are asked to do. This continuous change further complicates things. Elements of recent Medicare reform proposals, together with alternatives for existing federal agencies, suggested that there are a variety of ways for administering the program.

Medicare faces a huge challenge. It accounts for more than $200 billion in spending in 2000, about 12 percent of the federal budget in fiscal 2001. It covers 40 million beneficiaries; it processes about 900 million claims on an annual basis submitted by nearly a million hospitals, physicians, or other providers. Its largest component remains the fee-for-service program, but the managed-care piece, which covers about 20 percent of the beneficiaries, is increasingly competing for attention. The difficulties with Medicare + Choice in recent years have suggested important issues about the management and the pricing of the program. All those things are the backdrop for what should be done to manage this extraordinarily large insurance program.

The Study Panel's Charge

There have been several proposals in recent years about the restructuring of Medicare that focused on the administrative activities of HCFA. There were a variety of proposals about whether to split it off and to create new agencies, a new bureau, and a new board.

Those proposals will certainly be at the core of some of the issues before the panel, which was established last summer to address these questions. Our intention is to release a report in the fall of 2001. The panel has thirteen members, who are politically and philosophically diverse. Some have been drawn from law and relevant industries; others are providers, former HCFA administrators, and former congressional staff. We are trying to listen to not only the intellectual interests but also essentially the players and the stakeholders who are going to have to live with the result of what ultimately occurs.

The final report will attempt to come to some consensus about what we want HCFA to do. The panel will identify issues that should be assigned to HCFA, or whatever the successor agency might be, as well as a range of policy alternatives. We may not come to closure and total agreement, but there is great value in laying out what the challenges, questions, and possible options are. What other models, for example, might be modified and might be put in place. Within its diversity the panel will attempt to make some recommendations among those options. Work will include discussion of issues at our meetings; conversations with invited guests, commissioned papers, with existing literature; and utilization of work that is out there.

Issues to be Explored

Papers on the problems of accountability and management that are facing Medicare's current structure of governance have been contracted. What is working? Why is that particular aspect of it working? A lot of time has been spent trying to establish a baseline against which to measure other alternatives.

Papers have been requested on the history of Medicare's administration. What was envisioned in 1965? What has transpired since then? What changes have been made? Technical papers have been commissioned on the contracting process, an issue that continues to be raised in terms of what stakeholders face, and on the activities to combat fraud, waste, and abuse. What kinds of expectations do we have about Medicare's procedures? We are analyzing examples of the different types of decisions that are made by HCFA in the course of carrying out its responsibilities.

What is the agency actually asked to do? What are the pluses and minuses of HCFA's current organizational structure? What are the alternative models? For example, are the Federal Reserve Board or the Federal Employees Health Benefits Program useful alternatives? What would be accomplished by making HCFA independent of the Department of Health and Human Services, as was done for the Social Security Administration?

The panel starts with no preconceived notions as to which of these options make sense. To whom should they be accountable in terms of Medicare within those structures? What should be the internal structure?

Should the same agency in charge of Medicare be in charge of Medicaid? One set of tensions in HCFA is the differing issues and challenges that face those two programs.

Should HCFA retain responsibility for the children's health insurance program, for the Health Insurance Portability and Accountability Act, for all the other additional activities that have been added in recent years, or do we just stand back at some point? What kind of research should HCFA do? Should it, in fact, be in the business of doing research or should it utilize the benefits of others' research?

Finally, the panel will look at issues such as coverage. There is a great push for people to be moved out of institutional settings, but there are questions about whether the services to support people outside of the hospital should be covered. Can HCFA respond to those kinds of questions? Is the agency facile enough to be able to deal with changing coverage issues in that environment and in a timely way?

The Policy Environment

Those are the kinds of questions that the panel is looking at. We aim to suggest options that Congress ought to consider, whether they need additional financial resources or not, and whether changes in administrative procedures could be made to make the program more efficient.

We are working in an environment in which work has been done and there is some history. There is some conversation in the public about these issues.

As I noted earlier, there are new chairmen on both the House and Senate sides. Senator Charles Grassley (R-Iowa) will obviously have strong views on this issue and has a history of interest in administrative issues, as was seen with the Internal Revenue Service. He has a strong commitment to rural areas and some of the challenges that rural areas face in the administration of this program.

The same is true of Senator Max Baucus (D-Mont.), who will also be new in that respect, although he has a long history with the committee and with the program and has views from a somewhat rural perspective.

On the House side we have in Representative Nancy Johnson (R-Conn.) someone who again has a strong interest in this program. Whether her views will be similar to those of Chairman Bill Thomas (R-Calif.) of Ways and Means remains to be discovered. Not knowing the base from which to start complicates things, but it also makes it easier. We start with a clean slate.

A forthcoming report on Medicare, governance, and management to be published by NASI will be timely in putting forward alternatives and actually give people something to work from. Individual papers will be prepared for release along the way. The final document will be released with public policy briefings. Meetings will be held with members on both sides of Capitol Hill. Essentially, we will try to provide something that, in fact, will be useful at the end of the day.

12

Medicare and Markets: The Need for a New Framework to Guide Reform

Mark Schlesinger

FORTY YEARS AGO, as the Medicare program was being considered, there was a clear consensus among policy leaders and the American public that, with respect to medical care, the situation for America's elders had become quite dire. There was also a consensus on an appropriate approach. The federal government's role was accepted to involve giving elders access to a sort of health insurance that was comparable to that available to working-age Americans. From that combined consensus was forged the Medicare program we have come to know (and half-heartedly love).

Today, forty years later, there is an equal and growing consensus that there are significant problems facing Medicare's beneficiaries with respect to their health care. Three core problems stand out. The first is inadequate financial security, induced by rapidly increasing health care costs that exceed the growth of elders' income. These costs are the combined product of copayment requirements and the various services, like prescription drugs, that are not covered by Medicare.

The second core problem involves quality of care. Medicare has failed to exercise its authority to improve the American health care system to deal with the issues of people with chronic illness. That is reflected in a variety of different contexts. We finance a hospital system that has inexcusable rates of dementia and other iatrogenic illnesses among the elderly. We pay for an outpatient treatment system that lacks even the most rudimentary geriatric orientation in its care. We have a health care system that depends on patient-

This chapter makes some bold statements about Medicare's performance and prospects for reform. These comments are not as yet the consensus of the study panel. The National Academy of Social Insurance does not in any way endorse these conclusions. These are my assessments of the future direction for the study panel and the real challenges that we face.

initiated treatment for a population in which many people lack the cognitive capacity or the physical mobility or emotional resources to initiate their own care.

The third pressing problem involves inequities in treatment, producing disparities in outcomes between rich and poor, well educated and less educated, and whites and racial minorities. These disparities are also reflected in terms of the sorts of care people receive and Medicare finances. We have a strong sense that the Medicare program, beloved as it is, important as it has been to the American people, is seriously deficient in these various ways.

There is an equally strong consensus, although in this case limited to pundits within the Beltway, as to the sort of solutions that ought to be pursued. This consensus was exemplified by the Balanced Budget Act of 1997. It embodies a belief that we ought to be introducing market principles to Medicare, once again making it more like the sort of insurance that is available currently to working-age Americans.

There is one important distinction between today's consensus and the consensus of the early 1960s. By any realistic assessment, there is no possible way that policymakers' preferred strategy for reform—introducing market mechanisms—can successfully deal with any of the three core problems facing Medicare beneficiaries. That being the case, it does not necessarily mean market-based mechanisms should not be further introduced to Medicare or existing arrangements further refined. There may be other good reasons for doing that in terms of program administration or finance. But we have to assess those reasons realistically and not be caught up in a set of illusionary promises that emerge from more ideological appeals for market reform.

The Charge to the Panel

The core mission of this panel is to provide a more grounded understanding of the potential for markets in Medicare. This is a very challenging mission, in part because the evidentiary base for market choice by elders remains incomplete and, in part, because the full implications of reform will not be realized for years, perhaps decades.

Because many past claims for and against markets have been based on ideological arguments, a balanced assessment will require considerable dispelling of illusions. We must make clear the need for a more nuanced appreciation of markets. An overly simplistic introduction of markets will most likely exacerbate many of the problems facing Medicare beneficiaries. Equally problematic, simplistic reforms may undermine the very attitudes and behaviors upon which efficient markets depend.

It is to this objective—to explain to policymakers in a clear, comprehensive, and balanced way what can and cannot be reasonably expected from market mechanisms—that this panel is directing its efforts.

Addressing Medicare's Core Problems

This section describes why the challenge has been posed in this way and illustrates with some examples how we might go about trying to accomplish that task. The three core problems are discussed sequentially.

Inadequate Financial Security

The first problem, the lack of adequate coverage and adequate financial security for Medicare beneficiaries, has been well documented by Marilyn Moon's recent evidence on the share of beneficiary income that goes to health care (see chapter 10). This was a problem that market proponents had hoped could be addressed in a variety of ways by allowing elders to choose among private health plans. They predicted that, by producing market-based competition, efficiency would be improved in the health care system. Plans facing competition to attract beneficiaries would expand their coverage in various ways, offering better protection than the core fee-for-service Medicare program provides.

At least initially, evidence suggested that market reforms were making real accomplishments on this front. Through the mid-1990s, as Medicare beneficiaries enrolled in managed-care plans, they often had better financial protection and lower copayment obligations. They reported on surveys considerably higher satisfaction with their financial protections than did beneficiaries in conventional Medicare.

A number of plans offered expanded benefit packages. These included, most notably, prescription drug coverage, which is available in about two-thirds of all the plans offering Medicare managed-care benefits.

Moreover, in those counties where managed care had been most actively introduced, it was found that the number of people who could afford some kind of supplementary coverage to their basic Medicare plan actually increased. The proportion of the population without any supplementary protection fell from about 17 percent in counties where there were not managed-care choice options to about 13 percent where there were.

More recently it has been discovered that the benefits that seemed to be emerging out of a choice-based system were either illusory or temporary. Temporary in the sense that, as the insurance cycle for profits has turned

downward, managed-care plans have dropped a lot of the supplementary benefits or implemented premium increases for the benefits they previously provided. Illusory in the sense that what had appeared to be better financial
protection for the elderly was often offset by utilization review requirements and
other managed-care techniques that essentially excluded any access to care. In
these cases, elders were forced to use services outside of planned auspices and
pay for that out of pocket or to disenroll from the plan entirely. Studies have
found that disenrollees from Medicare's managed-care plans had health care
expenditures ranging from 15 to 40 percent higher than otherwise comparable
fee-for-service populations. They had simply deferred spending and subsequently faced the copayment requirements for this deferred treatment.

Finally, and most important, it is essential to recognize that in the absence
of a broader set of core coverage in Medicare fee-for-service, plans will not be
under long-term pressure to sustain broader coverage. When private plans
offer a variety of benefits, it is often difficult for elders to choose among a set
of different plans. The inconsistent packages of benefits make it difficult for
them to decide which ones are actually good deals. The cost pressures that
emerge in those circumstances turn out to be relatively mild, providing little
incentive for more efficient delivery of medical care.

Quality of Care

The second problem concerns quality of care issues. Proponents of the
market had hoped by giving elders choices among plans and consistent
information about plan performance, beneficiaries would choose among plans
in ways that would weed out the ones that were not performing well and would
encourage innovation among the better plans.

Research on beneficiary choice among health plans finds little evidence of
quality-enhancing decisions. The most recent study suggests that no more than
about 10 percent of the Medicare population is actively pursuing information
about health care plan choices. Among those who do seek information, few
appear able to actually recognize relevant bits of information to identify high-
quality plans.

Even the most basic attributes that experts agree represent signals of a good
quality plan, including providing various kinds of health promotion services
that have been demonstrated in their efficacy for the elderly, have little impact
on elders' plan choices.

Most important, it should be recognized that the incentives in a managed
competition system to deal with people who are seriously and chronically ill
are not going to produce the kinds of market outcomes that are suitable for

Medicare beneficiaries. Indeed, paying health plans a fixed payment for each beneficiary creates an incredibly perverse set of incentives for health plans. Elders who are best able to assess the quality of the plan are those who have been sick and have used services. But these are the enrollees the plan least wants to keep, because they tend to be enrollees who have very large or extended health care costs. To avoid these higher future costs, the plan would benefit financially by *not* providing these elders with good care, so that they become dissatisfied and disenroll. In other words, the best informed elders can be expected to be treated the least well. This is hardly the formula for an efficiently operating market, let alone one that will promote high-quality, gerontologically oriented care

Disparities

The third problem involves inequities in health care use and health outcomes, by race and socioeconomic class. Because these disparities have long persisted in Medicare's fee-for-service program, markets seemed a promising alternative. If people are given choices among plans, then those who are being treated not as well, such as racial minorities and low-income groups, could get out of situations in which they faced discrimination. They could seek other plans that would be more responsive to their needs.

Once again, however, there is little evidence that these hopes have been realized. The limited research that has compared disparities in outcomes by race or class within Medicare manage care plans finds gaps as large or larger than those found in conventional Medicare. These are two factors that might account for these failed expectations.

The first factor involves access to information to help make informed choices among health plans. Studies of the knowledge that people have in making plan choices have found that it is consistently low-income people, low-educated people; people with the most serious health problems; and racial and ethnic minorities who have the least effective information about health plan choices.

That is not because they do not care. Disadvantaged beneficiaries are the ones who express the greatest need, the greatest desire to get that information. But they cannot figure out how to do it in large part because resources such as the Internet are beyond their financial abilities. Past research on health education suggests that public education campaigns will only exacerbate these disparities because they reach highly educated groups more effectively.

The second factor producing disparities involves interactions with health plan officials. Although there is relatively little evidence on this yet for the elderly population, studies for younger Americans suggest that enrollment in managed care is very likely to exacerbate disparities of outcomes between rich and poor, high- and low-educated racial minorities, and the white majority. Disadvantaged groups have a more difficult time negotiating the administrative requirements needed to get services under managed care arrangements.

Exacerbating the Problems

For all these reasons, the core problems facing Medicare beneficiaries do not make for the most persuasive rationale for pursuing market-oriented reforms. Equally important, if we pursue markets as the fundamental direction for Medicare reform, we run a serious risk of exacerbating the very problems that need to be addressed. This can happen in two ways. First, we may get distracted. We may become so concerned with the way markets are functioning that we do not look at the other ways that Medicare as a program can improve quality. For example, many past reports on market reforms in Medicare have gotten so caught up in the details of risk adjustment mechanisms and the like that they do not pay attention to whether beneficiaries are actually getting the care they need.

Medicare has developed some wonderful initiatives for improving the quality of managed care for the elderly. The Program for All-Inclusive Care for the Elderly initiative, known as PACE, is built on the On-Lok model from San Francisco and has had some wonderful results. But those results have come not by turning lose the market and letting plans innovate. The results come from targeted government investments to induce better quality care by providing guidance and a clear model for improved plan administration. These innovations depend on a directed approach to improving quality, not waving the market wand and expecting quality to magically emerge. They call for government to guide the market, not passively observe its performance.

The second risk involves the ways in which market reforms may subtly alter the goals for the program in ways that mask some of its current shortcomings. For example, as we move to the market model there is a serious risk that norms of fairness will be transformed to undermine concerns for disparities. When there is a single Medicare program, there is a strong expectation that it treat everyone equally. Rich and poor, black and white, all beneficiaries should be treated on equal terms by both the program and heath care providers.

In contrast, as more beneficiaries become enrolled in managed-care plans, the presumption of equal treatment and standards of equal outcome no longer become as powerful. Because people are choosing different plans and making their own choices, while plans are providing different benefit packages and mixes of services, it is no longer clear what equality should mean or how it should be applied. Under this scenario, disparate outcomes can be rationalized as a consequence of individual choice. It is noteworthy that as federal policymakers have debated the scope and slope of various market reforms since 1997, the issue of disparities has virtually disappeared from political discourse.

The Real Potential for Markets and Choice

Although it is important to recognize the limits and consequences of market reforms, markets may offer other administrative or fiscal benefits. Moreover, it should be emphasized that this does not mean we do not want to have markets in Medicare. Even if they cannot address the three core problems just described, we may well want to give elders and disabled beneficiaries choice. Choice can be empowering in its own right. Studies of working-age Americans find that people who are given choice are more satisfied with their health plan and more satisfied with their health care.

But if we are to realize the potential benefits of markets, we must do so in a manner that reflects the implications for beneficiary well-being. To do this, reforms must be sensitive to the important differences between the Medicare population and the working-age population. Three considerations need to be emphasized.

First, although choice may be empowering for some beneficiaries, evidence suggests it is not empowering for the majority of current beneficiaries. Many elders are scared about choice. They find it a source of insecurity rather than security. To protect their interests, we must preserve a fee-for-service program that beneficiaries can take for granted, trusting to provide good medical care. We need to have a Medicare program in which the most vulnerable, least informed people can say, "I'm going to stay with this program and I'm not going to worry about it. I'm not going to make a comparison to the managed-care system. I'm not going to have to worry about what plan I get." Beneficiaries deserve this option because the costs of decision making in and of themselves are high. Ensuring security requires that we offer elders the right not to choose.

That means that Medicare fee-for-service cannot be a backstop, backwater program for those who simply have not been smart enough to go into managed care. It is the program that will get the most insecure, least capable, most vulnerable, and sickest people. It has to be the best program, not the lowest common denominator. It has to be the market leader, not the market follower. The need for this leadership role has important implications for a variety of the issues that Sheila Burke has described as Medicare's administrative challenges (see chapter 11).

Second, a Medicare market system has to be designed in ways that create incentives for plans that are compatible with providing better quality care to chronically ill people. That may mean disenrollment penalties when people get dumped out of the plan. (That is, the plan that has been treating them might be expected to pay part of the cost of the care once they have been disenrolled.) It may require incentives for long-term contracting so that plans do not jump in and out of markets, disrupting continuity of care for elders. There are a variety of specific recommendations that can be identified. The essential feature is that the program has to be adapted to the particular health needs of the population that it serves, not made to mimic the practices of employers that are responsible for the health care of working-age Americans.

Third, if we are seeking markets as a way of providing greater empowerment for the elderly and disabled, then we have to also recognize that there are ways of empowering people other than having them switch plans. Better grievance mechanisms and better mechanisms of consumer voice can be provided to empower those who are unable or unwilling to switch among plans as a matter of choice. This is an important adjunct to the consumer protections that currently exist in the program.

Conclusion

The task of this panel is not easy. This report has to convey a different message to an audience, many of whom seek in markets an easy solution, a solution that has cost savings and avoids having the government make hard choices about the quality of care.

In fact, adding effective market-based systems in Medicare requires exactly the opposite—it calls for an expanded, proactive role for government. To make Medicare work well, fee-for-service benefits must be expanded to eliminate the disincentives for disenrollment of healthy enrollees. To make Medicare work well, the Centers for Medicare and Medicaid Services must have the administrative capacity to adequately monitor quality of care in these managed-care plans. This demands a more active and capable role for the program administration, not a less active one. That is not going to be an easy message to sell. It will produce a lot of cognitive dissidence among policy analysts. It will be a struggle to find the right language to convey this conclusion.

In many ways we face a situation like that noted by Francis Bacon centuries ago. Contemporary policy discourse is dominated by what he called the *idols of the market*—the images of market beliefs, not the reality of market performance. We somehow have to strip away that idolatry and put the discussion of markets and Medicare back on a basis of evidence and realistic predictions.

If policymakers endorse markets under those conditions, all well and good. If, in fact, they have been endorsing markets simply because they think they are getting a free lunch or, more disturbingly, because they are trying to divert attention from some of the more fundamental problems facing Medicare beneficiaries, then that has to be addressed clearly and frankly. It is not going to be an easy task, but it is a task this panel will relish undertaking.

13

Chronic Care
and Medicare

Gerard Anderson

THE CHRONIC CARE PANEL was formed when all four previous panels of the National Academy of Social Insurance (NASI) recognized that consideration of chronic care was not being given appropriate levels of attention in Medicare policy recommendations, and chronic care was not being given appropriate attention by the Centers for Medicare and Medicaid Services. The purpose of the NASI panel is to educate policymakers that Medicare is a program for persons with chronic conditions, although it does not know it. An intention of this panel is to increase awareness of the problems encountered by Medicare beneficiaries with chronic conditions.

This chapter explains the mandate of this panel and shows why caring for people with chronic conditions should be the major priority of the Medicare program.

A Focus on Acute Episodes, Not Ongoing Chronic Care

The Medicare program's focus has historically been acute episodes of care. When the program started in 1965, it was organized based upon a Blue Cross model for the under age sixty-five population. The Medicare program was not oriented to the needs of the elderly with chronic conditions in 1965, and it has become only slightly more oriented toward the elderly with chronic conditions in the last thirty-five years.

In terms of chronic care benefits, for example, the private sector has expended benefits to meet the needs of people with chronic conditions. Individuals insured by the private sector are much more likely to use prescription drugs and long-term care benefits than Medicare beneficiaries. The Medicare program, which is much more likely to represent people with chronic conditions, has not expended benefits for these services, while the private sector has.

There are a number of definitions of a chronic condition. How it is defined determines how many people have a chronic condition in the United States. One definition of a chronic condition is one that lasts, or is expected to last, a year or longer; limits what a person can do; and may require ongoing care. Using that definition, there are approximately 125 million persons in the United States with a chronic condition—almost half the U.S. population.

At Johns Hopkins University we have examined the percentage of the Medicare population with a chronic condition using the above definition. Physicians were asked to review ICD-9 codes to determine which are chronic and which are acute. The 1998 data for Medicare beneficiaries was examined, and it was found that only 18 percent of Medicare beneficiaries had no chronic disease. That group represented 1 percent of Medicare spending. Nineteen percent of Medicare beneficiaries had one chronic disease, and this group represented 4 percent of Medicare spending. People with two or more chronic diseases (in two different organ systems) represented 63 percent of the Medicare population, and they comprised 95 percent of Medicare spending. Medicare has become a program for people with multiple chronic conditions.

In terms of expenditures, the level of expenditures increases with the number of chronic conditions, disabilities, and functional limitations. If you are fortunate enough not to have a chronic disease, expenditures for Medicare covered services are less than $1,000. If you have at least one chronic disease, the expected cost is more than $6,000. If you have a chronic disease and a disability, the expected cost increases to $11,000. If you have a chronic disease, a disability, and a functional limitation, expected costs are more than $17,000 per person. Coinsurance and deductible amounts increase with Medicare expenditures, so Medicare beneficiaries with chronic conditions pay more out-of-pocket.

The Panel's Charge

The panel on chronic care and Medicare will explore how Medicare can ensure access to appropriate care for people with complex, chronic, and long-term health conditions and disabilities. This orientation would represent a fundamental change in how the Medicare program is organized.

The four previous panels focused on two issues that are important to people with chronic disease: *benefit design* and the *payment system*. All four panels essentially came to the same conclusion—the current Medicare benefit program is inadequate for people with chronic conditions. They identified four areas that this panel is going to address.

The first one is a broader set of benefits. The Medicare benefits package needs to recognize that Medicare really is a chronic disease program. Prescription drugs are an obvious need, but long-term care benefits are needed as well.

A survey of the Fortune 100 companies has been conducted at Johns Hopkins, and it was found that every one of those companies had a better benefit package than the Medicare program for people with chronic disease.

Cost sharing is a second problem for people with chronic conditions. The purpose of cost sharing is to discourage unnecessary utilization. Preventing unnecessary care is not the fundamental issue for people with chronic conditions because these individuals require more medical care. They pay higher amounts because they have more utilization, not because they abuse the system.

A third area is greater flexibility in disease management programs. Most disease management programs are not designed to deal with people with multiple chronic diseases. Most of the disease management programs are around a single chronic condition, such as diabetes or Alzheimer's. Most people in the Medicare program, however, have two or more chronic diseases. A different approach to disease management is needed for people with multiple chronic conditions.

A fourth area is payment. Many physicians are concerned that current payment systems do not encourage the provision of ongoing care or coordination of care. One endocrinologist, for example, has argued, "Anytime I take care of a diabetic and keep them healthy, I don't get paid very much money and the hospital and the medical system doesn't make any money. On the other hand, when something goes wrong, we make a lot of money. That just doesn't make sense." The Medicare payment system needs to be restructured to encourage more treatment for ongoing care.

Additional Concerns about Chronic Care and Coordinated Care

An area that was not raised by any of the previous four panels but is important to examine is the definition of medical necessity. Private insurance and the Medicare program pay for services when they believe a person will get better, and coverage stops when it is determined that the person will not improve. That makes a lot of sense for acute illness but not for chronic disease. The goal of chronic disease is to maintain a certain level of functioning or to slow the progression of chronic disease. A recent public opinion survey asked who is the most well-known person with chronic disease. It turns out to be Ronald Reagan, followed by Michael J. Fox. In either case, the purpose of their treatment regime is not to get well. Ronald Reagan is not going to be cured from Alzheimer's and Michael J. Fox is not going to be cured from Parkinson's. The goal is to keep them as healthy and functional as possible. However, physical therapy and other Medicare benefits stop when the doctor says the person is not going to improve. The interpretation of medical necessity needs to change if we are going to provide better care for Medicare beneficiaries with chronic conditions.

In terms of payment, there were five topics that the previous committees discussed. The first was bundling Medicare and Medicaid payments. Programs such as PACE and On-Lok, which combine medical and long-term care benefits, have not increased rapidly. More investigation is needed on why this has not happened and how the payment system may be slowing diffusion of such programs.

Another payment issue concerns carve-outs of specialized services, mental health, and a variety of things that are occurring in the private sector. This is something that the task force will examine. Supplemental insurance and risk adjusters are two other issues that impact coverage of chronic care that the task force should examine.

Coordination of care is a critical issue. It was not discussed by the previous panels. If you are a Medicare beneficiary with a chronic condition, you are probably going to see eight different physicians in the course of the year. Who is coordinating those eight different physicians? Is it the internist? Is it the geriatrician? Care is worse when clinicians do not talk to other clinicians about a patient's care. Unfortunately clinicians report, "We don't get paid for coordination of care." In the Medicare program, coordination of care is part of an evaluation and management fee. Because they are explicitly reimbursed for coordination of care many physicians argue, "We don't have the time to talk to the other seven physicians taking care of a particular patient."

Team approaches are key, but they are not encouraged by Medicare. Johns Hopkins had a geriatric assessment clinic, and it has gone out of business. It was clinically the right thing to do; all the clinical evidence suggests that geriatric assessment clinics assist people. But only one doctor can get paid for providing care at geriatric assessment clinics, not the whole team. Financially, many geriatric assessment clinics cannot be sustained.

People with multiple chronic conditions present very complex cases. Ronald Reagan recently broke his hip. It is harder for an orthopedic surgeon to take care of somebody who has a broken hip and Alzheimer's than it is to care for somebody who has just a broken hip. It takes longer and more expertise. Medicare does not make adjustment for those kinds of things, and physicians who specialize in Medicare beneficiaries with chronic disease suffer. So do their patients.

Public and Policymaker Concerns

In a survey of American policymakers in Washington, a very low level of awareness about chronic disease was found. The policymakers reported that the issue lacks focus and needs a framework for solutions. This issue of poor care for Medicare beneficiaries with chronic conditions needs to be made much more prominent to the American public. The NASI task force will, hopefully, address this need.

A national survey of the American public was conducted by Harris Interactive. It was found that the American public experiences chronic disease on a very personal basis. When a cross-section of Americans was asked if they suffer a chronic disease, 36 percent said that they have at least one chronic disease. When people who did not have a chronic disease were asked if they thought they were going to get one sometime during their life, two-thirds said yes.

There is a lot of personal concern about this issue. According to the survey, people believe the government should do more to take care of people with chronic disease. They know through their personal experiences as caregivers or as persons with a chronic disease that the government does not do enough. The surveys suggest that people are willing to pay higher taxes to get services that benefit people with chronic conditions.

The public recognizes that chronic conditions affect all ages, ethnic groups, and income levels. It is not something that affects just the poor or the elderly. Policymakers in Washington perceive that chronic disease is an issue primarily affecting the poor. Thus there is a very different perspective between what the policymakers think and what the American public thinks.

Conclusion

A core message from this panel could be "different conditions, common problems, and shared solutions." Alzheimer's, diabetes, and asthma present different clinical conditions. The scientists and the clinicians view them as very different conditions. The media reports them individually. However, when you talk to the people who have a chronic condition, whether they are children or seniors, they recognize that they have common problems. The problem is that the system is oriented to acute episodic not ongoing chronic care. The goal is to try to convince the American policymaking community that there are shared solutions. Shared solutions are policy and clinical initiatives that benefit a wide range of people with chronic conditions. This project will examine the Medicare program, a program where the majority of beneficiaries have multiple chronic conditions.

PART VII

Philanthropic Initiatives in Health Security

THE FINAL SESSION of the conference looked at some possibilities for extending health insurance coverage beyond Medicare and Medicaid through public policy. The session was designed to bring lessons from successful and not-as-successful experiences in local communities to those making national policy. Lauren LeRoy led the session and describes in chapter 14 how health foundations have moved into the public policy void to support community-based responses to those without health insurance.

Chapter 15 by Ruth Lyn Riedel describes San Diego County's partnership of private philanthropic dollars, business acumen, and countywide political organizing. Chapter 16 by Henrie Treadwell compiles lessons around the nation from the Community Voices programs for the uninsured that her foundation supports.

14

Health Foundations
Respond to the Uninsured

Lauren LeRoy

THIS CONFERENCE OF the National Academy of Social Insurance focused attention on the question of whether improvements in health security would come by incremental action or fundamental reform. The history of policy change related to access to care and insurance coverage, two components of health security, has been consistently incremental in nature. It has involved both the government at all levels and the private sector.

The problem of the uninsured seems to have remained intractable even with a number of recent policy, economic, and environmental conditions that would suggest that there could be improvements, including:

—rapid growth in the economy

—reduction in unemployment in recent years

—the slowing growth in healthcare costs

—restraint on health insurance premium growth until recently

—the enactment of the Health Insurance Portability and Accountability Act in 1996 and the State Children's Health Insurance Program (SCHIP) in 1997

—state activities to reform the insurance market, develop risk pools, and subsidize the cost of health insurance

These all would appear to be promising developments. At the same time, however, there have been declines in both Medicaid coverage and private nongroup coverage, along with declines in employer-sponsored coverage for higher-income employees.[1] These conditions have offset some of the progress the country might have made in reducing the uninsured population. The United States remains a nation with more than 40 million uninsured, having experienced only a modest dip of one percentage point in the rate of uninsurance during the prosperous year of 1999.[2] We find ourselves today looking into an

---

1. Holahan and Kim (2000, p. 188).
2. Fronstin (2000).

economic crystal ball that raises concerns about sustaining the strong economy and enduring renewed increases in health insurance premiums. There are also concerns that less favorable economic conditions might stimulate employers to take a harder look at the kind and generosity of coverage that they offer in the future.

Survey data indicate that there are serious misconceptions about the uninsured: who they are and why they do not have coverage.[3] Many do not know that most of the uninsured are working. In fact, eight of ten uninsured people work or are children whose parents work.[4] Many are also unaware that the uninsured are more likely to have health problems and that they are four times as likely as the insured to delay or forgo care.[5] The costs associated with being uninsured due to lost days at work or school, delaying care until problems become more serious and expensive to treat, and use of safety net providers are borne not only by the individual but by the entire society. And yet, many do not make the connection between individual experience and societal consequences.

Public misconceptions about the uninsured are also likely to mirror the misconceptions among at least some policymakers who have to vote on these issues but do not work on them on a daily basis. Those who seek to improve access and expand insurance coverage cannot neglect the importance of basic education on the issue of the uninsured. It is imprudent to assume that people truly understand the causes and dimensions of uninsurance simply because of the persistence of the problem.

In the absence of a comprehensive, national response to the millions of uninsured, the number of people with insurance coverage varies considerably across states and localities. Economic performance and the impact of welfare reform have varied across the different states and regions. The interplay of these factors, along with the public and private insurance options that are available in different geographic areas, has created an evolving profile of who has insurance coverage and what that coverage includes, both nationally and within different states.[6]

Most of the uninsured do receive medical care. Those without coverage still have some access to care, but they get it by paying out of pocket, going to safety-net providers, or obtaining primary care in more costly emergency room settings. It comes at a relatively high cost to them, given their incomes, and in ways that are ultimately inefficient and costly to the health system and to our society.

3. Henry J. Kaiser Family Foundation (2000).
4. Institute of Medicine (2000).
5. Alliance for Health Reform (2000a).
6. Zuckerman et al. (2001, p. 169).

Public debates on coverage for the uninsured make clear that there is little appetite among both policymakers and many taxpayers for a comprehensive single national plan. Yet there are a number of incremental national and state approaches that are being put forth as potentially credible options for further policy change. They include such policies as expanding SCHIP and Medicaid to currently ineligible populations, providing tax credits for purchasing private insurance, subsidizing primary care safety-net providers, creating pooling mechanisms for small businesses to join together to purchase health insurance at more favorable group rates, implementing employer mandates, and opening up Medicare to those under the age of sixty-five, for a few examples.[7]

Preferences of the new Bush administration were expressed on the campaign trail, including such options as tax credits and pooling mechanisms for small businesses.[8] There are clearly different views about what are the appropriate next steps among various members of Congress. One thing to be sure of in these early days of a new Congress and a new administration is that there is no clear consensus among policymakers or taxpayers regarding what would be preferable or feasible in this area.

As the problems of the uninsured have grown, local actions to address those problems have also grown. The human cost of being uninsured is witnessed most palpably at the local level, and communities do not have the choice of ignoring the issue. They cannot wait. They have to do something to respond to their local circumstances. There are hundreds of community coalitions working to improve access and coverage in the country today.[9]

A number of community organizations focus their work on a particular aspect of this issue for a specific constituency. For example, health centers may structure and carry out special programs to address particularly neglected problems, such as mental or oral health. Churches and other faith-based organizations play a key role in both serving their congregations and offering community programs. Organizations serving different racial and ethnic groups also are actively involved. Foundations play a critical role in supporting these kinds of activities and organizations. They also design their own initiatives to increase access and coverage, particularly for such vulnerable populations as children, the working poor, people from different racial and ethnic minorities, immigrants, and residents in underserved rural areas.

Local efforts around the country, which often draw on foundation support, provide laboratories from which policymakers can learn as they shape federal

---

7. Alliance for Health Reform (2000b).

8. "George W. Bush on Health Care" (www.issues2000.org/george_w_bush_health_care.htm [January 7, 2001]).

9. The Access Project (1999).

and state policies. They provide examples of what works and what does not, and why. From the array of community programs, common themes regarding both needs and effective strategies often emerge that can inform policy development. Grassroots efforts can also pinpoint implementation problems that well-designed policies can seek to mitigate. Local programs also provide lessons about where government involvement is essential because of the resources needed, the regulatory framework required, or the accountability and expertise that the government can contribute. Community interventions offer examples of how to bring together different stakeholders who need to be part of the mix in order to make progress in covering the uninsured. The ways communities respond to the needs of their uninsured populations may give policymakers a new perspective on what taxpayers will support when they come face to face with these issues and they can see the results of their collective response in their own communities. Effective programs that improve coverage and access can have a real impact on people's attitudes toward what they are willing to pay for.

In many cases, foundations and the community organizations that they work through are not experimenting. They are working strategically to address a serious problem. When policymakers look at their experiences, they can view those initiatives as learning laboratories for state and federal policy.

Health philanthropy can play a key role in both facilitating and supporting community initiatives. Those not familiar with philanthropy may think of foundations as being similar to one another when, in fact, the field is extremely diverse in its resources and capabilities, its geographic foci, the priorities that foundations pursue, and the strategies grant makers use to advance their mission. Many also tend to assume that foundations are solely grant makers, but they actually play a number of other extremely important roles. Their role as a neutral convener is particularly important. Health foundations also are coalition builders. They conduct and support research, needs assessments, and public surveys that provide the underpinning for program development. They serve as information brokers. They play key roles in public education and informing policy development. There are also many legitimate and legal forms of advocacy that foundations can engage in. It is important to recognize this vital role, which is often overlooked.

Foundations also provide technical assistance to community groups, nonprofit organizations, and government. They pilot innovative approaches to improving health and health care, and they move agendas by collaborating with government both formally and informally. Each foundation determines the appropriate mix of these different strategies and the type of actions that it feels it is best positioned to pursue. Each one finds its own niche. It is not possible to make assumptions about the entire field after getting to know just one or two foundations.

The Grantmakers In Health database on health grant making provides evidence of the extensive interest among health foundations in access and insurance coverage. There are foundations throughout the country working on these issues. Even among the sample of programs contained in the database, there are more than 100 foundations that have been involved in SCHIP outreach, for example.

The specific approaches that foundations have adopted to improve access or expand insurance coverage include efforts to improve the delivery system by both providing better access to existing providers and trying to improve the availability of providers in areas where their numbers are insufficient. Foundation programs support research and policy analysis, train community organizations to mobilize and inform the policy process, support local coalition building to design programs and change policies, educate consumers, support government efforts to understand the issues and develop policy solutions, and both extend coverage and ensure that those eligible for public programs are enrolled.

There are many examples of foundation-supported activities to choose from. Some are national in scope, and many are locally focused. Among the national initiatives is the Robert Wood Johnson Foundation's "Communities in Charge," which supports community planning, design, and implementation of new systems of financing and delivering care to the uninsured. The W. K. Kellogg Foundation's "Community Voices: Health Care for the Underserved" supports community-based, collaborative efforts to reduce the number of uninsured people through such actions as developing systems of care, enhancing outreach to increase enrollment in public programs, and educating policymakers and the public. The Alliance Healthcare Foundation, Consumer Health Foundation, and the Rhode Island Foundation are among those focused at the state and local level that have made systemic change to expand coverage a priority.

Foundation support can make it possible to extend insurance coverage to vulnerable groups that are ineligible for public insurance programs. For example, the Riordan/CaliforniaKids Project of the California HealthCare Foundation subsidizes health insurance for children who are ineligible for public coverage due to income or immigration status. There are some exciting models from both national and local foundations of newly created programs to cover segments of the uninsured through partnerships with government. With foundation support for currently ineligible populations, these partnerships have the advantage of providing coverage for additional vulnerable populations within the framework of existing public programs.

There are foundations that are committed to enhancing the public's understanding of the issues and potential solutions related to insurance coverage, including the Commonwealth Fund, with its task force on health insurance for working families; the Henry J. Kaiser Family Foundation's Commission on Medicaid and the Uninsured; and the California HealthCare Foundation, which supports research to understand the characteristics of different groups comprising the uninsured and to develop model programs targeted to meet the specific needs and characteristics of those different groups. The Robert Wood Johnson Foundation also recently provided funding for a three-year study that the Institute of Medicine in Washington, D.C., has begun to assess the health, economic, and social consequences of being uninsured and to raise public awareness and understanding of those issues. The David and Lucile Packard Foundation has joined with the federal Agency for Healthcare Research and Quality to support research that will inform the future design of health insurance and health services delivery systems for low-income children.

Foundations can be innovators. They can support innovators. They can be partners in implementation, research, and policy design. The programs they undertake and support are impressive, but what ultimately can be expected from their contributions should be viewed with a note of caution: it is important to remember that foundation resources pale by comparison to public resources. The potential role of health philanthropy in solving a problem of the magnitude of today's uninsured must be kept in perspective.

There are hundreds of local initiatives. Many of those programs and the local foundations that support them, however, turn to national foundations or government for partnerships because they do not have the resources to sustain the different kinds of programs that they help put in place. At the same time, the activities that are being undertaken in communities all around the country and supported by foundations are evidence of local capacity to play a significant role. They also bring the gaps that government needs to fill into focus; these gaps require a broader policy response.

What policymakers can learn from local initiatives may define the terms for sharing responsibility, locally and nationally, and between the public and private sectors. Much can be gained from a closer look at these experiments and programs around the country. Let us not lose the opportunity to take those lessons and make health insurance coverage a reality for all who need it.

References

Access Project. 1999. *Action Where It Counts: Communities Responding to the Challenge of Health Care for the Uninsured.* Boston: Access Project (June).

Alliance for Health Reform. 2000a. "How Much Does Insurance Matter?" Washington (May).

———. 2000b. "Closing the Gap: State and Local Efforts to Cover the Uninsured." Washington (November).

Fronstin, Paul. 2000. Testimony before the Health, Education, Labor and Pensions Committee hearing on Health Insurance Coverage and Uninsured Americans, U.S. Senate. Washington: Employee Benefit Research Institute (October 4).

Henry J. Kaiser Family Foundation. 2000. *"NewsHour* with Jim Lehrer/Kaiser Family Foundation National Survey on the Uninsured." Publication 3013. Washington (April).

Holahan, John, and Johnny Kim. 2000. "Why Does the Number of Uninsured Americans Continue to Grow?" *Health Affairs* 19 (July/August): 188.

Institute of Medicine. 2000. "The Consequences of Uninsurance." Washington.

Zuckerman, Stephen, and others. 2001. "Shifting Health Insurance Coverage, 1997–1999." *Health Affairs* 20 (January/February): 169.

15

The San Diego County
Health Coverage Initiative

Ruth Riedel

T HE EXPERIENCE OF our philanthropy—the Alliance
Healthcare Foundation—is one of incremental action in
one region of the country: San Diego, California. The county's population is
2.9 million, of which an estimated 22 percent—more than 638,000 individuals—are uninsured.

The foundation's goal in this advocacy campaign has been to increase
access to health care by increasing health insurance coverage. We want to
reach the uninsured, whether they are working or not. We want to find out
whether employers are interested in commercial low-end insurance products in
which they and their employees may participate. In addition, we are interested
in documenting the eligibility of uninsured individuals for public benefits that
they are not receiving.

At least four groups had to be won over to achieve this goal. A major
obstacle in this work has been the apathy of the county board of supervisors, a
long-standing problem in this local health care system, especially in public
health. We also have a hostile and creaky public benefits enrollment system in
the county. Eligibility workers have been incentivized for various reasons for
nearly twenty years not to enroll people in Medi-Cal or other programs, even
though they are eligible. The voters were uninformed and did not know about
the uninsured issues, and community leaders are similarly uneducated. We
knew that educating these key groups would be an important part of our job in
increasing health insurance coverage.

We convened a countywide coalition called San Diegans for Health Coverage, a multisectorial collaborative to energize and promote our proposed
solutions. The coalition supports and enables legislation in a number of ways.
Proposed legislation will fund a business health-access resource center, called
the Business Health Connection. In addition, the collaborative is lobbying for
a substate 1115 Medi-Cal demonstration waiver.

The Alliance Healthcare Foundation has supported the development of this waiver through research providing accurate data to inform the debate, enriching the process for determining solutions that are expected to result from the implementation of the waiver. In addition, some of our staff members who are experts in managed care were assigned to this work and have promoted the waiver actively, along with other solutions, in a media campaign.

Our successes in the last few years include the design and implementation of a low-cost health insurance product for the working uninsured, and subsequent subsidization. We have reached out to many participants from different sectors of the community, such as the Business Health Connection and Medi-Cail demonstration 1115 waiver, and have generated options for financing this product or similar products.

We reached out to a nonpartisan team of eight legislators who are currently championing the issue of the uninsured. These legislators are well informed and are asking for more information from us and from other people in the region and statewide. They are drafting bills on their own and vying to cosign legislation to move the health insurance coverage agenda forward. This has been an exciting development over the last year, as all but one of our elected officials are actively involved.

The Context for the Initiative

The Alliance Healthcare Foundation was established in 1988 and has become the county's largest health foundation. We provide grant making, advocacy, and public education on San Diego's critical public health issues. Our priorities include the uninsured, substance abuse, communicable diseases, mental health, and environmental and community health issues.

Our work is a central influence on the development of a public health agenda in San Diego. San Diego as a region has the second highest uninsured rate in the state despite the lowest unemployment rate in forty years. Only Los Angeles County has a higher proportion of its population without health insurance. Overall the uninsured rate in California has not declined significantly even with the economic boom of the last five years.

More than 30 percent of the estimated 638,000 San Diegans without health insurance are eligible for public benefits but are not enrolled. Creaky methods and procedures, such as a twenty-three-page application form, the need for reenrollment in some of the programs every thirty days, and the relative indignities of the enrollment system discourage many people from trying to use it effectively.

Another 80,000 of the uninsured are employed adults with incomes below 200 percent of the federal poverty level. In California they are not eligible for public benefits. The remaining working uninsured have incomes above 200 percent of federal poverty. We surveyed them, and 64 percent responded that they simply could not afford commercial health insurance products. Eight percent—mostly the "immortal" young men—said that they were not interested because they did not believe they needed health insurance. The remaining uninsured individuals are either between jobs or trying to transition from welfare to work.

San Diego's cost of living is 24 percent above the national average, which makes it difficult for low-wage workers and their families. The housing market generates a significant part of the high cost of living. Currently the average price of a single-family, detached home in San Diego is above $330,000, and low-wage workers cannot afford adequate housing. Food expenditures for San Diegans are about 20 percent higher than in East Coast cities, and the electricity, gasoline, and natural gas prices are exploding. These high costs impact the ability of all San Diegans to afford health insurance. A summary of critical issues affecting the San Diego area appears in box 15-1.

Creating Low-Cost Health Insurance

The Financially Obtainable Coverage for Uninsured San Diegans (FOCUS) product, which provides low-cost insurance for working uninsured individuals and their dependents, was created through our partnership with Sharp HealthCare, one of San Diego's largest health care systems. Ninety-five percent of the businesses in San Diego are small businesses. We received crucial support from the San Diego Regional Chamber of Commerce, the leading business organization in town. They assisted in market research and helped market the FOCUS product.

Local brokers assisted in marketing by offering the FOCUS product at no charge in their ordinary books of business. We received free media coverage, especially broadcast media, TV, and radio, in the promotion of the FOCUS product. All this voluntary help in marketing the product caused it to sell out very quickly.

The FOCUS product has no deductibles and no lifetime maximums. The copayments are very low: $5 for a routine service and $50 for emergency care. Copays are much lower than other products in our region. At this time, mental health and chemical dependency services are included, although dental health is not.

The Alliance Healthcare Foundation subsidizes 50 percent of the premium, which is about $150 per member per month. Employers pay approximately 25

Box 15-1. *San Diego: The Regional Perspective*

The following is a summary of the critical issues affecting the San Diego region:

— Despite the lowest unemployment rate in forty years, 22 percent of San Diegans have no health insurance.

— San Diego County has the second highest uninsured rate in California, after Los Angeles County, with 638,000 uninsured persons.

— As many as 210,000 (117,000 children and 92,000 parents) are eligible for but not enrolled in public programs, which employ antiquated administrative procedures and are paranoid about fraud and abuse.

— The region includes 78,000 working adults with incomes below 200 percent of the federal poverty level, who are still not eligible for public benefits.

— The remaining 313,000 working adults have incomes above 200 percent of the federal poverty level; 64 percent report they cannot afford health coverage.

— The persistently high rate of uninsured in California is alarming given the low rate of unemployment and the booming economy; there was only a 2.1 percent decline in the uninsured rate statewide in 1998–99 (versus a 5 percent expected decline).[1]

— Statewide and in San Diego, employers cite high cost as the reason for not offering benefits.

— With the average price of a single-family, detached home reaching $330,500 in October 2000, the cost of living in San Diego is 24 percent higher than the national average—a strain on low-wage workers.

— Of 638,000 uninsured San Diegans, 150,000 are children.

— Of all adults, 84 percent work or are in working families, and nearly all uninsured workers are employed by small businesses (that is, fifty or fewer employees).

— Over-represented in the unemployment statistics are young adult men; single parents who are women; those between jobs; and those in transition from welfare to work.

— The county supervisors have just recently recognized health as a critical problem.

1. Todd Gilmer and Richard Kronick, *New Data Shows 6.8 Million Uninsured Californians* (University of California, San Diego, 2000).

percent of the premium, and the rest is borne by the employees who pay, depending on family annual income and family size, between $24 and $49 per month.

National health economist Richard Kronick and his colleagues at the University of California San Diego are conducting the evaluation, funded mostly by the California HealthCare Foundation. The early evaluation results are positive, showing that only one business had dropped out. A surprise in implementing this product was that 50 percent of the families who chose to enroll in FOCUS were below 150 percent of the federal poverty level. It was discovered through evaluation research that many of these families were eligible for public benefits, but they believe that FOCUS is an easier and more dignified alternative.

Sparking Business Interest

The FOCUS product has generated a lot of interest in the business community and among legislators. The Alliance provided staff and technical assistance to set up the Business Connection, a business health resource center for small employers who need to know more about commercial products and other potential benefit programs available for their employees. The center was set up to assist employers with accurate information and give them assistance, administrative support, and guidance. Many of these small employers are "mom-and-pop" shops that feel overwhelmed by the administrative aspects of commercial products. The center can assist them to enroll employees who are eligible for public benefits or those for whom they would like to help pay for health insurance. Enrollment can be done on the job site by community outreach workers.

Publicizing the Initiative

The Alliance Healthcare Foundation's media campaign was the core of informing and educating San Diegans and business leaders about the uninsured problem. A nationally known public affairs company, Burson Marsteller, was engaged to work with us to design an effective media campaign, because we did not have that expertise in-house. The public affairs group designed a straightforward print and broadcast media campaign that included speaking engagements, radio shows, media kits, news releases, feature stories, by-lined articles, and features on our foundation website.

The campaign was launched in September 1999 with a documentary that was essentially underwritten by two local television channels and shown eight times in the region. The first showing included a phone bank to direct people to potential sources of help and fielded more than 1,000 calls. The campaign also included one-page ads in the local subscriptions of three magazines: *Time, Newsweek,* and *U.S. News and World Report.*

The San Diegans for Health Coverage coalition was first convened in October 1999. It has been the energy behind our strategy. The business community comprises one-third of the coalition and the remainder includes faith-based and community organizations, community clinics, hospitals, health systems, county government, the San Diego Regional and Hispanic Chambers of Commerce, and the Vietnamese Foundation.

A speakers bureau made up of a group of San Diegans in the coalition and "key influencers" kept this issue on the front burner with the California legislators. Two public opinion polls were commissioned, one of 1,000 high propensity voters and a second of community leaders. Another forty high-profile business leaders were added to the advocacy group during the second poll. The first poll showed that 68 percent of our voters were willing to pay another $35 in taxes a year to create a fund to subsidize health insurance coverage for the working uninsured.

Political Support for Continuing and the Medi-Cal Demonstration Waiver

The demonstration waiver, if approved, would provide the opportunity for another 170,000 people to enroll in public programs. Subsidy dollars for lower cost commercial products would be provided to the Business Health Connection through state legislation, as a part of the Medi-Cal demonstration waiver to assist small employers to cover low-wage workers with existing commercial products like Sharp HealthCare's FOCUS. The county supervisors have just recently recognized the problem of the uninsured as critical. (They had made no significant allocations to health until the previous summer, when $65 million of tobacco tax money was committed to match the state's contribution to the 1115 Medi-Cal demonstration waiver for five years.) All but one of San Diego's legislators cosigned a bill to support the center. The uninsured problem is one of the few things they could agree on as a nonpartisan team. The critical element in all this work has been the strong support and involvement of San Diego County's business leaders.

16

Community Voices: Health Care for the Underserved

Henrie M. Treadwell

THE W. K. KELLOGG FOUNDATION is honored to be included in discussion of the future of social insurance. We can contribute the idea that, for some vulnerable groups, the central question is not whether reform is fundamental or incremental. Both types of reform may fail them. Thus a variation on the theme might be: Incremental action or fundamental reform: Will either be enough? Lack of health insurance threatens life, livelihood, quality of life (namely early morbidity), income earning potential and financial stability, the ability to save for retirement, and the ability to live long enough to collect Social Security and deferred savings. Social insurance is predicated on designing a system that protects from birth to the end of life.

Philanthropy can "remind" the public and private sectors of another America, where people are not adequately mainstreamed to enable them to benefit from their labors and contributions to the economy and tax base. Social insurance does not provide adequate health-care protection for millions of people in America who are either uninsured, underinsured, or underserved.

The reminder for those with this awareness is that the unprotected are *not* an undifferentiated mass. They belong to subgroups with distinctive characteristics that affect—and, indeed, determine—whether, how, and with what services they must be reached and served. The full panoply of these groups of underserved and uninsured people and their characteristics must be kept in the forefront of the awareness of policymakers and experts on social insurance whenever they think about design, organization, financing, and delivery of health care services.

Design, organization, and *delivery* have been included along with *financing* because those committed to health security must also be aware that financing alone is not enough. Financing for coverage creates the possibility of financial access. It is totally necessary, but it is far from totally sufficient. It does not

278

make people aware of or enroll them in coverage for which they qualify. It does not remove the fear and perceived stigma that turn people away from enrolling. It does not lower nonfinancial barriers to access by meeting needs for translation, transportation, and child care. It does not make services appropriate for people belonging to diverse, nonmainstream cultures, thereby increasing the chances that they will seek care. It does not shift the focus of services away from budget-breaking, tertiary sickness care to primary care, broad-based prevention, and facilitated self-management of chronic conditions. And it does not fill significant gaps in covered benefits, especially oral and mental health services and pharmaceuticals.

We cannot as a nation expect to fill gaps in any type of insurance simply by educating people better, as America will always have low-wage workers—the U.S. economy expects and demands this cadre, structurally. The solution to adequate social insurance lies, therefore in protecting *all* people—not just "people like us"—from the temporal and lifelong costs associated with preserving health. The initiative discussed here seeks to serve those at risk of being overlooked by analysts, actuaries, insurance experts, and decisionmakers as they craft health and social policy intended for all America. The initiative is Community Voices: HealthCare for the Underserved—A National Demonstration of Local Visionary Models.[1] It comprises thirteen communities in eleven states that serve as learning laboratories to demonstrate viable options for achieving four broad outcomes:

—sustained increase in access to health services for the underserved

—preserved and strengthened safety net

—stronger services-delivery system with a focus on primary care and prevention

—established models of best practices

The Kellogg Foundation has invested $55 million over five years, a time that may be sufficient to demonstrate at least efficacy, if not sustainability, in view of volatile market forces. One intent is to solve problems in communities—since communities can wait no longer for the nation to choose between fundamental reform and incremental action. Another intent is to fill the information gaps and potentially inform public will and action.

The Kellogg Foundation does not prescribe target underserved populations or strategies; these are the province of the grantees. We expect only that access to comprehensive, integrated primary care that includes oral and mental health services be achieved.

---

1. Materials on the initiative are available at www.communityvoices.org.

Community Voices projects use many strategies to implement three basic approaches. First, by enrolling eligible people in public programs, they are increasing both individuals' financial access to care and safety-net institutions' cash flows. Second, by creating insurance products or health plans for small businesses, low-income workers, and others they are compensating for a shortage of available, affordable coverage in the marketplace. Third, by strengthening the delivery system, they are seeking to support health by filling unmet need and focusing on prevention and primary care. They provide new services (such as oral health care and case management) and more accessible sites of service (such as school-based health centers).

The strategies that each Community Voices learning laboratory implements vary, but involve generally:

—outreach using community health workers to increase enrollment in all available payment programs and connect people with the health system

—case management

—coverage for immigrants

—development of managed care plans (or organized systems of care)

—development of simplified enrollment forms for Medicaid and the State Children's Health Insurance Program (SCHIP)

—work with departments of social services to expedite the processing of applications and problem-solving around denied applications

—special services for difficult-to-reach populations (for example, poor men of color)

—oral health care service initiation

—mental health service initiation

—funding stream analysis

—exploration of ways to provide coverage for the working poor who are employed by small businesses

Several striking innovations are also being pursued, such as exploration of development of a novel way to determine eligibility for public coverage using income tax filings.

A revisit to the history of social and health policy may be instructive to indicate achievements to date and the path yet to be traveled. The Social Security Act, passed in 1935, established a federal role in social welfare and income security. Although intended to create a broader safety net for society's vulnerable populations, the act was passed only when provisions for a minimum level of family subsistence and comprehensive national health insurance were eliminated. As a result, the Social Security Act created a dual system for federally supported income maintenance, which assigned poor children, and therefore their mothers (not their fathers, too) to largely unpopular and financially precarious assistance programs.

It is important to remind all of us of where we are, and of how far we have yet to travel, if we are to provide social insurance for all of America. A recent Census Bureau report provides the following information:

—Both the number and percentage of uninsured poor remained unchanged from 1998.

—Young adults (eighteen to twenty-four years old) remained the least likely of any age group to have health insurance coverage.

—The proportion of people without health insurance ranged from 24.1 percent for those in households with annual incomes of less than $25,000 to 8.3 percent for those in households with incomes of $75,000 or more.

—The proportion without health insurance was higher for Hispanics (33.4 percent) than for non-Hispanic whites (11.0 percent). The noncoverage rate for African Americans was 21.2 percent, not statistically different from the 20.8 percent for Asians and Pacific Islanders.

—Based on a three-year average, 27.1 percent of American Indians and Alaska Natives were uninsured.

—The foreign-born population was more likely than the native population to be uninsured (33.4 percent versus 13.5 percent).[2]

The focal points for action by Community Voices have been determined by analysis and experience with respect to the uninsured, who are described by these numbers, but also with respect to underserved people who may have coverage or receive limited care without coverage. Community Voices addresses what vulnerable people need in order to have access to comprehensive, integrated primary health-care services.

Immigrants

The numbers on uninsurance often do not include the numbers of immigrants living and working to the benefit of the U.S. economy, without the benefit of adequate (or any) health insurance coverage for themselves or their families. Serving immigrants is a vital function of a number of Community Voices projects. The following are a few telling stories about the needs and circumstances of immigrants and what seeking to serve them entails.

2. U.S. Census Bureau (2000).

Interventions

The Oakland Community Voices project is a partnership of Asian Health Services and La Clinica de la Raza and serves many immigrants. The data resources in the area that can be used to count and profile populations of interest are fairly extensive, and the project is augmenting data with a special survey. Nonetheless, the project director was able to construct, with comparative ease, a hypothetical family that would be missed by both routine data collection and the survey. The fragmented structure of both families and social insurance programs in the United States already means that a single determination of status and eligibility often cannot be made for a single family unit; each member's status and eligibility must be determined separately. Immigration adds to the complexity. In the hypothetical uncountable family, each member has a different status.

In El Paso, the challenge of reaching pregnant teens early with prenatal care is complicated by the fact that a girl may live in Juarez and only cross the border to deliver. Meanwhile, insured U.S. citizens cross into Mexico to buy prescription drugs for less than their copayments would be at home.

The rural North Carolina project has a program for immigrant children whom state policy disqualifies for SCHIP. One family referred to the plan had fled Mexico when a child was kidnapped and raped. Only the child born in the United States was eligible for Medicaid, but this was to be terminated because the father, who was working under an assumed name, could not show proof of income. The other children had severe untreated problems.

The Florida Health Insurance Survey equates "black" with "African American," thereby vastly diminishing its utility for the Community Voices project in Miami, which is a major entry point for immigrants from Latin America and the Caribbean. The work in northern Manhattan, which is home to both African Americans and African-heritage Caribbean immigrants, encounters the issues both of counting subgroups and of competing subgroups.

Oral Health Care

One-third of elderly adults have no teeth, while more than 85 million out of 218 million U.S. adults over eighteen years of age have no dental insurance.[3] In the next half-century, the number of men and women over sixty-five is projected to increase by 126 percent. In addition, African Americans, Hispanics, and Native Americans generally have the poorest oral health of all ethnic groups in the United States (see figure 16-1). While most of the affected are

3. U.S. Department of Health and Human Services (2000).

Figure 16-1. *Untreated Decayed Teeth, by Race*

Percent

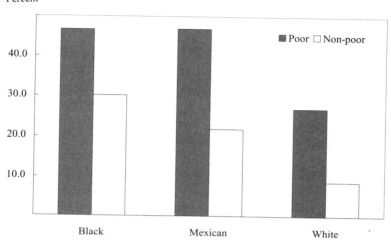

Source: Third National Health Examination and Nutrition Survey, NHANES III, 1988–94.

poor, there are many indications that even when people of color have insurance (Medicaid or others), they still lack access to care. The issue has implications for social practices and stereotyping issues that imply need for culturally aware providers and cultural competence.[4]

States have the option of providing dental coverage through Medicaid for adults. And while most states cover emergency services, fewer states cover preventive or restorative care. Medicare only covers dental services needed by hospitalized patients with specific conditions.

Interventions

All Community Voices sites must improve access to oral health care. Following are some specific examples:

—Northern Manhattan Collaborative: community- and school-based oral health care, with mobile vans to schools but no stationary infrastructure

—Northern Manhattan Collaborative: Mannie L. Wilson Health Center for the Elderly

—FirstHealth of North Carolina: provides school-based health services for children and three dental clinics

4. General Accounting Office (2000).

—West Virginia: reallocates Temporary Assistance for Needy Families dollars to provide care for custodial parents (mainly women) who are transitioning from welfare to work

—Alameda Health Plan: coverage for oral health care regardless of immigration status

—New Mexico: hired the first dentist (using Community Voices and Department of Public Health funds) to initiate services to the poor and underserved

—Baltimore (Sandtown-Winchester): established a men's health clinic that provides complete dental/oral health services, as well as provides sealants to all children in the second grade in the public schools, through a partnership with the University of Maryland

—Voices of Detroit: formed a partnership between university, city public health department, public health department, and hospital services (using Community Voices and the Federal Community Access Program funds) to initiate comprehensive services for adults and children

Mental Health Care

The Mental Health Parity Act of 1996 imposed new federal standards on mental health coverage offered under most employer-sponsored group health plans. However, the law does not affect employers who do not offer mental health coverage, and employers are also exempt if the law would result in excessive costs to them. Current research suggests that because of its narrow scope and reduction in mental health benefits that employers have made to offset the required enhancements, compliance with the Mental Health Parity Act may have little effect on employees' access to mental health services.[5]

Facts concerning the state of mental health coverage follow:

—Less than one-third of adults with a diagnosable mental health disorder receive treatment.

—Approximately 70 percent of children and adolescents in need of treatment do not receive mental health services.

—Ethnic minorities face both linguistic and cultural barriers to care.

—Rural populations face additional obstacles with the scarcity of providers in rural areas.

—The indirect cost of mental illness imposed approximately a $79 billion loss on the U.S. economy in 1990, with $63 billion in morbidity costs (loss of productivity due to disease), $12 billion in morbidity (loss due to death), and

5. Pascula and Sturm (2000).

Figure 16-2. *Estimates of Population Ratios for Clinically Trained Personnel*

Number/100,000

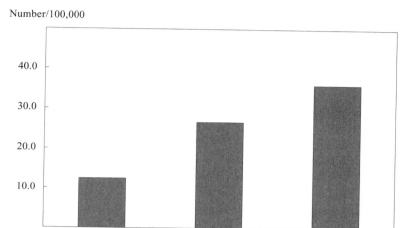

Source: Ivey and others (1998).
a. 1995.
b. 1996.

almost $4 billion in the productivity losses of incarcerated individuals and the caretakers of individuals with mental illness.

—In a recent survey regarding the causes of mental illness, 71 percent of the respondents believed that mental illness is caused by emotional weaknesses; 65 percent believed that mental illness is caused by bad parenting; 35 percent believed that mental illness is caused by sinful or immoral behavior; and 43 percent believed that mental health is in some way caused by the individual.[6]

—Studies indicate that people with mental disorders are at least twice as likely to abuse alcohol and other drugs as people with no mental disorder.

—The number of providers is very limited (see figure 16-2).

—Stigma perpetuated by popular culture and sensationalization in the press has disastrous consequences.

Interventions

New Mexico Community Voices and its sponsor, the University of New Mexico Health Sciences Center, received a national award for the UNM Care

6. Hinkley (1999).

Plan for 15,000 uninsured residents, which features accessible neighborhood-based care and one-stop shopping, including social services, case management, community outreach, and behavioral health.

Northern Manhattan will implement an integrated mental health services program to meet the needs of its mainly minority population, including immigrants.

Baltimore (Sandtown-Winchester) has supported the placement of mental health counselors in schools in the target area.

Denver Health provides mental health counselors (in collaboration with other providers) in schools in the area.

Gender Issues

There are a number of aspects of health security that directly affect women, especially those aged fifty-five to sixty-four:

—Women aged fifty-five to sixty-four are more likely than men to be uninsured (16.2 percent compared to 12.8 percent).

—Of widowed or divorced women in this age group, nearly one in five is uninsured.

—More than 11 percent of women aged fifty-five to sixty-four have annual incomes below $10,000, compared with 7.8 percent of men in this age group.

—Among all people under the age of sixty-five, 13.8 percent of whites are uninsured compared to 27.8 percent of minorities.

—Among women of fifty-five to sixty-four, 13.2 percent of white (non-Hispanic) women are uninsured compared with 26.5 percent of minority women (see figure 16-3).

—Among widowed or divorced women, 15.8 percent of whites are uninsured compared with 25.1 percent of nonwhite women in this age group.

In sum, nearly one in five widowed or divorced women aged fifty-five to sixty-four is uninsured and may have difficulty in finding good quality, affordable health-care coverage. Widowed and divorced older women with low incomes are most likely to be uninsured or to face problems gaining access to health insurance. Insurers may refuse to sell them a policy, especially if they have a history of health problems or a chronic or disabling condition. When a policy is available, it is likely to be expensive and may be unaffordable for those most in need of coverage. Those policies that may be more affordable often have limited benefits and sometimes exclude coverage for preexisting conditions.

The availability of public coverage is also quite limited for this population. Medicare is only provided to people under age sixty-five if they are very

Figure 16-3.   *Uninsured Women, 55 to 64 Years, by Race*

Percent

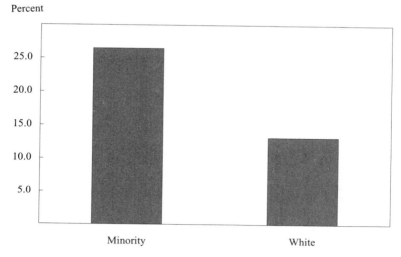

Minority   White

Source: Families USA (2001, p. 5).

disabled. Medicaid coverage is generally only available to older adults if they are disabled and have very low incomes.

Without changes to both the private insurance market and public programs, the number of uninsured women in this age group is likely to grow as the proportion of the population belonging to this age group grows.

Interventions

All Community Voices projects are serving women without insurance. Many can capture the costs of serving these women when they are present in the emergency room. None can capture costs of those who need care but do not come in for preventive primary health care.

Many sites cannot identify the number of women in their service area who do not have insurance due to the deficits in current governmental data-collection systems.

Men of Color and Men Living in Poverty

Among men, those who are of color and/or economically disadvantaged have greater risks. The difference in the life spans of African-heritage and European-heritage men in the United States (7.8 years) is greater than the difference between life spans of women and men (6.8 years). Black and Hispanic men also have a higher prevalence of preventable diseases. Furthermore, men of color are less likely to receive adequate care within the health care system and are more likely to face barriers than white males. Add to this the greater likelihood that men of color may experience unemployment, undereducation, poverty, incarceration, and racial discrimination, and, indeed, there is a crisis requiring a social insurance safety net.

Interventions

A forthcoming publication from Community Voices will attempt to tell the story of not just lack of coverage, but of other social and environmental factors that limit the ability of many men to access coverage and regular primary health care.[7]

Baltimore (Sandtown-Winchester) has opened a men's health clinic in cooperation with the city health department. It serves men from across the city and served 6,000 uninsured men in six months. This full-service clinic offers all services. The concern remains as to how this program will be paid for in the long-term.

In Denver, Denver Health is providing special services and screenings for men.

Pharmaceuticals Access

The lack of or limited coverage for prescriptions is a significant treatment barrier. For individuals with insurance coverage, access to pharmaceuticals is often restricted by formularies that carry limited name-brand pharmaceuticals and generic drugs. Uninsured individuals must pay out-of-pocket and do not receive any discount for their prescriptions.

For the low-income population with coverage, access to the appropriate drugs may be further limited due to cost-sharing. The issue of prescription drug coverage particularly affects the elderly without Medigap coverage, the uninsured, and consumers whose plans have limited drug formularies.

Interventions

In Washington, D.C., Community Voices is working with Unity Health Care and Catholic Charities to develop a pharmacy program for the district's

7. Rich (forthcoming).

uninsured residents. The project will include a prescription drug resource central and a central distribution center.

In Detroit's $80 million pharmacy access program, six to eight pharmaceutical companies are agreeing to participate in a single coordinated system that will be a source of benefits in the project's plan for care of the uninsured.

Other Major Areas of Work

The Community Voices program is trying to promote health security in other areas of U.S. society. The following are a few notable examples.

Small business coverage remains a thorny issue and is not easily resolved by and within states. While Community Voices sites in California, Colorado, New York, and North Carolina are actively pursuing or implementing small business plans, their work is limited by the financial ability of the small businesses to afford coverage for workers and their families and by the ability of the current policy environment to accommodate the needed changes.

Managed care plans are being developed and implemented in New Mexico, Texas, Michigan (Ingham County), Oakland (Alameda County Family Care), the California Rural Indian Health Board (Sacramento), and North Carolina. While these plans may run the same risks as established for-profit plans, they are attempting (variably) to demonstrate additional features such as coverage for immigrants (regardless of residency status), access to oral health care, and access to mental health services. A publication for Community Voices by the Economic and Social Research Institute illuminates the details of the plans and their anticipated opportunities and challenges.[8]

Conclusion

Community Voices works to address and integrate the complex needs and issues affecting those that work with no benefits, are paid too little, or are paid without income verification. To improve health security and ultimately a system of social insurance, the adequacy and reliability of any current "system" of employment insurance should be considered to determine if basic reform is needed relative to employment policy and practice. Far too many people work but have no network of insurance of any type available to them, short of national programs for which they may not qualify.

Philanthropy cannot and should not direct community action. Its appropriate role is to support the work that people in communities feel they need to

8. Meyer and Sillow-Carroll (1999).

implement to achieve their own goals. But philanthropy can, and should, shine a light on documentable evidence of human suffering, human misery, and a diminution of the human condition and human spirit. Community Voices may be one light that can bring into view persistently forgotten groups of individuals who live in the United States but have yet to realize the American dream.

Philanthropy should provide options for action that decisionmakers can examine for their utility in serving the public good. Philanthropy can disseminate and replicate the lessons learned and best practices developed by grantees. The public, not-for-profit, and marketplace sectors have an option, and perhaps a moral and ethnical responsibility, to examine, implement, and expand the work that people in communities have validated.

References

Families USA. 2001. "Too Few Options: The Insurance Status of Widowed or Divorced Older Women." Study conducted for the W. K. Kellog Foundation (Battle Creek, Mich.). Washington.

General Accounting Office. 2000. "Report of Congressional Requesters. Oral Health: Factors Contributing to Low Use of Dental Services by Low-Income Populations." GAO/HEHS–00–149. Washington (September).

Hinkley, R. H. 1999. "American Opinions on Mental Health Issues." Results of a study conducted by Research Strategy Management, Inc. (Fairfax, Va.) for the National Mental Health Association (Washington). *Mental Health Issues National Monitor*, i–99.

Meyer, Jack, and Sharon Sillow-Carroll. 1999. "Increasing Access: Building Working Solutions: A Proclamation of Community Voices." Battle Creek, Mich.: W. K. Kellogg Foundation, Community Voices (www.communityvoices.org).

Pascula, R. L., and R. Sturm. 2000. "Datapoints: Mental Health Parity and Employer-Sponsored Health Insurance in 1999–2000: II. Copayments and Coinsurance." *Psychiatric Services* 51 (12): 1487.

Rich, John R. Forthcoming. "The Health of Men of Color: Clearing a Path to Access and Care." Battle Creek, Mich.: W. K. Kellogg Foundation, Community Voices (www.communityvoices.org).

U.S. Census Bureau. 2000. *Current Population Survey.* Washington (March).

U.S. Department of Health and Human Services. 2000. *Oral Health in America: A Report of the Surgeon General.* Rockville, Md.: National Institutes of Health.

Comment by Jack Meyer

There are three roles that foundations can play to help develop effective social insurance policies. First, foundations can provide seed money to nurture promising reform strategies. Second, they can fund evaluations of these initiatives. Third, they can assist creative policy thinkers who are trying to develop the implications for national policy of a series of case studies of several local initiatives.

Instead of debating whether the safety net should be strengthened or coverage expanded, we should learn how to promote new insurance products to help the local angels who try to fill in the health system's gaping holes. While we support these angels, we also need to learn how to cope with the politics of gradually moving away from the current system toward providing health coverage to people in the first place.

While the economics of this transition are fairly simple, the politics are dreadful as one gradually moves resources away from the angels toward an insurance-based system. When one does that, one gets accused of being unsympathetic or unappreciative of the role of the angels, which of course is not the case.

Here is an example. I was recently on the phone with a physician who runs a health center in Washington, D.C. We were discussing the issue of increasing access to pharmaceuticals for indigent patients who use community health centers. While on the phone, I heard her say to someone else in the room, "Please put the bag over there in the corner." She then said to me, "Actually, it's funny that I'm talking to you now because the guy that brought in this bag is a local physician, and the bag is filled with pharmaceutical samples."

This physician practices in the neighborhood. Because it does not have enough drugs to meet the demands of its patients' many chronic illnesses, the health center has been fortunate to discover a few physician angels in the community who are willing to throw all their samples that they do not need into a bag and drop them off.

This is a wonderful story. However, without taking anything away from good-hearted people, acts of charity and many other local initiatives are not solutions to the problem of people not having access to all the medications they need.

We have to think more globally. In doing so, we need to avoid the temptation of thinking that the problem is merely a lack of money. We have plenty of money; it is just terribly allocated. The real problem is reallocating funds toward front-end investments in improved public health, preventive health care, and supporting social services.

There is an incredible amount of waste in the health-related tax subsidies and inappropriate care in the U.S. health system. The tax system distributes more than $140 billion a year to predominantly middle- and upper-income families. It also underwrites the cost of inefficient health plans. Moreover, this health care system makes disproportionate share hospital (DSH) payments that are not always well matched with the needs of communities.

As Ruth Riedel mentioned in chapter 15, the tobacco settlement presents a wonderful opportunity for financing health initiatives. But look where that money is going, because it is not always being targeted to good public health initiatives. In Washington, nearly $38 million of tobacco money was available this year to help address problems, but instead, at the last minute, the city government decided to use the money to reduce the debt. Sounds like a microcosm of the national debate in Congress, where one side wants to pay off the entire national debt with the putative $5.6 trillion surplus and the other side wants a huge tax cut.

Politicians are tripping over each other deciding whether to give the surplus back to the taxpayers or to pay off the national debt. Each has some worthy sentiments behind it, but little is heard in this $5.6 trillion surplus—which will not be around for long—about targeted investments. Here is all this tobacco money available to the District of Columbia, and the politicians want to put it into a "rainy day" fund while I am on the phone with a woman at a D.C. health clinic waiting for a doctor to bring in free pharmaceuticals. For that clinic, it is raining now.

Foundations can step in and fill a substantial void by providing seed money for local initiatives that government officials have failed to cultivate properly. If Medicaid funds, DSH funds, tobacco settlement funds, and other sources of available health financing are examined, a lot of money is found, but not necessarily money well spent on primary and preventive care. There is a lot of excess hospital capacity at the same time as shortages in staff, supplies, and facilities in the primary care setting.

Miami is an excellent example of this problem. All the money from a local sales tax for indigent care goes to one huge tertiary care center. The center does good work, but there is precious little money left over for the migrant health centers and community health centers in Miami-Dade County.

A second role that foundations can play in the social insurance arena is to fund evaluations of the kinds of state and local initiatives about which Riedel spoke. The term *evaluations* does not mean just quantitative impact analysis, but also qualitative analysis—case studies, interviews, focus groups, and stories that bring to life the impact of these initiatives on real people and their lives.

Foundations should help fund the qualitative analysis that unfortunately is often dismissed by the academic world as not rigorous. While I have great respect for more rigorous quantitative impact analysis, many of these initiatives do not lend themselves to that.

Foundations can help finance research that is more of this case study nature, glean the lessons learned and the policy implications, and figure out how one adapts what is being done in a variety of localities, from San Diego, California, to Muskegon County, Michigan.

Even more important, foundations can play a third significant role in social insurance by funding policy thinkers who can draw the proper links between successful community health initiatives and potential solutions to the nation's health care challenges. While they have done a wonderful job financing local initiatives, foundations have fallen short on probing the relationship between demonstration projects and the need for national reform.

For example, no group could be better than the National Academy for Social Insurance to tackle the question of why employer health care contributions are not treated in a social insurance framework, the way Social Security and unemployment insurance (UI) are treated. Germany, Japan, and France all treat health care contributions as part of their social insurance systems, so why is this not the case in the United States?

As a small business person, I have eight or nine researchers and policy analysts who work for me. I provide them with health coverage, but why am I not required to do that, just as I am required to pay Social Security and UI taxes? There would, of course, be adverse consequences that involve some wage cuts or jobs lost. But how big are these effects? Do they offset the gains from broader health coverage?

These are interesting questions. Unfortunately, it is very unpopular to raise these questions in today's market. One is considered to be somewhat wacky to do so. However, if we do not raise tough questions like these now, then in ten years we no longer will be talking about 43 million uninsured people. Instead, we will be talking about 53 or 63 million, because this problem is not going to solve itself. It is only going to get worse.

We should have an open debate on the role of subsidies. If we do not like a social insurance approach, should we have tax credits? How generous would the credits need to be to have the intended effect? Under what kind of purchasing mechanism would a taxpayer use the credit?

These questions are raised because it is not as simple as receiving a $2,000 tax credit and taking it into the individual market, where an insurer is going to say, "Thank you very much. Your family will need an $8,000 policy. That will cost you $6,000." The people about whom we are most concerned only make

$18,000 or $22,000 a year, and they cannot afford to pay $6,000 for that $8,000 policy.

We need to be realistic about this issue and bring discussions of employers' responsibility, the tax system, insurance market reforms, and other major reforms into the mix. Foundations do not need to present these ideas themselves, but they should provide seed money to policy people who are thinking about them so that community reforms and national issues can be linked.

That is a tough challenge, and Henrie Treadwell and her colleagues at the W. K. Kellogg Foundation deserve credit for taking on that challenge through their program. They are some of the few who are even thinking that way.

Comment by James Tallon

These were excellent presentations about philanthropic initiatives in health security, especially community-oriented initiatives within a broader context of other policy and programmatic initiatives undertaken by a range of philanthropic organizations.

Let us think about what is known about financing, service delivery, and strategy. We start with a fragmented financing system in which government and employers provide major components. The economists remind us that employer contributions theoretically belong to the employees. Both employer and employee contributions are tax-advantaged by the government.

As we look at initiatives to cover the uninsured, a simple central question is: Who pays? Follow the dollars to evaluate the strategy.

While it may be possible to squeeze some greater coverage on a marginal cost basis, our real choices require increased expenditures. Who will pay?

A second question is whether the approach is going to be voluntary participation in a program or whether it is going to be automatic or mandatory. This is very important because health insurance is a unique product. Health insurance assembles risk and, therefore, who participates makes a big difference. The simplest way to make a buck selling health insurance is to sell it to healthy people. The quickest way to lose money is to sell it only to sick people. Therefore, the nature of the product is unlike other products that we may purchase, and we have to think about how this affects intervention strategies. From the individual's point of view, health insurance is a discretionary expenditure, paying for future protection.

There are obviously a number of other questions. Whether we are going to build on the existing employer-based system; whether we are going to create expanded public programs; whether we are going to shift some greater responsibility to the individual.

Now, back to the first question. Who pays? When it comes to community initiatives, it is important to understand who is putting the money on the table.

Ruth Riedel, in discussing the San Diego presentation, talked about future funding initiatives and working with the state and others (chapter 15). But the alliance is subsidizing 50 percent of the premium right now.

Is it a viable strategy for private philanthropy to subsidize 50 percent of the premium cost? While this approach may work as a start-up in a pilot project, private philanthropy is not capable of providing half the dollars to solve the problem of the uninsured.

The second component of this issue is service delivery. In the organization of service delivery you see the real strength of many of the community initiatives that are sponsored by the Kellogg Foundation and by the Robert Wood Johnson Foundation.

In San Diego the effort at the community level gives voice to the problem in a credible way. The effort says we have a problem on behalf of our community and it brings diverse interests to the table to try to resolve them. It also speaks directly to the question of discrete services or individual groups in underserved populations. To design a service delivery system to get at those discrete problems requires a strong local effort.

It will be much more successful if you can bring together local health care groups and local community organizations, representative of those you are trying to serve, and design the service delivery mechanisms to get at specific problems. There is a powerful role to be played locally in terms of reorganizing the delivery of health care services. That is a role that is separable from designing the financing structure that is necessary to support this kind of innovation.

What does this tell us about strategy? Who are these people who are uninsured? A couple of myths show up in the polling. Myth number one: The uninsured are unemployed. No, they are not. A remarkably large number of the uninsured— as high as 80 percent—are employed.

This is, then, an employed population by and large. There are other groups. There are kids in transition, late teens who fall off their parents' policies at age eighteen. There are people aged fifty-five to sixty-four who drop out of the work force for whatever reason before Medicare kicks in. But this is by and large a working population.

The second myth is that the uninsured get care. There are many charitable efforts in the health care system, supported by hospitals and other organizations that seek to provide safety-net services.

There is a clear and uncontrovertible body of literature that says whatever care they get is not as good as the care that everybody else gets. Uninsured people get less care, and it usually comes later in the course of illness. They also pay a lot more for it out of their pocket. They have less access. They have measurably worse outcomes. People without insurance do not receive good health care.

Even if you hold everything else constant and just look within safety-net organizations, such as people being cared for in community clinics, there is a demonstrably different set of outcomes between insured people and uninsured people in the way in which they get care.

In addition, as the new Bush administration takes office, health care costs are going back up. The pharmaceutical industry has given us all sorts of new products, often with a significant price tag associated with new therapies. Ten years ago, when the economy was softening and cost numbers were going up, managed care was invented. We had a breather from dramatic cost increases during the 1990s, perhaps because of the onset of managed care—but there was a significant backlash at the end of the decade. In addition, I think it is fair to say that the first two years of the Clinton administration scared the hell out of the health care system and people behaved in a little more controlled way.

A central question then is: Where do we go next to control cost growth? One approach is to put more cost on individuals. The rhetoric of this change is to give us all a lot more choices. When you hear the word *choice* be careful. It is often part of a strategy to place more cost on the individual patient. And for many people, those costs will be simply unaffordable. Needless to say, there are many unanswered questions about how Americans will pay for health care in the future.

To come back to the community initiatives, which are the focus of this session, their strength is that they give voice to the problem, include communities in developing solutions, and design delivery systems in a way that links the resources of that community to underserved populations. This is a powerful mix.

The weakness in community strategies is that they cannot solve fundamental financing problems. That is the point about which I am exceedingly skeptical.

Epilogue

The Future of
Social Insurance

Susan Dentzer

W E AT THE *NewsHour with Jim Lehrer* could not do what we consider our stock-in-trade—to illuminate for the public some of the critical issues of our time—without the help of organizations such as the National Academy of Social Insurance. One of the participants at the conference noted, "Deliberation does improve knowledge among the public." We believe that at the *NewsHour.*

Because I was asked to address the issue of the future of social insurance, I went down the hall at the *NewsHour* to the closet where we keep our crystal ball. This device, of course, predicts the future with perfect accuracy, much like the people on the *McLaughlin Group.* Unfortunately, the crystal ball was being used by another of the correspondents. I was forced instead to haul out the *NewsHour* retrospectoscope, a device that I frankly find more informative in the way it sheds light on issues. We use it to look back on some recent events and try to reason from them what we might see in the future.

With the benefit of the retrospectoscope I reviewed some of the things we have lived through recently. For example, I thought of the Balanced Budget Act (BBA) of 1997 and the spending limits we imposed then on the Medicare program. I thought of the debate over reforming Social Security that has taken place over the last several years, and in particular of some public forums in which I was a participant that were sponsored by the Pew Foundation under the rubric, "Americans Discuss Social Security."

In thinking of all these things an old joke kept coming to mind. In this joke four people are assembled: a lawyer, a doctor, an engineer, and a politician. They begin to argue about what really is the oldest profession. The lawyer says, "Well, God handed down the tablets to Moses; that was clearly passing on the law. Therefore the oldest profession is that of lawyer." The doctor says "No, not at all. God created woman by taking a rib out of man; that was evidently an act of surgery. Therefore the oldest profession had to have been that of physician." The engineer says, "This is complete nonsense. It says in the Bible that God made the earth out of chaos; that was clearly an act of engineering. Therefore the oldest profession is that of engineer." To which the politician smiles and says, "You guys! Who do you think created the chaos?"

It is especially hard for those of us who have been close to the two major social insurance programs, Social Security and Medicare, not to think about politicians' role in bringing chaos to bear on many of these programs. Just think about some of the events of recent years.

In 1997 the Balanced Budget Act was enacted to expedite the balancing of the federal budget by, among other things, curbing Medicare's growth. You will recall that the numbers put in place at the time were $130 billion over five years; $130 billion was going to be carved out of the Medicare budget. It turns out years later that this $130 billion was not $130 billion; it was going to be closer to $200 billion, perhaps more than that.

As former Illinois senator Everett Dirksen would say if he were here today, "$100 billion here, $100 billion there, soon it adds up to real money." So we had to step back and pass the Balanced Budget Refinement Act in 1999 to pump about $17 billion back into the program, once it became clear that the rural hospitals, skilled nursing agencies, and home health agencies were on the brink.

We then came back again in 2000 and passed what is known as BIPA—the Medicare, Medicaid and SCHIP Benefits Improvement and Protection Act of 2000—to pump about $35 billion more back into Medicare over the next five years to offset still more of those Balanced Budget Act cuts. Chaos? I leave that to you to determine.

Then, of course, there was the Medicare + Choice program, which was put in place around the same time. The expectation was that having Medicare enrollees have greater options to enroll in health plans would not only save a lot of money, but it would also give Medicare beneficiaries infinitely more choices about how to receive their medical care. A few years later, more than 1.5 million enrollees are affected when plans pull out of the markets, complaining that they are not getting paid enough.

We then turned around and decided in the aforesaid BIPA to pour in an extra $6 billion into the program over several years—because it is clearly not saving money if no one is in it. The health plans are saying that they will need even more money to survive in business in future years. Not bad in the chaos department.

Now we look ahead, into what the great writer E. B. White cautioned us never to refer to with that nonsensical phrase "the foreseeable future"— pointing out that the future is probably foreseeable for about ten minutes and beyond that there is not much that can be foreseen. In our feeble attempt to look ahead, even the most die-hard believer in the necessity of reforming Social Security and Medicare would acknowledge that there is a great deal of opportunity for mischief. There are opportunities for many bad or unworkable policies to be adopted; there are many chances for unintended consequences to play out that could injure the public weal.

As a news person, I am excited about this potentially large stock of hair-raising stories. However, as a citizen and a person who is familiar with the memories of legislation past, and who has learned that the ratio of policy failures to policy successes in Washington is probably in the two-to-one range, all of this gives me pause.

I would like to discuss what I think is in store for us, on the basis of having this eye to the retrospectoscope. I would like to draw some lessons about what students of social insurance systems might be alert to in the days and years ahead.

Despite my opening joke about politicians and chaos, this is not a rant against politicians. All you have to do is watch a few hours of C-SPAN to understand that Barney Frank, the Massachusetts representative, was right when he observed that although people complain a lot about the politicians, the voters are not so hot either.

Although many ignoble people go into the noble profession of politics, it really is a noble profession. It involves the application of our deepest values, hopes, and dreams for humanity in an effort to govern our conduct and instill social order on our very existence. Nowhere is this point expressed more compellingly than in Joseph Ellis's terrific book *Founding Brothers* (Knopf, 2000), which is a story of the real heroes of the American Revolution. Their names are well known: Thomas Jefferson, Alexander Hamilton, John and Abigail Adams, James Madison, Aaron Burr, Benjamin Franklin, and George Washington. The book concerns their role in the early days of the founding of the American republic, and Ellis tells this story in the way you wished you had learned it originally in high school. It is a much more interesting portrait of the founders than the rather stuffy and idealized story we all received back then.

Ellis, who is a historian at Mount Holyoke College, does an especially masterful job of going over some of this very old ground in new and illuminating ways. He elucidates the early contradictions apparent in the founding of the republic, in what we have come to refer to, on the one hand, as the Jeffersonian tradition, versus the Hamiltonian tradition on the other hand.

The Jeffersonian tradition, as Ellis writes, "depicts the American Revolution as a liberation movement. The core revolutionary principle, according to this tradition, is individual liberty. It has radical and, in modern terms, libertarian implications because it regards any accommodations of personal freedom to governmental discipline as dangerous. In its most extreme forms it is a recipe for anarchy. Its attitude toward any energetic expression of centralized political power can assume paranoid proportions."

Ellis contrasts that with the opposing Hamiltonian interpretation of the revolution, in which the core principle is "collectivistic rather than individualistic, and which sees the true spirit of 1776 as the virtuous surrender of personal, state, and sectional interests to the larger purposes of American nationhood. It has conservative, but also proto-socialistic implications. It does not regard the individual as the sovereign unit in the political equation, and it is more comfortable with governmental discipline as a focusing and channeling device for national development. In its extreme form it relegates personal rights and liberties to the higher authority of the state which is us and not them, and therefore has in its most extreme form communal and despotic implications."

Ellis then makes the point that we are all still living out the legacy of this great tension between these two traditions. For most of us, he observes, taking sides in this debate is like choosing between the words and the music of the American Revolution. Most of us are drawn in some sense to aspects of both. Ellis says the key point is not that the debate has ever been or could be resolved, but that it has been built into the fabric of our national identity. If that means the United States is founded on a contradiction, so be it. Lincoln once said that America was founded on a proposition that was written by Jefferson in 1776, but, says Ellis, we are really founded on an argument about what that proposition means.

Does any of that sound in the slightest way familiar? Do concerns with individual liberty, resentment of governmental discipline, and distrust of centralized schemes have any applicability whatsoever to the great debate over social insurance programs? Or, on the other hand, is there a collectivistic impulse, as well as concern about the good of the many rather than the exercise of individual rights or liberties by an especially independent-minded few?

Does this conflict remind you of the debate over the proposition that Medicare should be structured to set people free from the shackles of government bureaucracy, to allow freedom of choice, and to surf the options of the glorious private insurance market? Or does this Jeffersonian and Hamiltonian debate remind you of the argument over why Social Security should be at least partly, if not wholly, privatized? Does it presage the argument that individuals should be given lots of investment choices based on their own personal preferences, that they should be free to sink or swim in the rushing water of speculation, and that they should be free to own the fruits of their investments and bequeath them later to their heirs? On the other side, does it remind you of the contrary view, that a collectivized social safety net, protecting people from the vagaries of the market, is the way the system should be structured?

The point I am driving home is that if we wander into some serious debates over social insurance programs, as I suspect we will over the next few years, we will be recapitulating this long-standing national debate once more. Personally, I worry that the needs of the American public may be lost sight of in the process and that the public well-being may be harmed in ways that we cannot begin to imagine at this point. There are three specific examples of the types of fears that I have.

With respect to Medicare reform, we now have a president who has embraced the version of reform set forth by a majority of the Medicare Commission in 1999, if not by the then-requisite supermajority. The proposal is part of legislation in Congress proposed by Senator John Breaux of Louisiana, a Democrat, and Senator Bill Frist of Tennessee, a Republican.

There are parallels between this proposal and our earlier experience with Medicare + Choice, and the compelling question about whether policies that are written down on paper have a chance of flying in the real world. A critical piece of any Medicare reform, from the perspective of those who are pushing plans such as the Breaux-Frist proposal, is how to contain the budgetary costs of the program over the long term. However laudable that goal may be, the Balanced Budget Act and its aftermath constitute a reminder of the need to stay focused on the real world impact of these cost-containment policies.

Posted on the American Hospital Association's website are various accounts about how member hospitals have fared under the cuts imposed under the Balanced Budget Act. Even discounting 50 percent of what is said there as special interest pleading and parochial interest at play, which is probably a fair thing to do, stories like the following emerge. Two years ago in Montpelier, Idaho, a remote rural area, there were three home health agencies making 14,000 visits a year to persons in need of home health care. Today there is one, and the number of visits has dropped to just 2,000 a year as a consequence of some of the pain imposed by the Balanced Budget Act cuts.

Are we prepared to believe that all those visits could cease taking place with no impact on the local population in need of care? I do not think so. This, again, is a very strong and compelling example of the fact that these policies have real world implications.

Consider this story: In a rural part of Upperville, Ohio, a ninety-one-bed hospital opened up a primary health care clinic for Medicaid and uninsured patients several years ago. Hospital officials knew all along that it was going to be a money-losing venture, but they did not think it was going to be an institution-destroying venture, which is basically what it became. The rest of the hospital fell into serious financial difficulty, in large part because of some of the constraints imposed by the Balanced Budget Act. That clinic, which in its first year saw almost 6,000 uninsured patients and patients on Medicaid, is now closed. Where are those patients going today?

This is not to say that every health care institution in this country is a precious resource that must be preserved and protected at all costs. I sit on the board of trustees of an academic medical center; I know better than that. I would nonetheless argue that health care institutions in this country have been buffeted about to an intolerable degree by the BBA and other policy initiatives over the last three years.

Reexamining this history might cause us to ask the following: What would happen if the entire Medicare program was restructured wholesale—encouraging Medicare beneficiaries to exert this precious freedom to pick and choose from among competing health plans? What if that approach were coupled with some sorts of limitations on payment—leading in turn to shifting enrollments among plans, fluctuating levels of payments to providers in charge of caring for these individuals, and thus changing dynamics all the way down the health care food chain?

Do we even begin to understand what all this would mean to the system? Do we understand how much Medicare beneficiaries want choice? A new study by the consulting firm Mathematica reported that only one in seven Medicare beneficiaries in a Medicare + Choice health plan had ever considered making a change and shifting to another plan—and only half of those had actually changed.

By citing studies such as this I am not saying, "Don't do a sweeping Medicare reform." I am asking, once again, have we begun to think through the consequences? The same is true with Social Security reform, which, according to the newspapers, we either will or will not see set forth as a Bush priority in the president's first year in office.

Some of you may have seen excerpts of an interview with the president, published January 15, 2001, in the *Wall Street Journal*, in which the subject of Social Security was addressed. Bush seemed to say that he favored setting up a bipartisan commission to set forth reform proposals. A bipartisan commission—how is that for a new idea? The president went on to fret in the interview that "a commission sometimes provides a lever for no action." (Think about that for a moment: "a lever for no action." It made me think of the surrealist painting by the artist Magritte, *Ceci n'est pas un pipe* [This is not a pipe]; this is not a lever, it leads to no action.) Whether we get a commission that is a lever for no action or a lever for action, perhaps a reform bill of some sort will eventually come out of the White House. That means we will see a playing out, at least at some level once again, of this Hamiltonian and Jeffersonian debate.

On the Jeffersonian side, is it important to carve out a piece of Social Security and declare that for each of us it is our own private island of double-digit investment returns? Should all good citizens be prepared to follow the path forged by the president's top economic adviser, Larry Lindsey, who embraces partial privatization even as he acknowledges that he has pulled every dollar he has out of the stock market for fear of a crash? Or, on the Hamiltonian side, is it important to preserve a collective social safety net at all costs, even at the substantial political peril that could ensue in the future as millions begin to grumble about their nonexistent or negligible returns?

Many questions remain about any reform proposals. How will people living in the real world respond to them? Is it conceivable that reforms could to any degree accomplish each side's sought-after economic, ideological, or other goals? What are we to make of a president who insisted on advancing a "carve-out" partial privatization proposal over the course of the election campaign—but without telling anybody how much he wanted to carve out or how he would finance Social Security in the event of this carve-out? Why have we not seen the president expend some political capital raising some of the well known—if politically unpalatable—ideas that we all are pretty darn sure would improve the program's solvency over the long run? For example, he has not attempted to muster support for ongoing increases in the retirement age, coupled with major improvements in the Social Security Disability Insurance program, which could protect those who might not be able to work to a more advanced age?

If we are talking about personal freedoms, why not speak about personal responsibility—that maybe we all have a duty to work longer than we thought we would have to in order to accommodate ourselves to the demographic realities of the twenty-first century?

I allow that it is still early in this administration, and we may yet see some of these thoughts or themes come forward. We all will be waiting for them as persons keenly interested in where we are going.

Let me turn now to another social insurance issue that warrants our attention: long-term care. Many will recall that, about twelve years ago, there was a debate over whether to enact just such a social insurance program. There were a number of events around the 1988 political conventions—pressing a campaign known as "Long-Term Care '88." At the time, people were predicting passage of a long-term care social insurance program that would be put in place just a few short years later. I remember gearing up to cover the great national debate about long-term care that would follow the 1988 election. Needless to say, this did not happen.

It is striking how completely the subject has fallen off the table ever since. More than twelve years have elapsed and we are further down the road to the retirement of my generation, the baby boomers, and presumably to a rise, and possibly even an explosion, in the number of persons who will be needing what we think of as long-term care.

All this came rushing back to me thanks to a woman named Gabriella Anderson, who was featured in a story we recently aired on the *NewsHour*. I would like to share her story with you.

I met Gabriella in the course of reporting a story about a very small demonstration project run by the Health Care Financing Administration, along with several states and the Robert Wood Johnson Foundation. The program is called Cash and Counseling, and it is aimed at people with disabilities who are on Medicaid. The program grants participants relatively small sums of cash, on the order of $300 or so a month, to pay small stipends to caregivers of their own choosing, rather than forcing them to have services delivered by agency personnel and paid for by Medicaid. As a consequence, most of the individuals who get these small grants turn around and hire people they know—often, their relatives. These workers provide personal care and assistance to the disabled, including assistance with bathing, grocery shopping, transportation, and other services that home health care agencies cannot provide under Medicaid.

Arkansas is one of three states in this very small pilot program, and when we went there last year, one of the program participants we interviewed was Gabriella Anderson. She is a forty-one-year-old woman who suffers from multiple sclerosis. In her level of need and disability she is quite similar to the average elderly person who is in need of assistance with virtually all activities of daily living.

Here, in brief, is Gabriella's story. She's a married woman with a child. She has lived much of her life as a productive wage earner, working at a collection agency. She suddenly becomes very ill in her late thirties with a disease that at first nobody can diagnose correctly, but which is eventually diagnosed as multiple sclerosis. She is forced to quit her job because she simply cannot perform it; most mornings she cannot even get out of bed.

Fortunately, her husband still works full time, but because Gabriella must leave her job, her family income of roughly $60,000 a year is immediately cut in half. Her medical bills quickly run up to $48,000 a year, but her family cannot pay them because her husband's job does not come with health insurance. So she concludes after considerable deliberation that she has no choice left but to divorce her husband and go on Supplemental Security Income (SSI) and Medicaid.

By the way, the maximum income one can have in Arkansas to qualify for Medicaid is identical to the SSI level: $6,000 a year. Translation: If your income is more than $6,000 a year, you are too well off to qualify for Medicaid in Arkansas.

So Gabriella divorces her husband and goes on Medicaid, which begins to pay her medical bills. Then she learns, happily, that she is eligible for two state programs: the Cash and Counseling program, as well as another program that is run under a home- and community-based care waiver for Medicaid and is designed to help keep people out of nursing homes, if possible.

In a nutshell, these two programs end up paying Gabriella's ex-husband and caregiver about $25,000 a year to stay home and take care of her. It does so because that is at least $10,000 a year cheaper than putting her in a nursing home and having the state pick up the tab in Medicaid.

How crazy is this? Add up what she is receiving annually from various public programs: $6,000 from SSI, $48,000 or thereabout for her medical bills under Medicaid, and $25,000 in payments to her husband to care for her. Collectively it costs nearly $80,000 a year in public resources to pay for Gabriella's care. Multiply that by the estimated 40 million Americans now with disabilities and you get a sense of the gargantuan financial needs we face now and will face in the future.

I don't begrudge Gabriella a penny of this, by the way. But is it reasonable to put a woman like this in a position where she has to get a divorce and then hire back her ex-husband so she can stay out of a nursing home? Is this any way to run such a system now, let alone twenty years from now when instead of 40 million people with disabilities we will possibly have more in the range of 80–100 million with disabilities?

Twelve years have passed since that 1988 long-term care campaign, and virtually nothing has happened. Not only has nothing happened, but it is also true that very little if anything has even been talked about.

In addition to having concerns about things that might be done in the way of reforming social insurance, I would like to see the nation contemplate still other measures—such as putting long-term care back on the table. I would like to see us start talking more about a range of possible public and private approaches to the issue. And, at the risk of sounding like a total dinosaur, one of the things that ought to come back on the table is discussion about a formal social insurance approach on long-term care. I have no expectation whatsoever that such an approach would fly in the current political climate. But at least putting such an approach out for discussion might generate greater examination of the exigencies that may await us.

At a minimum, discussion of this issue might spur creation of some real community-based services for people like Gabriella Anderson. These are seriously lacking in various parts of the country and are made worse by current labor shortages. These are circumstances that, among other things, force home health agencies to hire ex-convicts to help deliver service to the elderly and the disabled. It can only be hoped that close scrutiny of such facts might lead to more services for the chronically ill and disabled.

Then again, perhaps we will not have a serious national discussion about the issue. Maybe we will just sit back and punt for a few more years, or bank on medical researchers to help find a cure for Alzheimer's that could help roughly 40 percent of those currently in the nation's nursing homes. Maybe cures will be found for some of the other debilitating conditions that force people into those facilities today. Perhaps we will not end up in a future where millions of elderly baby boomers are homebound or institutionalized with serious disabilities. Frankly, I would not want to bank on it.

In closing, it is well worth having a Jeffersonian and Hamiltonian debate over how to face the issue of long-term care—just as it is with Medicare and Social Security reform. These are among the most pressing public policy issues our nation faces. They are urgent issues to take up for those of us still engaged in this debate about what life, liberty, and the pursuit of happiness really mean, and what they will mean for those of us who will live out our lives in the twenty-first century.

I look forward to a very vigorous debate, and I hope it is a debate that leads to a more rational order instead of chaos.

Contributors

Gerard F. Anderson is with the Johns Hopkins University School of Medicine and is also the national program director for the Robert Wood Johnson Campaign on Chronic Illness and Senior Fellowship Adviser to the Commonwealth Fund's Harkness Fellowships in Health Care Policy. He has also held various positions in the Office of the Secretary, U.S. Department of Health and Human Services, where he helped to develop Medicare prospective payment legislation.

Richard Berner is Chief U.S. Economist at Morgan Stanley Dean Witter, responsible for directing the firm's forecasting and analysis of the U.S. economy and financial markets. Before joining Morgan Stanley Dean Witter in 1999, he was Executive Vice President and Chief Economist at Mellon Bank and a member of Mellon Bank's Senior Management Committee.

Jeffrey R. Brown is with Harvard University's John F. Kennedy School of Government. He is also a faculty Research Fellow of the National Bureau of Economic Research.

Sheila Burke is Undersecretary for American Museums and National Programs, Smithsonian Institution. Previously, she was Executive Dean at the John F. Kennedy School of Government at Harvard University, as well as Chief of Staff to Senator Robert Dole. She helped shape the 1983 Medicare prospective payment system law and much of the health care cost containment legislation of the 1980s.

Ann L. Combs was Vice President and Chief Counsel at the American Council of Life Insurers. Previously, she was with William M. Mercer, Inc. She was a member of the 1994–96 Advisory Council on Social Security. Combs was Deputy Assistant Secretary for Policy for the Pension and Welfare Benefits Administration and Senior Legislative Officer in the Congressional Affairs Office of the U.S. Department of Labor (DOL).

Fay Lomax Cook is at Northwestern University where she teaches in the School of Education and Social Policy as well as the Department of Political Science. Her research focuses on the dynamics of public support for older Americans, the interrelationships between public opinion and social policy, and the politics of public policy.

Craig Copeland is with the Employee Benefit Research Institute. Before joining EBRI in 1997, he taught economics at Southern Illinois University–Carbondale

Albert B. Crenshaw has been a reporter, editor, and columnist at the *Washington Post* for more than 25 years and has written about the future of Social Security, as well as about the transition of much of the nation's private pension system from traditional defined benefit plans to investment-based defined contribution arrangements.

Susan Dentzer is a correspondent for *The NewsHour with Jim Lehrer* on PBS. She covers such issues as Medicare and Social Security reform and health care and health policy. She also has written for *U.S. News and World Report* and for *Newsweek.*

William C. Dudley has served as Director of the U.S. Economic Research Group at Goldman, Sachs and Company since October of 1995.

Peter Edelman is a Professor of Law at Georgetown University Law Center. He also has served with the U.S. Department of Health and Human Services and as a partner at Foley, Lardner, Hollabaugh, and Jacobs. In his early career, he served as legislative assistant to Senator Robert F. Kennedy and as a law clerk to Supreme Court Justice Arthur J. Goldberg.

Howard Fluhr is President and CEO of the Segal Company. He is a Fellow of the Society of Actuaries, the Conference of Consulting Actuaries and the Canadian Institute of Actuaries. Mr. Fluhr is Chair of the Employee Benefit Research Institute (EBRI).

Heidi Hartmann is the founder and Director of the Institute for Women's Policy Research, a nonprofit, scientific research organization on policy issues of importance to women. Previously she was the Director of Women's Studies at Rutgers University, a member of the graduate faculty at the New School for Social Research, and a staff member at the National Research Council/National Academy of Sciences.

Ron Haskins is a Senior Fellow with the Brookings Institution. Prior to this, he served as Staff Director for the Subcommittee on Human Resources of the Committee on Ways and Means, U.S. House of Representatives. He has taught at the University of North Carolina at Chapel Hill and at the University of North Carolina at Charlotte.

Lawrence R. Jacobs is an Adjunct Professor with the Hubert H. Humphrey Institute and an Associate Professor of Political Science at the University of Minnesota.

Kilolo Kijakazi is Senior Policy Analyst in the Income Security Division at the Center on Budget and Policy Priorities. Before joining the center, she was with the Food and Nutrition Service of the U.S. Department of Agriculture, the National Urban League, and George Washington University.

Pamela J. Larson has directed the National Academy of Social Insurance since it began in 1986. First as Executive Director, then as Executive Vice President, she continues to work closely with the Academy's Members and Board and staff to implement its programs on leadership development, public understanding, and international training as well as develop its services to social insurance professionals and its fund-raising initiatives.

Lauren LeRoy is President and CEO of Grantmakers in Health. Previously, she was Executive Director of the Medicare Payment Advisory Commission, having earlier served with the Physician Payment Review Commission, the Commonwealth Fund Commission on Elderly People Living Alone, the Institute for Health Policy Studies, University of California–San Francisco, and the U.S. Department of Health, Education, and Welfare.

Jack A. Meyer is the founder and President of two research and policy organizations: the Economic and Social Research Institute (ESRI), which pursues a broad range of studies evaluating health and social welfare programs, and New Directions for Policy, which develops, analyzes, and evaluates health care issues and other social policies for business and government.

Marilyn Moon is a Senior Fellow in the Health Policy Center of the Urban Institute and served as Public Trustee of the Social Security and Medicare Trust Funds from 1995 to 2000. She has worked at the Public Policy Institute at the American Association of Retired Persons, Congressional Budget Office, and taught at the University of Wisconsin–Milwaukee.

Cecilia Muñoz is Vice President for the Office of Research, Advocacy and Legislation for the National Council of La Raza. She also has worked for the Catholic Charities of the Archdiocese of Chicago and has served on the boards of the National Immigration Forum and the National Coalition for Haitian Rights.

Janet L. Norwood is a consultant on unemployment compensation. She was a Senior Fellow at the Urban Institute from 1992 to 1999. She served as Chair of the Advisory Council on Unemployment Compensation from 1993 to 1996. She was the U.S. Commissioner of Labor Statistics under both the Bush and the Clinton administrations.

Eric Oxfeld is President of UWC-Strategic Services on Unemployment and Workers' Compensation and UWC's research arm, the National Foundation for Unemployment Compensation and Workers' Compensation. He has served with the American Insurance Association, the U.S. Chamber of Commerce, and the U.S. Department of Labor.

Wendell Primus is the Director of Income Security for the Center on Budget and Policy Priorities. At the U.S. Department of Health and Human Services, he served as a Deputy Assistant Secretary in the Office of the Assistant Secretary for Planning and Evaluation. For the House Ways and Means Committee he served as Chief Economist and as Staff Director for the committee's Subcommittee on Human Resources.

Ruth Lyn Riedel serves as President and Chief Executive Officer and a Trustee of the Alliance Healthcare Foundation, San Diego's largest independent health care philanthropy. She has operated her own consulting firm and worked for national philanthropies such as the Robert Wood Johnson Foundation and the Kaiser Family Foundation.

Robert Rosenblatt has written for the *Los Angeles Times* since 1976. He covers financial and economic issues, with a specialty in Social Security, Medicare, pensions, and the aging of the baby boom generation.

Dallas L. Salisbury is President and CEO of the Employee Benefit Research Institute (EBRI) and Chair and CEO of the American Savings Education Council and the Consumer Health Education Council. He has been an Assistant Executive Director of the Pension Benefit Guaranty Corporation. At the U.S. Department of Labor, he was an Executive Assistant to the Administration of Pension and Welfare Benefit Programs and an Acting Assistant Administrator for Policy Planning and Research.

Mark Schlesinger is Associate Professor in the Department of Epidemiology and Public Health at Yale University Medical School. Previously, he was Assistant Professor of health policy at Harvard Medical School.

James R. Tallon Jr. is President of the United Hospital Fund of New York. He has been a member of the New York State Assembly. First elected in 1974, he was Health Committee Chair from 1979 to 1987 and Majority Leader from 1987 to 1993. He is currently Chair of the Kaiser Commission on Medicaid and the Uninsured and a member of the Joint Commission on the Accreditation of Healthcare Organizations.

Henrie M. Treadwell is a Program Director at the W. K. Kellogg Foundation of Battle Creek, Michigan. She began her career as an Assistant Professor of biology at Morris Brown College in Atlanta, Georgia, and became Department Chair of the Division of Science and Mathematics in 1976. She conducted research in molecular biology under a visiting faculty research fellowship at the Harvard University School of Public Health.

Jack L. VanDerhei has been a faculty member at Temple University's Fox School of Business and Management since 1988. At the Wharton School of the University of Pennsylvania he served as Research Director of the Pension Research Council. Currently, his research agenda primarily focuses on analyzing a proprietary longitudinal database of eight million 401(k) participants from 30,000 plans.

Wayne Vroman is an Economist at the Urban Institute. Previously, he held positions at Oberlin College, the University of Maryland, and the University of California–Berkeley.

Charity C. Wilson is a Policy Analyst with the AFL-CIO. Her areas of specialization are immigration, low-wage worker issues, and the unemployment compensation program. She was previously a Deputy Director of the Washington office of Pennsylvania Governor Tom Ridge and a Counsel to the Senate Committee on the Judiciary for Senator Arlen Specter.

Conference Program

National Academy of Social Insurance
13th Annual Conference

The Future of Social Insurance: Incremental Action or Fundamental Reform?
January 24–25, 2001

The 2000 election debate offered very different future visions for Social Security and Medicare. As the new administration and the 107th Congress begin their work, this national forum takes a fresh look at issues central to the public policy debate about how to cover the economic risks people face throughout their lives.

Conference sessions examine emergent ideas for Social Security, Medicare, unemployment insurance, retirement income, and health insurance. Conferees will learn about the latest research, discuss new conceptions of old problems, and exchange fresh ideas to be considered by policymakers in Washington and in state houses and legislatures around the country.

Wednesday, January 24, 2001

9:45–10:30	Welcome and Introduction Opening Address William C. Dudley
10:35–12:15 p.m.	Session I. Issues in Social Security Reform Moderator: John L. Palmer, Maxwell School of Citizenship and Public Affairs, Syracuse University

Presenters:
What investment returns to expect for the future?
  How much needs to be done?
Richard Berner, Morgan Stanley Dean Witter

Low earners: How far to go?
Kilolo Kijakazi, Center on Budget and Policy
  Priorities

Public views on Social Security: Incremental action
  or fundamental reform?
Fay Lomax Cook, Institute for Policy Research,
  Northwestern University
Lawrence Jacobs, University of Minnesota

Discussants:
Howard Fluhr, The Segal Company
Cecilia Muñoz, National Council of La Raza
Robert Rosenblatt, *Los Angeles Times*

12:30–1:30   Luncheon Address
                    E. J. Dionne, Brookings Institution

1:45–3:15   Session II. The Changing Face of Retirement
                    Benefits: What Role for Guaranteed Income?
                    Moderator: Thomas Paine, Independent Consultant

Presenters:
The Changing Face of Private Retirement Plans
Jack VanDerhei, Fox School of Business
  Management, Temple University

How Should We Insure Longevity Risk in Pensions
  and Social Security
Jeffrey R. Brown, John F. Kennedy School of
  Government, Harvard University

Discussants:
Ann Combs, American Council of Life Insurers
Albert Crenshaw, *The Washington Post*
Heidi Hartmann, Institute for Women's Policy
  Research

3:30–5:15   Session III. Issues in Unemployment Insurance
                    Moderator: Richard Hobbie, Interstate Conference of
                    Employment Security Agencies

Presenter: Janet Norwood, Chair, 1993–96 Advisory Council on Unemployment Compensation

Discussants:

Eric J. Oxfeld, UWC—Strategic Services on Unemployment and Workers' Compensation

Wayne Vroman, The Urban Institute

Charity Wilson, AFL-CIO

5:30–8:00pm   Dinner and the John R. Heinz Dissertation Award presented by Robert B. Hudson, Boston University, Chair of the Award Committee

Speaker: Susan Dentzer, *The NewsHour with Jim Lehrer*

Thursday, January 25, 2001

9:00–10:00   Roundtable Discussions

Advances in Understanding and Measuring Access, Costs, and Quality of Workers' Compensation Medical Care

Jay Himmelstein, University of Massachusetts Medical School

Long Term Care in the New Millennium: Report from the Academy's Task Force

William Scanlon, General Accounting Office

Social Security Reform and the World Bank: Reflection From a Decade of Transition

Robert Brown, University of Waterloo

Social Insurance Research-in-Progress

John Williamson, Boston College

Gloom and Doom vs. Boom and Bloom: Examining the Trustees Long Range Projections for Social Security

Ronald Gebhardtsbauer, American Academy of Actuaries

10:15–10:45   Opening Address

11:00–12:15 p.m.   Session IV. Medicare: Government, Markets or Partnership?

Moderator: Robert D. Reischauer, The Urban
Institute

Panelists:
Medicare's Long-Term Financing
Marilyn Moon, The Urban Institute

Medicare's Governance and Management
Sheila Burke, Smithsonian Institution and Kennedy
School of Government, Harvard University

Medicare and Markets
Mark Schlesinger, Yale University

Chronic Care and Medicare
Gerard Anderson, Johns Hopkins University

12:30–1:30   Luncheon Discussion
"Reflections on Welfare Reform After Five Years"
Moderator: Peter Edelman, Conference Co-Chair

Panelists:
Wendell Primus, Center on Budget and Policy
Priorities
Ron Haskins, Brookings Institution

1:45–3:30   Session V: Philanthropic Initiatives in Health
Security
Moderator/Presenter: Lauren LeRoy, Grantmakers in
Health

Panelists:
Ruth Riedel, Alliance Healthcare Foundation of San
Diego
Henrie M. Treadwell, W.K. Kellogg Foundation's
Community Voices
Catherine Dunham, Robert Wood Johnson
Foundation's Access Project

Discussants:
Jack A. Meyer, Economic and Social Research
Institute
James R. Tallon Jr., United Hospital Fund

3:30pm   Conference Wrap-up

Index